Toxic Feedback

Helping Writers Survive and Thrive

JONI B. COLE

University Press of New England   Hanover and London

Published by University Press of New England,
One Court Street, Lebanon, NH 03766
www.upne.com
© 2006 by Joni B. Cole
Printed in the United States of America

5   4   3

Interview excerpt from Julia Alvarez copyright © 2005 by Julia Alvarez. Reprinted by
permission of Susan Bergholz Literary Services, New York. All rights reserved.

Library of Congress Cataloging-in-Publication Data

Cole, Joni B.
Toxic feedback : helping writers survive and thrive / Joni B. Cole.
   p.   cm.
ISBN-13: 978-1-58465-543-5 (alk. paper)
ISBN-10: 1-58465-543-7 (alk. paper)
ISBN-13: 978-1-58465-544-2 (pbk. : alk. paper)
ISBN-10: 1-58465-544-5 (pbk. : alk. paper)
1. Authorship—Psychological aspects.   2. Authorship—Evaluation—Psychological
aspects.   I. Title.
PN171.P83C66   2006
808'.02019—dc22   2006002882

Toxic Feedback

For the writers in my workshop,

and for Stephen, who is always there for me

Contents

☞ In the Company of Writers

Toxic Feedback

Introduction: Every Writer Has a Story

When my husband was in graduate school and I was still trying to figure out what to do with my life, I decided to take a continuing education course in fiction writing. My professor had all the markings of a genius, literary and otherwise. His novels broke ground and enjoyed dismal sales. Like fellow geniuses Norman Mailer and Joyce Carol Oates, he assigned a mystique to the sport of boxing that is lost on me. And his course cost $2,432, an amount roughly equivalent to the annual earnings of a freelance writer, which I happened to be at the time.

Once a week, every student submitted a story to the professor, who then judged whether it was worthy of discussion by the group. If he chose your story for the class to discuss that evening, he insisted the writer remain anonymous, similar to how newspapers handle the coverage of crimes committed by juvenile delinquents. With great trepidation, I submitted my first piece to the professor. Because my entire self-worth (at the time, anyway) depended on the professor's reaction to those twenty pages, I cheated, naturally. I submitted a story I had been working on diligently for over a year. This was a story excavated from the mines of my personality, roiling in turmoil yet tinged with bittersweet humor. This was a story forged in the traditional framework of conflict, crisis, epiphany, resolution. This was a story I had received an "A" on in a community college creative-writing class I had participated in a few months earlier.

This was *not* the story the professor chose for discussion. That evening, our class critiqued a short piece that consisted entirely of messages on a suicidal woman's answering machine. In hindsight, I realize that this was the more sophisticated story, actually quite powerful, but that's not the point of this anecdote.

After class, the professor summoned me and the other writer-rejects to his podium, and wordlessly returned our submissions from the previous week. The teacher's stigmata of academia: the shapeless brown corduroy blazer with blue slacks, the faint odor of a tobacco shop from the 1960s, the world-weary weight of his briefcase—all precluded me from wasting his time by asking, "Well?" Later, however, behind the lowered, green industrial shades that accessorized my apartment in married student housing, I extracted the manuscript from my backpack and searched the story page by page for his feedback.

Nothing. Nada. No red ink, no finger smudges, no telltale splotches of bourbon. Then I turned the manuscript over and there, on the back of the back page, I found it. The professor's feedback, three scrawled words: "It's all wrong." That was the professor's response to a year's worth of creative effort. *It's all wrong.* What was I to do with that? Outside my drawn shades, I could hear the barely muted roar of the university's lawn-care crew racing around on their riding mowers, charged with keeping the grounds of married student housing as close-cropped as Oliver North's head. Rrrr. *It's all wrong.* Rrrr. *It's all wrong.* To this day, whenever I hear the roar of a riding mower, the phrase "It's all wrong" reverberates between my ears.

Later, I calculated the cost of that professor's feedback: $810 per word, based on the class tuition. But his feedback cost me much more than money. Those three words confirmed what my own insecurities had been whispering to me all along: *I was an outsider; I had nothing of importance to say; I would never be a real writer.* The professor's response to my writing is what I call "toxic feedback." It made me lose ground and lose confidence as a writer.

That fiction-writing class is ancient history, but my experience with toxic feedback left an indelible impression on my psyche. I almost quit writing; but I didn't. I wrote more short stories, and I still call myself a freelance writer, though I've added other labels over the years: editor, author, fiction-workshop instructor, and temp, not necessarily in that order. Despite the professor's serious blow to my self-esteem (he never did choose any of my work for discussion in the class), I continued to write because writing for me, as is the case with so many other people, isn't simply a matter of confidence or success, but compulsion.

Something inside writers makes them need to put words on the page, regardless of their boot-stomped egos. Writers may ignore or deny that need for years out of fear or with good excuses or lame excuses, but the need remains, manifesting in a sense of excitement and agitation whenever an intriguing idea or character pops into their consciousness, whispering insistently, *"Write about me! Write about me! Wouldn't I make a great story?!"* You know this anticipatory, antsy feeling if you are a writer. You also know this feeling if you have ever taken Dimetapp Cough Suppressant.

For twelve years, I have been teaching fiction writing to adults in my community. Some of the participants who come to my writing workshops are new to the craft, others have been publishing for years. Some join the group because they are in the throes of working on their latest novel or short story; others join because they need help getting started. Regardless of these differences, most of them arrive at that first meeting ready to bolt. As the participants introduce themselves to the other members in the circle, they begin to apron-wring and apologize for their narrative failures before they have even shared one word of their writing in class. They admit they are nervous wrecks about submitting their stories to the group for feedback. Where is this coming from? These people are not wimps. By day, they take on much riskier tasks: brain surgery, childrearing, insurance billing. So why would a writing workshop intimidate them? Of course, I knew the answer all along.

It's all wrong.

Almost every writer has a story, some sad tale about how a teacher, fellow writer, critique group or workshop, friend, boss, spouse, parent, agent, editor, or rogue reader provided them with toxic feedback that made them doubt their abilities, distrust their own voices, sabotage their stories, or just feel really, really lousy. Once exposed to toxic feedback, some people stop writing, sometimes for years, sometimes for a lifetime. Others keep scribbling away, but avoid feedback for fear of harsh criticism, burying their unread novels or poems or essays at the bottom of their sock drawers, alongside other shameful secrets like those leftover European Royalty diet capsules and miracle wrinkle removers ordered from late-night infomercials. Still others continue to write and solicit feedback, viewing the process as a necessary evil.

Necessary it is. Evil, it isn't—because only feedback can answer the ultimate question: Are you connecting with your readers? With the exception of creating a secret diary or a grocery list, most writing is intended to communicate something meaningful to a person other than yourself, whether it is a life story in the form of a memoir or the power of forgiveness in a ten-line verse. Without the benefit of feedback during the drafting process, how do you know whether your words are achieving your intent? How do you recognize the weak passages or missed opportunities when your only perspective is the one inside your own head? How do you know if the reader is moved by your writing, or wants to move on?

The time has come to rid the world of toxic feedback so that writers can avail themselves of this invaluable but too often tainted resource. With the understanding that it takes two to create toxic feedback, we can move beyond pseudo-solutions for improving the feedback process, such as simply telling writers to toughen up, as if toxic feedback wouldn't be an issue if these artistic types would just get a backbone. We can also stop vilifying feedback providers, as if their lack of awareness of what motivates writers makes these critiquers inherently toxic. I suppose there are a few feedback providers who are truly malevolent, but my experience as a workshop leader has taught me that most feedback providers mean well, even when they are saying something horrifically insensitive. Even people in love, *especially* people in love, generate toxic feedback. Consider the true story of the once happily married writers who provided feedback to each other during their collaboration on a self-help book. The book was successful, but now the children only see their father every other weekend.

The intent of *Toxic Feedback* is to help writers not only survive criticism, but thrive in the feedback process. This book is for every struggling writer who wants to do less struggling and more writing (Can you imagine!). It is for feedback providers who want to empower writers, and enjoy the sense of satisfaction that comes from helping someone achieve a work of merit. And it is for writing workshops and critique groups that want to leave every participant informed and energized by this communal experience.

My own experiences receiving and giving feedback contributed to the insights and opinions that follow, as did my conversations with a diversity of writers, teachers, editors, and other knowledgeable people inside and outside the writing realm. This book also includes my interviews with thirteen successful authors, across genres, who generously shared their own feedback stories from the inspiring to the deranged.

Despite all the evidence to the contrary, the myth of the lone (and lonely) writer continues to loom large, and with it the unhealthy assumption that "real" writers toil in isolation. By offering instruction to writers and feedback providers on how to manage this vital but delicate dynamic, my hope is to dispel this myth once and for all. Yes, writing is a solitary effort, but it doesn't have to be a lonely one—and that is the real gift of feedback.

☛ RETHINKING FEEDBACK

What is Feedback?

It seemed like a good idea to start this book with an official definition of the term *feedback*. So I looked up the word on an online dictionary, and here is what I found.

I found the definition of feedback as it relates to cybernetics and control theory. I found how the term is used in electronic and mechanical engineering, economics and finance, gaming, organizations, biology, and nature. I found diagrams of feedback loops with lots of arrows pointing here and there. I found exotic-looking translations of the word (*terugkoppeling* . . . *Rückkopplung* . . . ανάδραση . . .). But what I didn't find was a definition for feedback as it specifically relates to writing.

How can this be? I knew writers had co-opted the term from some other realm (electrical engineering, as it turns out, circa 1920, according to the *Oxford English Dictionary*), but you would think that by now our application of *feedback* would have merited its own place in the dictionary, especially since we use the term all the time. "I joined a writing group because I want feedback." "I'm waiting for feedback from my editor." "Winston wants me to give him feedback on his story, but I don't have a clue what to say."

So with no dictionary definition to help us out, what exactly are we all talking about when we talk about feedback?

I think a lot of writers view feedback as someone telling them what's wrong with their writing in order to help them fix it. That may be one way to think of feedback, but it sure doesn't make me want to race out and get some. As a writer, just the thought of readers focusing on my imperfections takes me back to the junior prom, with everyone staring at the zit on my nose, but no one even noticing my dress. And, as a feedback provider, the responsibility of helping a writer "fix" his story only makes me feel desperate to find fault with it, even where there is none.

It seems to me that as writers and feedback providers we need to change the way most of us perceive feedback. We need to come up with our own definition of the term, one that distinguishes it entirely from feedback as it applies to electrical engineering, for example, with its dry references to input and output, and its awful association with that shrieking sound coming from the P.A. system. We need to put a positive spin on feedback as it relates to writing, and we need to do it quickly before it's too late for damage control. Otherwise, the term *feedback* is in real danger of going the way of *criticism,* a word once connoting praise as well as censure, but is now just a big, fat negative in most people's minds.

We can't let that happen to feedback. We just can't. Because the essence of feedback is nothing but positive (even when it is negative), and we are only hurting ourselves if we overlook its real meaning and value.

For a writer, feedback means you never have to write in a vacuum. It means that whenever you need or crave a connection to a real live reader, there it is, yours for the asking. And the beauty of feedback is—you can take it or leave it! Part of the reason we shy away from feedback is because we assign it the power of a mandate or a judgment. Feedback is neither of those things. It is simply a resource to help you create the poems or stories or essays you want to create; to help you be the writer you want to be.

Consider all the ways that feedback can serve you in achieving your goals. Feedback can help you polish your skills, hone your writerly instincts, and massage your words into shapely prose or poetry much faster than going it alone. Equally important, feedback can serve as a source of inspiration and motivation. It can energize you to go at it again, make it better, dig deeper, and discover for yourself what happens next and why. Creating an inspired and polished work can be a long and murky process. No wonder so many writers are plagued by two debilitating questions: What the hell am I trying to say here? And Who the hell cares anyway? Feedback is one of the best defenses against this kind of self-doubt and its parasitic sidekick, writer's block.

Writers need to come up with a definition of feedback that embraces all of these positive attributes. And while we are at it, we need to make sure that our definition takes into account the fact that feedback can manifest in a multitude of forms. Yes, feedback can be a critical response to a manuscript, someone telling the writer what is wrong with his writing. That may be exactly the form of feedback that serves the writer best, depending on where the story is at, and where the writer's head is at on any given day.

But feedback can also take the form of listening to a writer talk about his work. "Wow, tell me more about this sculptor in twelfth-century France." "Tell me why it matters to this old woman to live out her life in her own home." "Tell me how this chess fanatic uses the game to avoid the reality of his bad marriage." Letting the writer hear himself talk—and showing that you are interested in his subject matter—not only helps him crystallize his thoughts, but also helps to solidify his faith in the project.

Feedback can take the form of brainstorming. "What if you gave your narrator a secret crush?" "What if you set the story in an Alaskan village rather than downtown Seattle?" "What if you moved these seven paragraphs around?" This form of feedback stimulates the writer's creativity, reminding him that the story's elements are his to manipulate and recreate as he sees fit.

Feedback can be an affirmation. "You're doing great!" "I know you can do this!" "I can't wait to read more!"

Feedback can be a kick in the pants. "I want to see a second draft by next Thursday at four."

Or feedback can simply be a walk around the block with a friend because sometimes what you need more than anything is to get away from writing for a spell. Your conversation doesn't even have to be about the story because while you and your friend are debating whether you would want your dogs cloned, or complaining about those neighbors who let their kids run wild, your right brain will be doing its thing, quietly making connections, registering patterns, and solving your plot snarl for you.

So what is the definition of feedback as it relates to writing? Given all the positive things that feedback can help achieve, and all the useful forms that feedback can take, I would define feedback as *any response* to the writer or his work that helps him write more and write better. Better yet, I would define feedback as any response that helps the writer write more, write better, and be a happier person (because writers are always happier when they are writing successfully).

Now *that* is the kind of definition that would put a positive spin on feedback. That is the kind of definition that would encourage even the most timid writers to avail themselves of this terrific resource throughout the writing process. In fact, that is the perfect definition of feedback as it relates to writing, or at least the perfect definition according to me. But since you won't find a better one anywhere in the dictionary, let's all consider mine the definitive meaning of the word.

feed'back' *n.* (writing): any response to a writer or his work that helps him write more, write better, and be happier.

Doesn't it make you want to race out and get some?

EQ

People are not supposed to know their IQs. Schools, for example, go to great lengths to hide IQ scores from students and their parents, locking the records in remote file cabinets where only the guidance counselor and the janitor can access them when necessary. I can tell you from personal experience that this policy of secrecy should never be lifted.

I know my IQ and this knowledge has caused me nothing but grief. My husband, unfortunately for him, is to blame. Stephen is a clinical psychologist and when we got married he was still in graduate school. Part of his training meant learning how to give IQ tests, so one day I agreed he could practice on me. Big mistake. In retrospect, it's obvious that no couple should engage in this kind of behavior because there is some information—how you eat when no one is looking, the number of your former sex partners, and exactly how smart you really are (versus how smart you *think* you are)—that should remain outside the bounds of marital knowledge. Still, I was a starry-eyed newlywed at the time and wanted to help out my beloved. I also was sure I could nail that IQ test to the wall.

As part of the test, my husband read off a long span of digits and made me recite them backwards from memory. He showed me pictures that I had to arrange in a logical sequence. He asked me if I knew the name of the president during the Civil War. Up to this point in the testing I was doing great, imagining my IQ right up there alongside Einstein's and Dr. Seuss's and whoever the genius was that invented control-top pantyhose.

Then came object assembly, a test of spatial reasoning. My hubby handed me some puzzle pieces, told me to fit them together into a recognizable object, and started his stopwatch. I turned the pieces this way and that, assembling them in all sorts of permutations. Were they supposed to form an elephant? A tree? An elephant stuck in a tree? As the minutes ticked away, so did the points of my IQ. My husband finally had to pry the still-disjointed pieces out of my hands. From there, things went downhill fast.

After the testing, Steve combined all the subtest scores, scaled everything in accordance with my age, and calculated my full-scale IQ. He was reluctant to tell me the number until I threatened to adopt one of those Vietnamese pigs for a pet, which happened to be all the rage at the time. I wish he had opted for the pig.

EQ   11

For years, I suffered within the confines of my limited IQ. Like most people, I was conditioned to believe that intellectual intelligence is the best measure of human potential. As a result, I went through my young adulthood convinced I was doomed to only a slightly-above-average future. Then, in the early 1990s, came a burst of good news. Two psychologists named John Mayer and Peter Salovey introduced the concept of EQ in the *Journal of Personality Assessment.* In case you missed that issue, *EQ* stands for Emotional Intelligence Quotient, and it is an alternative way to assess intelligence. Like your IQ, your EQ is also a predictor of future success, only instead of assessing your intellectual abilities, your EQ measures your emotional intelligence—how good you are at acting appropriately, based on your understanding of your own emotions and the emotions of others. A high EQ indicates you are likely to perform well at work, at school, and at home. A low EQ means you should go into computer programming.

Well, as soon as I heard the news about EQ, I knew I had to know mine. For this testing, though, I was determined to get a more professional assessment, so I filled out an EQ questionnaire in a woman's magazine. That is how I discovered that my EQ ran circles around my IQ. Suddenly, I realized that I had just as much potential as all those brainiacs with higher IQs. In fact, I actually had *more* potential because, when it comes to success, EQ matters even more than IQ, at least according to some experts. Armed with this new insight, my approach to life changed forever and my future has never looked brighter.

There is nothing like a fresh perspective.

The time has come for a fresh perspective on the feedback process, as well—one that takes into account not only the intellectual factors that support good writing, but the emotional factors that also play a crucial role in the feedback process. "Emotions?" You ask. "What do they have to do with addressing weak characterizations, thin plots, and passive verb choices?" "Everything," I say, because if both the writer and the feedback provider are unaware of their own and the other person's needs, feelings, and motives, then the feedback process is likely to do more harm than good.

Consider a typical feedback scenario. On one side of the feedback process is the writer; and, let's face it, every writer is a basket case. Yet, like Tolstoy's unhappy families, every writer is a basket case in her own way, which is why one writer may find a particular comment helpful, while another writer may be crushed by the exact same comment and do something drastic, like chuck writing altogether and decide to become a life coach. On the other side of the exchange is the feedback provider. This person's first concern, naturally, is to sound smart, which is why so many workshop peers and writing instructors often end up trouncing around the submitter's psyche like Thing One and Thing Two in *The Cat in the Hat,* not intending to harm, but generating a lot of toxic feedback nonetheless.

I remember being in a workshop years ago with a twenty-something woman who felt compelled to tell an older writer in the group that her memoir wasn't "meaningful." Trying to be helpful, the twenty-something advised the woman to write about the child welfare system or overcrowded prisons, something that had some significance. Not surprisingly, this feedback provider went on to become a social worker. She is a good person. Only her feedback was toxic, causing the writer to doubt the value of her own existence.

In my roles as workshop leader and editor, I, too, have made plenty of toxic bloopers. Maybe I said too much or too little. Maybe I worried more about what I had to say than what the writer needed to hear. Maybe I was just having a bad hair day and was distracted by the fact that my head had suddenly sprouted a hay bale. Regardless of the specifics, in each of these situations I must have left my EQ in my other purse because the result of my feedback was that the writer ended up feeling overwhelmed, despondent, or wanting to kill me. It doesn't get much more toxic than that.

For both writers and feedback providers, applying emotional intelligence is the key to detoxifying the feedback process. Writers, if you want to use feedback to be a better, more productive writer, you need to pay attention to your feelings. What kind of feedback motivates you? What causes you to melt down? At what stage in the writing process do you often feel stuck? How can you manage the feedback process in a way that feels supportive and productive? How are you getting in your own way when processing feedback? Feedback providers, you need to be equally attuned to the emotional component of the process. What is your personal agenda? What impact are your words having on the writer? Are you paying attention to what the writer really needs to hear, right at that moment, to move his work forward? When writers entrust us with their works-in-progress, it is our responsibility to remember that there is an actual, living, breathing, sentient person on the other end of our wisdom.

Let me add here, in case you think I have gone off the touchy-feely deep end, that communication experts far more clinically minded than I'll ever be have weighed the relevance of emotion in the feedback process. As a result, we now have formulas such as "the feedback sandwich," which advises that when you are critiquing something, whether it is an employee's job performance or a writer's manuscript, you will meet with more receptivity if you start with a positive comment and end with a positive comment, sandwiching the downer comment in the middle. Other communication experts go even further, advocating a four-to-one ratio of positive to negative (or "kiss to kick") comments.

Goodness knows, all those feeding frenzies that pass as writing workshops would be well served if only there were some kind of formula to stop the madness. But formulas for doling out positives and negatives don't always help, especially since those terms can often be confusing. Here is what I mean. Most people think positive feedback is when a reader says something nice about a writer's story, and negative feedback is when the reader says something critical. An example of positive feedback might be, "Gee, you write just like Stephen King." An example of negative feedback might be, "Gee, you write just like Stephen King." Do you see the difference? Neither do I.

To address the problem of toxic feedback, we need to remember that feedback isn't simply an equation that can be solved with formulas and ratios, but an *interaction* between humans, one in which personality and temperament (not to mention alcohol, cigarettes, and chocolate) all have a significant effect on the outcome. Overlook the human factor during the feedback interaction, and you are ignoring the heart that gives writing its life.

As writers and feedback providers, one of the smartest things we can do is to be conscious of the emotional factors that inspire or undermine the creative process. Whether we are on the giving or receiving end of feedback, success comes from understanding our own feelings and the feelings of others, and acting accordingly. Maybe computer programmers can function in their work just fine without emotional intelligence, but when the work involves humans, it's a different story. After all, it doesn't take an Einstein to figure out that humans are nothing if not emotional.

✍ Sarah Stewart Taylor *"Wow! This could be my job."*

When mystery novelist Sarah Stewart Taylor was in ninth grade, her English teacher, Mrs. Mongoluzzi, gave the class an assignment: take a Robert Frost poem and write a piece of fiction about it. Sarah chose "Fire and Ice," a nine-line verse that ponders how the world will end. Sarah created a story that took place after a nuclear holocaust, about a lone woman with her baby wandering across the apocalyptic landscape describing what happened. "From what I remember," says Sarah, "there's this revelation at the end of the story that survival is futile. A classic freshman mentality," she laughs.

Sarah also remembers that this was one of the first assignments that didn't feel like an assignment. "I wasn't thinking about how long it would take me. I was really on fire when I was writing" (no pun intended). A few days after Sarah turned in the assignment, Mrs. Mongoluzzi asked her to stay after class. The teacher walked Sarah out into the hallway. "I can still see her," Sarah says, "very elegant, very Talbot's. A formal person, but she loved literature. She told me, 'You know, *you're a writer.*' It was one of those really powerful moments. I remember so vividly standing in the hall of that high school and having this feeling of joy. I remember thinking, *Wow! This could be my job.*"

Sarah had a comparable defining moment at age twenty-two, during a creative-writing class at Trinity College in Dublin. She'd gone to graduate school to study literature, thinking she would be an academic, but still sought out writing classes, hoping for encouragement. At Trinity, her instructor was Thomas Kilroy, best known as a playwright, but also an award-winning novelist once short-listed for the Booker Prize. The class had been discussing Sarah's work, many of the students projecting their own styles onto her writing. "There was this guy writing a Faulknerian short story complaining I wasn't Faulknerian enough," Sarah recalls. "The sci-fi writer wanted more aliens. I remember near the end of the discussion, the instructor said, 'I'm not going to say I agree or disagree, but I am going to say that Sarah should just keep writing this novel and try to get it published.'"

After graduation, Sarah worked as a newspaper reporter and editor, an assistant to a literary agent, a teacher in a prison, and a community college professor. While working these jobs, she also labored for several years on a mystery novel, featuring amateur detective and art historian Sweeney St. George, who specializes in gravestones and funerary art. Published in 2003, that novel, *O' Artful Death,* earned her an Agatha Award nomination and has spawned three more Sweeney mysteries. *O' Artful Death* was similar to the novel Sarah presented to her creative writing class at Trinity only in the fact that both stories were set in a Vermont arts colony. But the two books—one published, one long-abandoned—are forged by a deeper connection.

"Basically, what Tom was saying in front of that writing class was, 'Don't listen to them.' He was saying, 'You can.' It was that same feeling of joy I had in ninth grade," Sarah recalls. "It was such a small thing what he said—'I think you should try to publish this.' He may have said it to twenty other students that term, but it hit some nerve. I remember walking home after class that day. I lived in this part of Dublin called Irishtown, and it was a long walk along the docks. I remember it vividly, this feeling of wanting to skip down the docks."

GETTING FEEDBACK

Is It You . . . or Is It Them?

When a feedback provider criticizes a writer's work—say he tells the writer his story could use some editing, or is pretty clever, or he didn't get around to reading it yet—a lot of writers react in one of the following ways. They either begin loathing themselves because they are obviously terrible writers, or they begin loathing the feedback provider because he is clearly mean and insensitive, and he deserves to be punched. If you are a writer yourself, you are likely to think these responses to feedback are perfectly normal. If you are a mentally sound individual, you are likely to recognize these reactions as *over*reactions that could be counterproductive when trying to write more and write better.

As a writer, you have no hope of surviving, let alone thriving in, the feedback process if you don't first recognize your own role in creating the kind of toxicity that can result in literary paralysis or an assault charge. Therefore, if either of these overreactions mirror your typical response to feedback, here is a suggestion. The next time you find yourself immediately feeling angry or defensive or despondent during a critique of your work, ask yourself the following question: Is it you . . . or is it them? Think about this seriously. Dig deep in your soul for a second or two. Soon, the answer will be obvious. It is you, of course. You. You. You. Definitely you.

Yes, you.

In fact, even when it is them, it is still also you because, when it comes to hearing feedback, most writers are chasms of hypersensitivity. At the mere whiff of a critical remark we lose any sense of perspective, not to mention humor. Chalk this up to our artistic temperaments, or maybe some atavistic fight-or-flight response left over from our cave-writing days; regardless, the truth remains the same. When it comes to our words, we are predisposed to overreacting to feedback, a characteristic as indicative of our status as writers as hemophilia is evidence of royal lineage in Russia.

Despite this reality, some writers profess to be perfectly secure in their abilities to respond rationally to criticism. To prove their point, these "secure" writers aggressively solicit negative feedback. "Tell it to me straight," they say to their fellow workshop participants or editors or spouses. "I want you to be brutally honest." When I hear someone say words to this effect, a big alarm goes off in my head. *Code H! Code H! This is an especially hyper-sensitive person!*

For this insight, I have Jim to thank, a pharmacist and gifted writer who took one of my first fiction-writing workshops. When Jim introduced himself to the group, he announced that he had been writing stories for years. He had shared his work with family and friends and they had all praised his efforts, but these were *nice* people—Jim dismissed them with a wave of his nail-gnawed hand. What he wanted from me and the other workshop members was *serious* feedback. To drive home the point that he could handle tough criticism, Jim also let us know that he was training for a marathon and restored vintage Mustangs.

Eager for this serious feedback, Jim was the first workshop participant to submit a manuscript for discussion. The piece was a short story about a character who, coincidentally, restored vintage Mustangs and was training for a marathon. Already, Jim had demonstrated his grasp of one of the most popular, albeit controversial, tenets of fiction writing: write what you know.

The following week, the group discussed Jim's story. The readers were generous in their admiration, and the tone of the discussion was upbeat. As usual when a good story launches the workshop, some of the other participants started issuing warnings about how their own future submissions were sure to pale in comparison. This, too, had to make Jim feel good.

A few evenings after the meeting, my phone rang close to midnight. The good news was that the late call did not mark the demise of a relative. The bad news was that the caller was a devastated Jim, who told me that he was going to drop out of the workshop. Clearly, everyone in the group had hated his story. He had decided to quit writing and focus solely on doling out pharmaceuticals, a far more rewarding pursuit, even in this age of Medigap. After about an hour on the phone, I managed to convince Jim to continue attending the workshop. He agreed, reluctantly, though it was clear he still had some doubts.

Was it me . . . or was it Jim?

My take on the discussion of Jim's story was that the other workshop members had clearly communicated their enthusiasm. Was I delusional? A good workshop leader is a master of attentive listening, yet I must have been replaying *Brady Bunch* episodes in my head to be so far off the mark in my recollection of what took place during that first evening of our workshop.

Because I provide typed, summary critiques for every submission, I was able to retrieve my comments to Jim off the computer. My two-and-a-half pages of commentary gushed with honest praise, all the more meaningful because I confessed that, as a rule, I can't stand stories about cars, especially muscle cars like Mustangs. In my notes, I had articulated my admiration for the psychological complexity of Jim's protagonist, his compelling plot, and the clarity of his language.

In one paragraph, I did suggest that Jim might want to edit with an eye toward trimming some of the "as you know, Bob's," related to the history of Mustang performance. Authenticating background information is terrific, I reassured Jim, but long, technical explanations inserted into a character's thoughts or dialogue typically feel contrived to the reader, and disrupt the flow of the narrative. I pointed out one example in Jim's story, in which the protagonist reflects, for no apparent reason, on how the Mach 1 was introduced in 1969 with a 351, 390, or 428 V8, and a stiffer suspension; how manual drum brakes were standard at the time; and how the average new car had a top speed of 125 miles per hour with 12 miles per gallon. A much better strategy, I suggested, would be to disperse some of this background information throughout the narrative, if and when it could be tethered to relevant moments in the plot.

"That said," I wrote in the conclusion of my critique, "a wonderful story!"

After rereading my feedback, I asked myself again— *Was it me . . . or was it Jim?* I reread my notes. I reread them again.

It was Jim. Definitely Jim.

Writers, even as you are reading this chapter, I invite you to take a moment to formally acknowledge your predisposition to hypersensitivity. Own this characteristic shared by writers from prehistoric times to Jim—especially if you are *serious* about your work. "I am hypersensitive!" Say it loud. Say it proud. If necessary, paint a big *H* on your forehead to remind yourself and others of your tendency to emotionally decompose.

The purpose of this admission is not to try to guilt feedback providers into going easy on you when critiquing your stories. In fact, professing your hypersensitivity as a writer may actually have the opposite effect because it can easily be misinterpreted as an invitation to flick you upside the head. The purpose is to acknowledge that when it comes to that all-important question—Is it you . . . or is it them?—the answer is you. Definitely you. You. You. You.

Yes, you.

And the sooner you own up to this fact, the sooner you will be able to see beyond the distraction of your own high dudgeon, and focus on the feedback with more attention, acuity, and even appreciation.

Post script. For those of you who are curious, Jim completed the writing workshop, sold his Mustang story to a car-related publication, and continued to write fiction. In fact, about five years later, Jim phoned me out of the blue, asking to enroll again in the workshop. Now he was writing an historical novel set during the French and Indian War. "Just one thing," Jim cautioned, as I enthusiastically welcomed him back. "Sometimes your group has a tendency to be too nice during the discussions, and I'm looking for *serious* feedback."

Processing Feedback

Here is what most writers forget: You are the boss of your own story. Not the other writers in your critique group. Not the famous author whose workshop you were lucky enough to get into at the Iowa Summer Writing Festival. Not even your mother-in-law who comes into your house while you are at work and vacuums the mattresses because somebody has to protect her grandchildren from dust mites. When it comes to applying feedback, you—and only you—are the one who gets to determine what stays and what goes in your story. And that is a good thing.

So why do most writers forget this fact? Why do most of us, when confronted with feedback, automatically relinquish authorial control and start scribbling copious notes all over our manuscripts like some junior intern on Red Bull, determined to meet everyone's demands. "Yes sir, I'll rewrite the whole novel in first person and add more sex scenes, no problem." "No ma'am, I don't need to kill off the grandfather in the end; I thought he was a nice guy, too." "Yes, sir, I'm sure my memoir would sell better if I were raised in a Chinese orphanage. I'll get on it right away."

When processing feedback most of us need assertiveness training, if not for the sake of our stories then for our mental health. For one thing, you will never be able to please everybody anyway. Newton's third principle of motion explains that for every action there is an equal and opposite reaction, and any given writing workshop underscores this same reality. For instance, if your well-respected writing instructor hates the scene depicting your main character's long bus trip to Reno, it is inevitable that another respected feedback provider in that very same workshop—likely the graphic novelist/performance artist whom you have had a crush on since day one—will drill his tortured eyes into your soul and insist that the long bus trip is the one part of your story that rocked his world. So now what do you do?

There is only one thing you can do. When processing feedback you must plant yourself figuratively in the corner office, plunk down one of those massive paperweights on your desk that reads "Head Cheese," and claim creative control. Because if you don't, whenever you sit down to revise your work you are likely to start second-guessing and compromising and rewriting by committee, until your story starts to read more like word salad than impassioned, polished prose.

Acknowledging that you are the boss of your own story makes processing feedback a lot more palatable, even when you are in the hot seat. Who doesn't have a silent meltdown when their writing is up for review, whether by a single reader or an entire writing workshop? I know when the time comes for my work to be critiqued, I always have a strong urge to toss back a few in the powder room, if only to stop the soundtrack in my head. *They're gonna hate it, I know they're gonna hate it . . . Oh, I can already hear the workshop star, Roberta, with her usual refrain, "Kill your darlings . . ." (which she keeps attributing to Mark Twain). And Lars, with that weary note of resignation in his voice, "It doesn't matter if it really happened, you have to make it convincing on the page," and Marilyn, throwing her fifty-thousand-dollar advance in my face by telling me, "Add more conflict. Only trouble is interesting."*

But then I remind myself that I am the boss of my own story so there is really no need to get all worked up in my head. If someone does trash my work—"Well, this is a sorry excuse for a story"—I can and should hold that person accountable. "What exactly do you mean by 'sorry excuse'? What part was sorry? Why was it sorry?" Like any good boss, I should strive to be inclusive, encouraging all my readers to speak up and be forthright. I can listen to their comments with equanimity, even appreciation, knowing that soon I will return to my corner office, shut the door on the cacophony, and continue to process all feedback on my own time and in my own way.

Over the years, I have calculated that feedback on any given piece of writing always falls into one of three categories, and breaks down into the following percentages: 14 percent of feedback is dead-on; 18 percent is from another planet; and 68 percent falls somewhere in between. I am not a statistician (actually, I am hopeless in math), but I find it reassuring to know that there is an element of predictability to the art of processing feedback.

Dead-on feedback is the kind of feedback that feels right the moment you hear it, usually because it confirms something you already knew on a gut level. *Oh, yeah,* you think when you hear dead-on feedback, *now I remember not liking that passage myself, but I was having such a good writing day I just kept going and forgot all about it.* Dead-on feedback is also the kind of feedback that can lead to those wonderful Aha! moments. For example, a reader might tell you that he isn't hooked by your story until the scene on page eight when the surgeon amputates the wrong leg. For weeks, you had been struggling with those opening pages that summarize the protagonist's medical school education, trying and failing to get them right.

Now, just like Archimedes in the bathtub, you see the solution all at once: *Cut the opening! Cut the opening! It only gets in the way.* Processing dead-on feedback is easy because a small region of your brain—the right hemisphere anterior-superior temporal gyrus—flashes you the instant message: *Eureka!*

The 18 percent of feedback from another planet is also relatively easy to process, once you catch on to the fact that the feedback provider has issues. See how long it takes you to figure out where this feedback provider is coming from: "I think your main character should kill off her boyfriend. Why? Because men are pigs! All men are pigs! They're born pigs, they die pigs, and in between they give you a promise ring on Valentine's Day, but then they make out with your ex–best friend Sheena at Happy Hour two Fridays ago, and I know this for a fact because my new best friend Heather saw the whole thing while I was out in the parking lot throwing up after we did all those two-shots-for-two-dollars . . ." Feedback from another planet should be discounted for obvious reasons, but make sure you don't discount the feedback provider along with it. She may surprise you when critiquing your next story.

Which brings me to the remaining 68 percent of feedback, which falls somewhere in between dead-on feedback and feedback from another planet. This category of feedback may include a timid suggestion that speaks volumes about a weakness in your plot. It may include a brilliant insight that ends up being wrong for your current story, but will certainly apply to another story down the road. Or it may include a blunt comment that raises your hackles, but also the level of your prose.

One of the first things to look for when processing in-between feedback is a consensus of opinion. Say you present your work to two or three trusted readers or members of a critique group, and more than one of them found your ending confusing—Did the father reconcile with his teenage son or didn't he? If your intention in the story is to clearly show a reconciliation then you should pay particular attention to any type of collective opinion on this point. This doesn't mean you should automatically change your ending, but it does mean you should scrutinize your motives if you don't change it. Are you preserving the ending because you really think it works and is perfect as is, or because you are being lazy or overly attached to the writing?

Now take the same story, but a different scenario. Let's assume half your readers "got" the ending, but the other half didn't understand your intent. If this is the case, first you should feel good about batting .500. Then you should take the time to process the feedback of your excluded readers more carefully, just in case they offer any insights about how you might tweak or

Tips for Processing Feedback

Be open: You can't begin to process feedback if you won't let it in. I know how hard it is to curb the impulse to defend your work against every little criticism, but try. If it helps, write a note on your palm as a reminder—*Hush up!*—and refer to it whenever you hear yourself going on and on. In a workshop setting, some groups institute a "no talking" policy to prevent writers from interrupting the critique, but I feel that's an extreme measure. Writers should feel free to ask questions or raise issues that inform the discussion.

Resist the urge to explain: A teacher I know who works with both writers and actors once noted that if you tell a performer something didn't work in his performance, he simply drops the line or fixes it; whereas writers have a natural impulse to explain why they wrote something a certain way, or what they were trying to do in the piece. As writers, we need to resist the urge to explain. Explanations give feedback providers too much information, making it harder for them to separate what is coming across on the page from what you have told them.

Little by little: It is easy to get overwhelmed when processing feedback, especially if you try to take it in all at once. After a feedback session, sift through all the comments once, but then put them away and only worry about addressing one issue at a time. For example, if a reader has told you that your plot is slow and your main character seems shallow, forget about the plot issue for the time being and concentrate on character. Or focus on moving your story forward, and worry about character development in the next draft.

Ignore feedback until you are ready for it: If you are on a roll with your writing, don't let feedback stop you. Some writers avoid feedback until they have taken their work as far as they can on their own. This makes sense if hearing feedback too soon interferes with your own creative vision. But feedback can also serve you in the midst of a productive period. The value of hearing feedback, and then putting it in your mental lockbox as you push forward, is that this allows your unconscious to quietly process the outside information in a way that informs your writing in sync with your instincts—without slowing you down.

Try out the feedback: Sometimes the only way to judge feedback is to play it out on the page where your own writerly instincts can react to it. For example, if a trusted reader is adamant that your first-person, coming-of-age novel should be written in third person, try writing a couple chapters this way. See for yourself what you lose or gain. If several readers think that your main character isn't likable, write a scene inside or outside the story that shows your protagonist doing something endearing. Whether you ultimately use the scene or not, this is a great exercise in character development. No writing is a waste of effort.

Give yourself time: If you are at a point in the revision process where you can't tell whether you are making things better or worse—stop! Move away from the computer with your hands in the air, before you do any permanent damage. Take a break from writing, or start something brand-new. It is remarkable how a good night's sleep or a short period away from the manuscript can restore clarity, and help you process feedback in a way that leads to enlightenment.

revise the ending to make it more accessible to a broader audience. For instance, Darla, the romance writer in the group, offers the following feedback: "If you want to make it clear that the father and son reconcile at the end of your story, why don't you just have them hug in the last scene?"

Your knee-jerk reaction to Darla's feedback may be to dismiss it outright because Darla writes genre fiction and you are a snob. But part of processing feedback is getting over yourself, as well as recognizing that sometimes feedback can be wrong in the particulars, but right overall. Okay, so the father in your story is not a hugger. But what if he did show some outward sign of love for his son at the end? What if he offered the boy his prized penknife, for example, the one that his own father gave him when he left home as a teenager? That scene would maintain the integrity of the father's character, add a wonderful symbolic gesture, and clarify the ending for more readers.

Two of the biggest mistakes writers can make when processing feedback is to categorize readers too quickly—"good reader"; "bad reader"—and to do the same with their comments—"good advice"; "bad advice." Sixty-eight percent of the time, that's not how feedback works. As writers, we have to be vigilant to fight the impulse to accept or ignore feedback wholesale. Just recently, someone gave me some heavy-handed advice that I thought was totally ridiculous, until I took the time to scale it down in service to my story.

Processing feedback effectively means being receptive to hearing a variety of opinions, but filtering it all through your own writerly lens. What serves your intent? What rings true? What is your own inner voice telling you to do? Sometimes it can be hard to tune in to your own instincts after a feedback session, especially when the comments have been coming at you like the arrows flying at St. Sebastian. But that's when you need to hightail it to your corner office and rest your cheek on the cool weight of your Head Cheese paperweight. Breathe. Give yourself some space and quiet. Listen carefully, and I promise you, your inner voice will speak up over time. And here is what it will tell you: 14 percent of the feedback feels dead-on; 18 percent is from another planet. And 68 percent feels like Darla, coming at you with good intentions and arms outstretched. Just remember, Darla can comfort you, or she can squeeze you. As boss of your own story, it is up to you to decide.

☞ Samina Ali *"I would have sold my soul."*

When Samina Ali had forty pages written of what turned out to be her first novel, *Madras on Rainy Days,* she sent them to four agents. Within a week, every one of them had phoned her, eager to take her on as a client. Third on the line was one of the top agents in the country, a woman based in Los Angeles, who started the conversation by gushing about Samina's writing. This agent repeatedly addressed Samina as "darling." She informed Samina she'd be sending a contract immediately—"just a formality." She promised to make Samina "the next hot thing."

"When I got her call I just flipped," says Samina, who was twenty-six at the time and a graduate of the MFA program at the University of Oregon. Samina had been writing scenes of the novel off and on since she was twenty, revising just the first chapter alone for two years. After graduate school, she stopped writing completely for a year—"I had so many demons in my head"—but ultimately returned to *Madras.* Forty pages later, Samina's phone was ringing. "It was so exciting to think this woman could be *my* agent," the author recalls. "I thought, you can't do any better than this."

"You know, Samina, darling," said the agent from L.A., "There's a new 'F' word. Do you know what it is?"

Samina, embarrassed by her naiveté, racked her brain. "No . . ."

"Fiction," said the agent. "Darling, nobody writes fiction anymore." Samina would have to change her novel, some of which was based on her experience as a Muslim woman in an arranged marriage, to a memoir.

"But a lot of the novel isn't true," Samina explained to the agent.

"Do you think Maxine Hong Kingston's memoir is true?" the agent countered. "Do you think Frank McCourt's *Angela's Ashes* is true? They're not true; they're just marketed as true. And I don't want your book to have anything to do with you and your arranged marriage. I want it to be about you and your father."

Samina's mind was racing. What could she write about her father? "The book's not about my father," she apologized.

"Just write anything you want about *a* father. We'll collaborate, just as I collaborate with all my authors. No writer writes a book alone. We'll call your memoir *Demon Lover*. We'll write *Demon Lover* together!" The agent wanted a manuscript from Samina in ten months. *Ten months,* thought Samina. *I can do it!*

"We're not just going to sell *Demon Lover*," the agent went on. "We're going to sell Samina. Just *Samina!* No last name. You're gorgeous, darling. We're going to put you on the cover of every magazine. I want you to think big! Big! Don't just think of yourself as a writer, think of yourself as a rock star." Samina was spellbound by the agent's exuberance. A rock star! *Demon Lover!* By *Samina!*

The contract arrived from California the next day. Samina signed it, but this was the weekend so she would have to wait until Monday to drop it in the mail. On Sunday, Samina received another call in the morning. This one was from the fourth agent she had queried. His name was Eric Simonoff, a vice president of Janklow & Nesbit Associates in Manhattan. Eric had spent the previous night reading Samina's forty pages, and was phoning her from his home. They spoke for over two hours.

"We talked about *my* book," says Samina. "It was the most refreshing, comfortable conversation. It was the first time I realized that stories are universal. It was startling to me that this white, Jewish man from New York related to a Muslim, feminist novel. I felt understood." Goodbye, *Demon Lover.* Welcome back, *Madras on Rainy Days.*

In hindsight, Samina can't believe how close she came to choosing the other agent, the star-maker from Los Angeles who called her "darling" and wanted her to write a memoir about a father, any father. "When you're young and impressionable, the process is very seductive," Samina cautions. "I remember thinking, this woman must know what she's doing; look at how famous her authors are; I can become *Samina!* When Eric called two days later," Samina says, "it was like this window opened up in my mind, and I felt like I'd been set free."

After their conversation that Sunday morning, Eric sent a contract to Samina the next day, and that's the one she unhesitatingly put in the mail. A very good move, Samina emphasizes, and not just because Eric later sold the completed manuscript to Farrar, Straus & Giroux, garnering her the largest advance this prestigious publisher had ever offered to a first-time author. The book also went on to be awarded the 2005 Prix Premier Roman Etranger (Best First Novel in Translation of the Year) by France and also was a finalist for the PEN/Hemingway Award in Fiction. "I really, really would have trapped myself in a very unhealthy relationship," Samina says of her near-seduction by the other agent. "Who would have taken me seriously? Would Farrar have even considered *Demon Lover?* Would I have been on the cover of *Poets and Writers?* My career would have been over by now," Samina says. "I would have sold my soul."

Twenty-Two Years

One time I went with a friend of a friend to lunch, my treat, so I could pick his brain about feedback. This man was a children's librarian and aspiring author who had just received a knock-your-socks-off publishing deal for his first novel. I'm talking about the kind of offer the rest of us scribblers fantasize about incessantly when we should be working on our own novels, or at least on our abs. I'm talking hard cover and paperback rights from a major publishing house, a two-book contract, and the one thing that every writer craves more than anything else in the world—an advance large enough to give us an excuse to quit our day jobs. This friend of a friend had already given his notice at story hour.

When I spoke with this man about *Toxic Feedback*, the first thing he did was criticize the title of my book. But right after that he claimed, with quite a bit of assertiveness, that when he was working on his own book he never solicited feedback from anybody.

"Never?" I asked.

"Never ever," he assured me, brandishing a knife over his blackened chicken Caesar salad. After all, he explained, how could an outsider possibly have more insight into his book than he did?

Never ever. The notion gave me pause. Maybe this friend of a friend had a point. If you are the one who is writing the book, why *should* you trouble yourself with other people's opinions? From this man's perspective, my own book's premise—that feedback is a terrific resource you should capitalize on throughout the writing process—now seemed entirely stupid, as stupid, for example, as adding Red Dye #3 to pistachio nuts. Who needs it? Why bother? In the end, you'll only end up with something unnatural, toxic, and needlessly messy. Suddenly, I experienced a crisis of confidence.

My crisis lasted until dessert. As this friend of a friend was enjoying his tiramisu, he casually mentioned that it had taken him twenty-two years to complete his novel. Yes, I had heard him correctly. Twenty-two years. That's two decades, going on three. Time enough to see five presidents come and go in the Oval Office, the advent of personal computing, and a film version of *Charlie's Angels,* plus a sequel. Such a span of time doesn't necessarily imply any dysfunction in the writer or his work habits (after all, writing is not a race), except for this one additional fact shared by this friend of a friend. During those two decades he labored on his novel, he also experi-enced extended, want-to-put-your-head-through-the-plaster bouts of writer's block, self-doubt, and boredom.

Nothing could have cheered me up more. In fact, now I recognized this man as a veritable poster child for *Toxic Feedback;* the embodiment of my book's target audience. I understand that novelists, or writers of any kind, need to allow time for their ideas and stories to gestate quietly, without in-terference from busybody, opinionated feedback providers. I am also not arguing the fact that this man is an excellent writer who should defer to his own editorial judgment during the revision process. But twenty-two years. Think about how much artistic pain he might have avoided, how many other novels he might have produced in those two decades, and how much happier the childhood of his now-grown sons might have been, if he hadn't been so fanatical about squirreling away his work-in-progress. Despite the cliché, time is not on our side. As this writer said to his own agent, whom he temporarily fired when the woman failed to send his manuscript to publishers at a pace to his liking, "I'm not getting any younger."

Certainly, there will always be dry spells during the writing process. In truth, I think short, agonizing episodes of writer's block, self-doubt, and boredom are actually healthy by-products of the creative process; your un-conscious's way of saying, *Hey, Mr. Thinks-He-Knows-Everything, stop pes-tering me for a while so I can sort out this plot in peace.* But I would suggest that *extended* bouts of writer's block, self-doubt, and boredom are not a healthy part of the creative process. I am talking about those bleak periods that go on for weeks, maybe months, maybe years, when writers find them-selves asking, *Why? Why am I doing this? Shouldn't I be spending my six min-utes of free time doing something that is actually important, like teaching my eleven-year-old to read?* These are the dark days when soliciting feedback is most important.

People typically turn to feedback for help with editing. For example, what could be better than an outside perspective to quickly alert you to the fact that your opening chapter, as precious as it is, is spoiled rotten and could use some solid discipline—say editing down the first seventy-four pages of description about the narrator's breach birth to a single declarative sentence? But the value of feedback isn't limited to advice about structure and wordsmithing. Feedback is just as much about bolstering the writer's faith in himself and excitement about his project along the way. It is about getting some external validation.

Let's say your manuscript is a mess and you don't have a clue where to go from here. At this point, the best thing you can do is to show your work to a feedback provider, maybe a trusted friend, or an online critique group, or perhaps even a lively, healthy workshop in your community. Once you do this, your readers will inevitably begin talking about the characters you made up as if they are real. (Okay, most of them are thinly disguised depictions of your relatives, but that's irrelevant at the moment.) Your readers will let you know, in no uncertain terms, that they collectively despise (in a most satisfying way) your story's antagonist, Frieda, the heiress who is determined to destroy your heroine's life. They will express grief over the secret past of your narrator, Martin, which prevents him from reuniting with his alienated son. The men in the group will passionately defend your complex characterization of Cindi, the flight attendant who successfully manages to land the plane curiously topless, while the women in the group will insist that her depth goes no further than her D cup. Debates will ensue, literary and otherwise. "What happens next?" the group will demand. "When can we see more?" they will ask.

With this kind of fresh perspective, a writer sees what is so hard to recognize when working in a vacuum. Your stories, even in the messy draft stage, can entertain people. Engage them in heated debates. Move them. Make them curious. Enable them to connect with someone or with an experience outside their normal realm. Writing—including writing-in-progress—nourishes and enlivens the human spirit, yours and your readers'.

Armed with these affirmations, you can return to your work with renewed confidence and vigor. You may make a lot of progress, or maybe just a little, but either way you will be better off than you were before, suffering in silence while the seasons changed. And every time you feel lost or bored for an unnatural period of time, you can renew your faith with more feedback—and more reminders from readers that your writing matters. It really does, and no one should wait twenty-two years to hear that.

Editing Your Editor

In the original version of the game show *Who Wants to Be a Millionaire,* the young man in the hot seat was stumped by the following question, worth $64,000: "What color does litmus paper turn when it comes into contact with acid—red, blue, green, or yellow?" The contestant stroked his chin and thought for a few, prolonged moments. Then he told Regis and millions of viewers he was pretty sure the answer was red. He had even worked one summer in a lab. But since $64,000 was at stake, he thought he had better use one of his lifelines to phone a friend. (The show gives contestants three "lifelines" to outside help, one of which is phone-a-friend.) So the contestant read the question aloud to his lifeline who responded immediately, "Blue. Litmus paper comes in red and blue, so when it comes in contact with acid it turns blue or stays blue."

"Are you sure?" the contestant asked. All his instincts were still telling him the answer was red.

"I'm sure about this, buddy; the answer is blue."

"Blue," the contestant told Regis and millions of viewers.

"Final answer?" asked Regis.

"Final answer," the contestant gripped his armrests.

Of course the answer was red. So it's only money, right? But that's not the point of this story. The point is that the lifeline spoke with authority. The lifeline only wanted what was best for his buddy. The lifeline is an intelligent guy (after all, you don't get selected as a phone-a-friend for your looks). Which goes to show that if your authoritative, well-meaning, intelligent lifeline can be wrong, then so can just about anybody.

Even your editor.

Editors are like lifelines to writers. They exist to save us from the embarrassment of obfuscation, sentimentality, saggy middles, misplaced modifiers, and other detractions that can cling to a manuscript like toilet paper to a shoe. What's more, editors read everything and know the market. This makes them book *experts,* and a perfect test audience for how your book is going to hold up when it is on a store shelf surrounded by thousands of eye-catching tomes, most of them written by James Patterson, James Patterson with a coauthor, or a diet guru who once helped Oprah run a marathon. So if your editor at the publishing house actually makes the effort to write you a single-spaced, six-page, editorial letter chock-full of suggestions, consider yourself very, very lucky. But remember, if she says "blue" and all your instincts say "red," don't feel like you have to go along with her suggestions.

I used to be intimidated by editors. Actually, I still am intimidated by editors, and with good reason, I might add. Editors have a lot of authority. After all, it was your editor who acquired your book in the first place, or at least ratcheted it up the wheel of decision makers. So who is to say that if you displease her in any way, perhaps by looking askance at her suggestion to make your ending more upbeat, that she won't have your publishing contract yanked faster than you blew through that first part of the advance on dinner and drinks at Red Lobster.

Editors even intimate this possibility in writing: "Should the publisher, in its sole judgment, conclude that the Work as first submitted cannot be revised to its satisfaction within a timely period, or after the agreed revision period, should the publisher find that the revised Work is still unacceptable for any editorial reason relating to the Work, the publisher may reject the Work by written notice to Proprietor." My goodness, no wonder I never read my publishing contracts. And no wonder one of the most common questions aspiring authors ask published authors is "Did your editor make you change stuff in your book?"

On the one hand, I think it is silly to worry in advance about whether some future editor is going to pull rank on your artistic integrity. That kind of fear will only hobble your courage to even try for publication. And let's get real. If you are that far along in the publishing process, you are probably a lot better off than you were a year or two ago when no editor cared about your depressing (read "unmarketable") ending, or the conversational style of your prose, or the unpronounceablity of your main character's name.

On the other hand, as the person who sweat blood over the manuscript and whose name will be on the cover, you are right to be paranoid, just in case there may be something to be paranoid about. I was eager for clarity on how much authority editors at publishing houses really have over manuscripts, so I called up Carrie Thornton, editorial director of Three Rivers Press (part of the Crown Publishing Group/Random House). Here is our conversation:

Me: "Can an editor make you change stuff in your book?"
Carrie: "No."
Me: "Really! Why not?"
Carrie: "I can't just say to authors, 'Do this' or 'Do that,' because, at end of the day, it's their work, so that would be doing a shady thing."
Me: "But what if it is something you *really* don't like?"
Carrie: "The most I've said is, 'Fine, if you want to get bad reviews, we'll do it your way.' But it takes a lot to get to that point. Most writers are open to suggestions, and I don't suggest anything without explaining why."
Me: "And if they still disagree?"
Carrie: "I'm happy to listen. I'm happy to be wrong when the writer convinces me his way is better. I understand what's at stake emotionally for the writer."
Me: "So you won't yank a contract over an editorial disagreement?" [Note: As you can probably tell, my style of journalism is to repeat the same question over and over, slightly reworded, until I am convinced of the answer.]
Carrie: "Editors can cancel a contract for nondelivery, or if a book is just not what was described in the contract. For example, if I commissioned a book on dog training and the writer turned in a book on how to buy a dog. But for an editorial dispute, I can't imagine canceling a contract. Once you've made the financial commitment to the writer, you want to do everything you can to publish the book because, honestly, we'd be the ones to lose money."

I found my conversation with Carrie tremendously reassuring. In retrospect, I realized that my own experiences working with editors had mirrored what Carrie had said. I have had editorial disagreements with editors at three different publishing houses (independent, giant, and academic), yet none of them ever acted the bully, and each one offered helpful suggestions. Most of the writers I talked to for this book also enjoyed good relationships with their editors. Yes, there were a few unhappy stories. One writer told me how the editor who had "inherited" her book (after the acquiring editor took another job) treated it like an unwanted orphan. Some writers were surprised at how little their editors actually edited. And, of course, every profession has its share of psychopaths.

Still, I think it is safe to assume that aspiring authors (and this includes authors like myself who aspire to continue publishing) can let go of their paranoia about editor-despots and focus on a more relevant question: "How can writers make the most of their working relationship with editors?" What follows are some suggestions that can be applied to working with *any* editor, whether at a publishing house or on a freelance basis, with the only real difference being that you will need to pay the latter for her expertise, and she probably won't mind if you call her at home (but be sure to check with her first).

Think collaboration: Don't forget, you and your editor are on the same side, sharing the mutual goal of producing the best book possible. You bring to the collaboration the vision, the voice, and a familiarity with the work that only comes from spending umpteen hours laboring over its creation. Your editor contributes a reader's perspective, professional editing skills, and a knowledge of how to size and price your book for the market. When your editor makes suggestions, be open. Be respectful. Aim to please, but don't pander.

Expect guidance, not fixes: Editors edit at two levels. They look at the big-picture issues such as pacing and development. And they look at the language—Is the wording clear? Where is there repetition or flab? In either case, most editors (with the exception of copy editors) are more likely to make general comments, pointing out patterns and a few supporting examples, rather than say, "Do this" or "Fix that." As one editor told me, "I expect and hope that writers will take a fair amount of responsibility in the revision process."

Wait: An editor once suggested a major structural change in my manuscript that I hated. Immediately, I composed an e-mail rebuttal, the gist of it being that she was WRONG! WRONG! WRONG! Thankfully, I didn't push "Send," partly because the stakes were so high I was afraid of her response. This gave me time to revise my note over the next few days, fleshing out my argument and toning down the vitriol. When I eventually did send the e-mail, my heart was racing. Only a few hours later the editor responded, "I see your point. I'm fine with the structure as is."

Picture your editor's life: Five new proposals just landed on her desk, adding to the five she didn't have time to respond to yesterday. She's got your book to edit along with several others, all with various production timetables that can't be compromised. At lunch, she needs to dash to Bloomie's to try on bathing suits under fluorescent lighting, then race to a three-hour meeting with sales and marketing. Oh, and last night she was up until two a.m. with a sick kid and a stack of trade journals that she never found time to read. Bear all this in mind when you consider her editorial judgment, and the pace at which she returns your phone calls.

Give and take: When it comes to making editorial changes, it never hurts to give a little. In fact it helps. Once you show your editor you aren't poised to fight every suggestion, she's likely to be more cooperative than commanding, especially when she hears the finality in your voice about the issues that really matter to you. "Throw 'em a bone, for Chrissakes," is how one author put it (but he writes crime novels, so that might be his police lieutenant talking).

Be a problem solver, not problem creator: "The most frustrating thing a writer can do is to consistently disagree with my suggestions, but not offer any alternatives," said one editor. "'I hate the subtitle. I hate the subtitle.' So then come up with an alternative," he advises. "The process is supposed to be an exchange of ideas."

Don't go to great lengths: I was surprised when an editor informed me that publishers feel as strongly about the length of a book as they do about its editorial treatment. That was until I learned that if a manuscript comes in just 10 percent over word count, the editor has to justify it to the folks in accounting. Books are made up of "signatures" of thirty-two pages each; adding just half a signature translates to higher production costs. Given this reality, be sure to take your contractual word count seriously and be open to trimming if your book comes in long. Publishers aren't likely to absorb the additional expenses of an oversized, over-budget tome unless, of course, it's written by Bill Clinton or Jane Fonda.

Show good manners: An author friend was working with her editor on revisions to her book. They had to work fast to meet her publishing deadline. My friend got behind on her rewrites by about a week, so she phoned the editor to tell her not to expect the new pages on time. The editor was stunned. "You're the first author who has ever called to let me know she's behind," the editor told her. "Usually they just stop taking my calls."

Bundle: As much as you would like to instant-message your editor every five seconds to make sure your revisions are on target and she still thinks the world of you, busy editors would prefer it if you bundle your reactions and questions into one longer e-mail or phone conversation. Otherwise, they really might stop loving you.

Be forceful and articulate: In my first book, my editor's boss wanted me to take out all the profanity, or at least replace the middle letters with asterisks. This would have been a great idea had I been shooting for the children's market, but this was a book of diaries from real women. So even though I was a nervous wreck about coming off as one of those pushy first-time authors, not to mention a gutter mouth, I reiterated my argument over the course of several weeks until my editor's boss reluctantly conceded. A few years later I was talking with my former editor (we no longer work together, but have remained friends) when she brought up this debate over swear words. "Thank you for being so forceful and articulate," she said. "Your arguments really helped me convince my boss." *Forceful and articulate.* This took me by surprise, and taught me a good lesson about working with editors. Because the whole time I was fighting to preserve my book's integrity, I thought my editor thought I was just being a pain in the a**.

✎ Ernest Hebert *"I wanted writing to be easy for me and it wasn't."*

In 1974, Ernest Hebert's wife, Medora, dragged him to the Bread Loaf Writers' Conference. They couldn't afford it—in fact, money was so tight they had to camp out for the two weeks of the conference—but Ernie knew he needed some instruction. "Something was wrong with my method of composition, but I didn't know what," Ernie says, "and I certainly wasn't making any progress in the material world." Ernie was thirty-three years old when he reluctantly agreed to go to Bread Loaf, and had published a single short story in college. Since then, he'd started a couple of projects, finished a lousy novel, and was drifting. "I would have quit," Ernie says, "but every once in a while I'd write one good paragraph and then I'd think, *If I can write one, I can write fifty.*"

Ernie's assigned faculty reader at Bread Loaf was the legendary writer and critic John Gardner. A few months before the conference, Ernie had submitted a manuscript for critique, a clean-typed first draft, sixty pages long, single spaced, "straight out of my id," he says. Gardner was scheduled to meet with Ernie to critique the work for a half hour on the last day of the conference. In the weeks before the meeting, Ernie was in a state of total anxiety, held together by his wife and another writer, Bill Atwill, whom he had met at the conference. "Some of the other writers there saw Bread Loaf as a vacation," Ernie says. "I hated them all because I was in a crisis and all these people were treating it like fun."

Ernie showed up at the appointed time for his meeting with his faculty reader. "I remember Gardner's face," Ernie says. "He was very blond and fair. From the profile, he looked almost pretty, feminine. Square on, he looked hard, Gestapo-like." The two men shook hands. Then Gardner picked up Ernie's thick, single-spaced manuscript, pointed to a spot about a third of the way down the first page, and said, "This is as far as I read. No real writer would write a sentence like that." End of meeting.

"It wasn't that I wanted to defend myself," Ernie says, "I was incapable of breathing. I could barely get up to leave. Gardner was happy to see me leave." Ernie never looked at that manuscript again.

When he returned home from the conference, Ernie thought about some of the themes from Gardner's lectures at Bread Loaf. *You can't just write a crummy first draft. Write every scene as if it's the only scene in the book. One bad scene is nothing but a take-off for the next bad scene.* "I began to see the wisdom of that," Ernie says. "I remembered that the things I'd written well had been written over and over. I wanted writing to be easy for me and it wasn't."

The meeting with Gardner changed Ernie's perspective. "I was hurt, but not tense anymore. I was born again." He decided he wasn't going to worry about writing a novel. For a while, an idea for a character had been insisting his attention—a small-town man outside the middle class. Ernie decided to find out more about this fellow. "I wrote longhand, typed, pencil-edited, retyped. I told myself I wouldn't move on until each section was brilliant, with at least one striking metaphor or turn on every page."

The character Ernie created was Howard Elman, the protagonist of his first novel, *The Dogs of March,* the cornerstone of the author's acclaimed Darby series, set in rural New England. The *Washington Post Book World* described the novel as "a human story in which each page offers some new insight into the human mind and heart." Twenty-five years later, *The Dogs of March* is still in print and continues to be taught at colleges and high schools across the country. The author's most recent novel, *Spoonwood,* is the sixth novel in the series, and marks Ernie's return to Darby after an almost-fifteen-year hiatus. Ernie is also the author of *The Old American,* hailed by *Kirkus Reviews* as "a brilliant work."

"Gardner was probably right," Ernie says, referring to that sixty-page, single-spaced first draft from thirty years ago. "The piece was hastily put together, not very good writing. Since then my rule has been never to show anything to anybody until I have done my best work. On occasion I've broken this rule, always to my regret."

Feedback Hotlines

One of the hardest things for me is finding the time to write. Kids, jobs that actually pay, *West Wing* reruns, life; all of these things conspire to whittle away at my writing time until I am lucky if I salvage a few hours per day for getting some words on paper. And if by some miracle I am able to sneak in some extra time at the computer, maybe after my youngest daughter gets home from kindergarten, I am well aware that the clock is ticking, *The Little Mermaid* runs for exactly eighty-three minutes (can't Disney make these movies any longer!), and I need to be an efficiency machine.

Sadly, I am not an efficiency machine, at least not when it comes to writing. This is partly because the creative process doesn't lend itself to efficiency, at least not in the same way that I can efficiently catch up on all the *People* magazines at the hair salon, or finish off a carton of mint chocolate chip ice cream without even dirtying a bowl. Even when I come to the computer with a clear vision of what I want to say, my brain often seizes up as soon as I try to translate my thoughts into standard English. Or I'll start out okay, but then find myself imprisoned in some tricky paragraph, writing it over and over again. Or I'll reread a finished chapter, but by this time it all sounds so predictable that I become convinced I must have plagiarized some tiresome author I was assigned back in junior high school. Meanwhile ticktock, ticktock, ticktock. I am stuck inside my own head, panic is setting in, and that little mermaid Ariel is downstairs racing through her movie like she's some kind of cokehead.

That's when I pick up the phone and call a feedback hotline.

If you have ever experienced a difficult writing session (and if you haven't, I don't want to hear about it), you know how a slow start or stall-out can feel like a minicrisis. And let's face it, most writers, by temperament, are not very good in a crisis because our first instinct at any sign of trouble is to do something desperate like take a nap or clean our toilets. Oddly enough, these mindless distractions can occasionally serve the creative process; but, to paraphrase Freud, sometimes a distraction is just a distraction; which is why a feedback hotline offers a great alternative. With one relatively quick, well-placed call, you just may get the information, or reality check, or spark of inspiration you need to push your way through to a productive work session.

As the name implies, a feedback hotline gives you direct access to help with whatever psychological or linguistical crisis you are facing *at the moment.* No, there is no national, toll-free hotline that provides this service to distraught writers (though now that I think of it, there should be). You can, however, easily establish your own hotline by engaging any friends who care about your mental health and want to see you succeed, or by availing yourself of other resources (teachers, workshop peers, experts in a field you are writing about . . .) who don't mind the occasional crisis call, or who are too cheap to spring for caller ID.

Here, I want to emphasize that even if the first number in your feedback hotline's speed-dial connects you to your best friend's cell phone, you should never use the hotline for social calls or a gabfest. This is a writing resource, one in which you scream *"Help!"* and the voice on the other end of the line obliges with the appropriate form of feedback. Maybe you are having trouble organizing your thoughts and could use some guidance as to how to start. Maybe you are stuck on a Gordian plot point and want to brainstorm "What if's." Maybe you have lost your sense of humor and need a reminder why you should *not* have that apple martini at ten a.m. (No, the garnish does not qualify it as part of any healthy food group). Regardless, both you and your feedback hotline need to stay focused on the writing issue at hand; the very second you feel like you have achieved any kind of breakthrough, you need to hang up the phone and push on with your writing. Don't worry about saying goodbye or other pleasantries. Your hotline will understand. Clarity is fleeting, so you don't want to waste precious seconds.

One of my own favorite feedback hotlines is my friend Nancy, whom I met years ago in graduate school when I sat one row above her in a tiered-seating classroom. It was the summer term and I had fallen off my bike the day before, which meant my raw, bloodied knees aligned exactly with her line of vision whenever she swiveled her chair. This made for a natural conversation starter that led to a long-lasting friendship. Nancy actually inspired the feedback hotline concept a few years ago when she was working as a researcher at a technology corporation and I was struggling with a big freelance writing assignment that was due all too soon.

For some reason, this particular assignment overwhelmed me more than most. One morning, in the midst of yet another frustrating, nonwriting session, I picked up the phone and called Nancy at work, partly to stave off panic and partly to see if she could meet me for an early lunch. But instead of debating the merits of Subway versus the new, cheap sushi place, I started ranting about my writing assignment. Nancy offered me a sounding board for my scattered thoughts. She didn't make me feel like an idiot for needing help. She asked questions and offered insights that helped me organize my thoughts. In essence, she turned my spontaneous rant into a productive work session. Toward the end of our conversation, when I was telling Nancy about my idea for a lead for the article, she responded, "Why don't you just write it down exactly like you told me?" So I hung up the phone and did just that.

That's when the value of having a feedback hotline first occurred to me. As insurance that I would continue to make progress on my assignment and meet my deadline, I asked Nancy if I could call her whenever I felt like I needed an outside perspective. This arrangement worked well for both of us because I couldn't afford to waste any time, and she hated her boring job. Unless I called during the minigolf tournaments her office held every Friday in the hallways, she welcomed my creative diversions. Sometimes I'd phone Nancy several mornings in a row to jump-start my thinking. Sometimes I wouldn't call for weeks because I was on a roll. Sometimes I'd just e-mail a quick question. Regardless, it always amazed me how even the smallest doses of feedback during a stagnant writing session could restore my emotional equilibrium and motivate my writing.

Unfortunately, a few months after Nancy started serving as my feedback hotline, she quit her boring job and found new, more fulfilling employment. This cut down on her availability during my working hours, and forced me to broaden my network of feedback hotlines as I moved on to new writing projects. The big upside of this change, however, is that now I can pick and choose among my hotline resources, depending on what type of feedback I require at that moment.

So now when my mind has gone blank, I often phone Meredith, because Meredith is a scientist-pagan-novelist who knows something interesting about everything.

Or I'll call Lois, who writes powerful poetry and is in her late eighties, because when Lois doesn't like something I've written she tells me bluntly, and how can I get mad at someone in her eighties?

Or I'll phone Deb, a no-nonsense editor who actually came over to my house in response to one of my calls and decluttered my impossible desk.

Or I'll call John, an academic, because he is the smartest book-person I know in real life, which makes him the perfect test subject for my half-baked ideas.

Or I'll e-mail Beth, an army sergeant once stationed at Saddam Hussein's presidential palace, because Beth writes honest, funny prose and stops me from being too writerly or sounding like Madonna with that faux British accent.

Or I'll call Steve, my husband, to ask him to pick up the kids and a pizza because I am *this* close to achieving a breakthrough on my own.

Or I'll call Mary, who wrote a critically acclaimed memoir and consults with companies about workplace discrimination, because Mary converses in eloquent, full sentences, and always, always knows just the right words. For example, when I was talking with her about this chapter, fumbling to explain what I meant by a feedback hotline, Mary easily responded, "Oh yes, I also relied on several interlocutors while writing my memoir." This perfectly exemplifies the value of feedback hotlines, and speaks to why you, too, should use them when you are immobilized at your desk and feel like you are going batty or wasting time. Because without *interlocutors* to help in a crisis, it would have taken me forever to think up that word.

"Danger, Danger, Will Robinson!"

So here I am in the bustling lobby of Big Time Publishers in New York City. I am here with my two partners in the book project *This Day in the Life* to meet with an editor from Big Time who told our agent she loves our proposal and wants to discuss it with us in person. As I am going through the building's security checkpoints, then standing in line to receive my identification badge, then elevating up sixty-seven floors at warp speed, then proceeding down a maze of halls to a tiny holding area with a wall of back-lit books and a male receptionist in a dazzling white shirt, I have to keep telling myself this is really real. An editor at Big Time Publishers loves our proposal!

In what seemed like a lifetime ago, I'd had an idea for a book. I had wanted to know what a day in the life was really like for women from all walks of life—young, old, black, white, rich, poor, stable, and high strung like me. How in the world, for example, can someone possibly be a funeral director? When I used to have an office job, I couldn't even stand being around coworkers, but at least they weren't corpses. And what about single moms? With those kinds of demands on my time I think I'd be getting high on glue sticks every chance I got. Or what about Miss America? The perks! But can you imagine sporting a crown whenever you went out in public? I feel self-conscious just wearing big earrings.

When I had first envisioned this book, I'd known I didn't want to interview women and write about their lives. What I wanted was to spend a day in their presence and in their heads. To that end, I decided I would ask hundreds of women across America to create a "day diary" on the very same day, jotting down not only what they were doing, but also what they were thinking and feeling as they went through the course of that day. The book would be a collection of these first-person, real-time accounts.

Of course, it is one thing to have an idea. It is quite another thing to turn that idea into a reality, especially given the logistics involved in putting together a book of this nature. To make sure I didn't give up before I even started trying, I invited two friends, Becky Joffrey and Bindi Rakhra, to be my partners in the project.

Now here the three of us are, in New York City, following the beacon of the male receptionist's dazzling white shirt into the Big Time editor's office.

I take a seat on her cozy couch under a voracious, potted palm with an overhanging frond that keeps grazing my forehead. The editor who loves our proposal arrives and sinks into the cushion next to me. She is the epitome of today's hot, young literati—five minutes out of a prestigious women's college, exuding self-assurance, and fashionably concave in her ribbed black turtleneck, skinny skirt, and pointy-toed boots. Next to this woman, I feel like her peasant grandmother who just arrived from the North Country. A copy of our book proposal rests on her lap. I peer under the frond and try to read the notes she has jotted in the margins.

"You have a fabulous concept for a book," the editor tells us. After having weathered an avalanche of rejections from other publishers, it takes all my reserve (of which I have painfully little, even in the best of circumstances) not to burst into joyful tears and kiss this woman's pointy-toed, black boots. In fact, I am a bit stunned by her manner, which is warm and hardly fakey at all. I don't know what I was expecting, but it wasn't this . . . this *humanity.* Not from someone who works at Big Time Publishers, perpetuated in the press as some bottom-line-driven megacorpglomeration sprung from so many mergers and acquisitions that no one is really quite sure who owns it anymore.

The editor makes a few more enthusiastic comments about our proposal and I beam beatifically. Maybe I am getting a little ahead of myself, but I start anticipating how I am going to let everyone in the world who ever thought I was a loser know that I am a Big Time author. That's right, *me,* a Big Time author, baby. *Big Time!*

The editor starts explaining how she envisions turning our proposal into a book. "Celebrities!" she announces brightly, and I sit up straighter, the frond poking me in the eye. At first, I think she means me and my partners are celebrities, but then I realize she is talking about our book. Only it is not our book, but a strange distortion of our book that she is describing. She elaborates, "Readers love celebrities. Readers don't care about ordinary people. Ordinary people don't sell books. Celebrities sell books. How about . . . *A Day in the Life of Celebrities!*"

When I was a kid, I used to watch a sci-fi television show called *Lost in Space.* Now, sitting here in this Big Time editor's office, a line from that show pops into my head, *"Danger, danger, Will Robinson!"* In my mind's eye, I can see perfectly the hokey little robot that used to spin and flail its metal arms in young Will Robinson's direction, trying to protect the poor kid from harm. Why is this editor talking about celebrities? I don't care about celebrities. I mean, I love celebrities (secretly, my favorite television station is the E! channel), but my book idea has nothing to do with celebrities. What happened to the book described in our proposal, the very same proposal this editor professed to love, and that is now resting on her lap? What happened to the book I envisioned?

Having had a few years to calm down after this meeting, I can tell you exactly what happened to that book I envisioned. It *almost* got lost in space. This Big Time editor, the one with the compliments and the cozy couch, really did love my book concept. Or rather, she loved the overall idea of using first-person, real-time accounts to reveal a day in the life. So this editor took my idea and creatively ran with it, supplanting my vision with hers. This editor was a vision supplanter, and out there—from big-city publishing houses to small-town critique groups—lurk thousands of others just like her.

Writers beware. Whenever you show a work-in-progress you are bound to encounter vision supplanters. These are feedback providers who can't help but view other people's ideas through their own creative lens. I see this happen all the time in my own writing workshops, with me being the biggest offender. Show me a draft with promise and I start burbling, "Play out the plot this way . . . make the character that way . . . now here's how the whole story should work . . ." When I am on a tear like this, saying vision-supplanting things, this is what the writer should be hearing: "*Danger, danger, Will Robinson!*"

Vision supplanters, myself included, don't mean you or your writing any harm. We are motivated by our excitement about the potential of your idea. We are sincere in wanting to help you make your work better, more marketable, more successful. This makes us all the more dangerous. I spoke with an editor at a small publishing house who often works with first-time authors of inspirational books. She told me that so many writers turned in manuscripts that failed to reflect the vision of their original proposal that she started telling the new writers she signed not to show their work to anyone during the writing process.

Obviously, I don't agree with this advice (and later in the conversation the editor herself endorsed the value of feedback), but it does speak to how susceptible writers can be to other people's opinions, and how natural it is for feedback providers to forget whose book it is. A perfect example comes from a business professor I know who is equally passionate about history and hostile takeovers. He envisioned a book that used the rise and fall of historical empires to illuminate strategies for contemporary global business empires. "Great idea!" enthused one of his colleagues after reading the professor's first draft, "Now lose the history and the book will really sell."

During the writing process, you can and should rely on outsiders to help you rethink and revise many aspects of your writing. But your vision for the work is the one aspect that should remain yours and yours alone. Just like you can't borrow someone else's prescription glasses to see things more clearly, you also cannot use someone else's vision for your own work and expect to write with originality or strength of purpose. Your vision is what motivated you to write about the idea in the first place. Your vision is what allows you to take one of the thirty-six dramatic situations (purported by French critic Georges Polti to represent the entire spectrum of literary plots), and make it uniquely your own. Your vision is what infuses your writing with passion and integrity.

Your vision is also what feeds your determination during the writing process. Even on the most discouraging writing days, when it feels like no one else believes in your idea, or like someone has rearranged all the letters on your keyboard to produce nothing but gibberish, your vision is the one thing that can compel you to keep trying. You know you have a compelling idea. You know there is something you really want to say. With your vision you can *see* it, even if you can't yet find the right words.

My vision for *This Day in the Life* was inspired by personal reasons. When I thought up the book idea, I was feeling blue and needed to connect with other women. I also saw the book as a way for readers to get to know women beyond the reductive labels society assigns them, or we assign ourselves. I wanted this collection of day diaries to show how unique and interesting we *all* are—in particular, those of us who are not celebrities.

When my partners and I left our meeting at Big Time Publishers, I really didn't know what to do. As a writer desperate for a publisher, I couldn't imagine turning down an offer from one of the biggest publishing houses in the world. But as a writer with a vision, I couldn't imagine accepting an offer that compromised everything that mattered to me about my book.

Danger, danger, Will Robinson . . .

In the end, I didn't have to make the choice. Two weeks after our meeting, Big Time Publishers turned down our book proposal. In an e-mail to our agent, the editor remained enthusiastic and gracious. "I love the idea behind *This Day in the Life* and think a book with this concept—especially one about celebrities—would be fantastic. Unfortunately, we just can't get our numbers to work so reluctantly we're going to be passing."

As a writer, it is never easy to get rejected, especially from Big Time Publishers. In this particular instance, however, I believe that out there, somewhere in the publishing cosmos, a little robot must have been spinning around and flailing its metal arms in my direction, making sure I didn't lose my way.

✒ Jennifer Crusie *"A story is a collaboration between a writer and a reader."*

In the summer of 1991 Jennifer Crusie set a goal of reading a hundred romance novels as research for her dissertation on the impact of gender in narrative strategies. The experience taught her two things: reading romance novels made her feel good; and she wanted to try writing one herself. A year later, she had quit her job as a high school English teacher to write full time, put her dissertation on hold, and sold her first book, *Sizzle,* to Silhouette. Next came over half a dozen books sold to Harlequin, including *Getting Rid of Bradley,* which earned her a Rita Award for Best Short Contemporary from the Romance Writers of America.

In 1995 Jennifer began to write mainstream novels for St. Martin's Press (*Tell Me Lies, Crazy for You, Faking It, Bet Me,* to name a few of her bestsellers), but don't assume that she turned her back on the genre she got her start in. Some of Jennifer's heroines wear glasses or could stand to lose a few pounds, but they all have what it takes to get the guy hot and bothered. On her Web site, the popular author makes her loyalties clear. "Trying to find something bigger and better than romance would be impossible," she writes. Also stupid, since the genre accounts for half of all mass-market paperbacks sold.

When it comes to feedback, Jennifer has experienced the gamut—"MFA feedback, Amazon feedback, editor feedback, you name it," she told me. And on top of that are the "Cherries"—an on-line community of readers and writers that is part Jennifer Crusie fan club, part gabfest on topics ranging from recipes to the best way to hide dead bodies, and part writing workshop—which the author relies on for critiques of her work. In the following Q&A, Jennifer shares her thoughts about feedback.

Do you think feedback is useful to writers?
Depends on the feedback. People who criticize pop fiction because it's not "as good" as literary fiction are like people who eat roast beef and complain it's not chicken. It's not about what's good, it's about their tastes and what they expect from a book. So that kind of feedback is pretty much worthless

because they're not criticizing what you wrote, they're criticizing you for not writing what they wanted. And this is the basis for a lot of reader criticism. One reader didn't like one of my books because the heroine's best friend was gay, and that did not fit into her world of admirable women. One reviewer didn't like another book because the heroine asked the hero for time to figure out her life before she settled down. In that reviewer's story world, women did not put relationships on hold, so the story failed for her. Clearly, these are not my story worlds, so the fact that these readers rejected the books is inevitable. You don't take that kind of feedback personally, and you don't change your world view. You just accept that not everybody thinks or sees the world the same way as you do, and move on.

What's your feedback process?
For professional feedback, I have a small pool of readers, including my daughter, my editor, my agent, and my long-time critique partner. The Cherries are also invaluable. A couple of them read my work when I've gotten it to the final draft stage. I don't always take their suggestions, but I always pay attention to the places they had trouble, and try to figure out what went wrong for them. If somebody says, "This section was boring" when I know it has good stuff in it, I figure I've buried the good stuff in too many words, too much dialogue, too much narrative, and I pare it down. My mantra is from Elmore Leonard: try not to write the parts people skip.

Do you have any good "bad feedback" stories?
I got a huge packet of PETA materials once from a woman who'd read *Bet Me* and was upset because the heroine was overweight. She believed fat people get that way by being cruel to animals, so she sent me brochures and handouts, and had circled key points in marker and made notes in the margins. I never did get the connection—overweight people eat meat?— but she was adamant that I join the crusade and never write another overweight heroine again.

Some reviewers are obviously dealing with issues of their own and, if your book hits one of those, it can also result in some pretty weird evaluations. I had one reader say that *Bet Me* was too close to formula romance, then added, "Where was the dog?" and a few other things that are often in my books. As somebody else pointed out, she didn't object to formula fiction, she objected because I hadn't written the formula she liked. But most of the criticism I get from readers is honest and thoughtful, and I pay attention.

Any feedback-related advice for writers?

Here's the key thing: A story is a collaboration between a writer and a reader. If the novel is constructed with enough white space for the reader to move into it, it becomes a visceral experience for her. She writes the story with you by filling in the blanks, seeing in her mind what the characters look like, sound like, what the setting looks like, what the characters are feeling, even what they want to a certain extent, even if you've put the goals clearly on the page.

Also, feedback is absolutely critical once you've reached the "finished" stage, the point at which you have solved all the problems you can see. Then you give it to others so they can find the weak spots and you can go back in and figure out the problem. I remember doing a critique for a contest winner, a really detailed analysis of where her strengths and weaknesses were and where the story needed work. I got back an e-mail, "LOL, Jenny, the book is finished." I wanted to write back, "LOL, in more ways than you know."

The Club

I know what it feels like to be an outsider, to be a wannabe in a world where everyone else seems to belong to "The Club." I understand this sense of isolation and dejection because that is how I feel whenever I listen to *Car Talk,* the National Public Radio call-in show that features two Boston-based brothers who work as mechanics and love to whoop it up on the air about other people's car problems.

I don't get the appeal of the show. All right, let's be honest here. I hate that show. Hate it! How can thousands and thousands of highly educated, upscale, influential listeners—*exactly* the kind of demographic profile in which I long to be included—enjoy the banter of these two brothers (who go by the irritating nicknames of Click and Clack), let alone call them on the air to ask about their stuck clutches and harrumphing engines?

Ratings don't lie, however, and apparently everyone in the universe—everyone but me, that is—loves *Car Talk,* whether they drive a Ram-tough pickup, or a rusty Civic, or a gas-guzzling SUV for the sake of the children. At no time am I more aware of my isolation than on my family's Sunday-afternoon drives, trapped inside our '96 Ford Taurus (or is it a '98? as if I care), while those two MIT-educated radio hosts entertain my yukking-it-up husband, as I sullenly work my crossword puzzle.

Yes, it is a terrible thing to feel like an outsider. Yet, in the writing realm, that is how about 99.9 percent of us feel. In our heads we envision an exclusive club—The Club of *Real Writers*—to which we don't belong. At the gates to The Club, discouraging our tentative approach, sneers a trivisage dog bearing the likenesses of Virginia Woolf, Gore Vidal, and that seventh-grade teacher who failed us in English composition because we started a sentence with "And." Inside The Club, gathered around the ponderous oak tables, the Real Writers laugh hysterically over their glasses of absinthe at our miserable attempts to associate with them. "Who do you think you are?" they nasal. "Where have you published?" they snicker. "Don't you make a living in sales?"

On a regular basis, I hear writers talk passionately about the stories in their hearts they feel compelled to put down on paper; the sense of satisfying exhaustion they experience after a good writing session; and the drive that lures them at four a.m. to their computer table tucked in a corner of their semifinished basement, where they struggle with that stubborn plot point before the kids wake up and the real workday begins. Yet most of these writers inevitably end the conversation by discounting their own genuineness. "Of course, I'm not a *Real Writer,*" they apologize, as if they have in some way overstepped their bounds.

Why do so many people who are writing feel this way? What propaganda have we internalized that leads us to believe that practicing the craft of writing is not enough to call ourselves "real"? And if we are writing, but we are not Real Writers, then what are we? Are we Fake Writers? Is there even such a thing? Doesn't that suggest we are simply going through the motions, waving our fingers above the computer keys or hovering our pencils over the writing tablet, but never making contact?

In the feedback process, our first challenge as writers is to stop listening to that collective chorus of naysayers who have lodged themselves between our ears, and who are incessantly whispering reminders of our illegitimacy— "You are not a Real Writer . . . YOU are NOT a Real Writer . . . YOU ARE NOT A REAL WRITER!"

Here, I feel obligated to warn you that if you are unpublished, if you have a life outside writing where people prefer it if you simply pack lunches and earn a decent salary, or if you are even just a tad insecure, it will not be easy to shut these naysayers up. Egging them on is a culture of literary snobbism with a long history of disqualifying potential members of The Club on totally subjective criteria, including gender, race, and other bizarre factors. For example, I once read in a writing manual (by an author whose first novel I loved) that you are not a Real Writer unless you know enough Latin to read Horace and Livy. Say what?! This advice was from the same author who also felt compelled to brag that the very first book she ever checked out of the library (at age five) was Strickland's *Queens of England* (volume one). I think this author has issues. I think perhaps she has a need to prove to her readers that she is very smart; in fact, maybe just a wee bit smarter than they are. She wants to prove she deserves to be in The Club.

Please don't misunderstand. I am not saying that learning Latin isn't a worthwhile pursuit. But what good does it do, for example, to tell a harried, at-home mom with three young kids, a husband on the road half the time, a desperate urge to write, and exactly five minutes to herself during normal people hours that she can't be a writer unless she manages to fit in a community college course on a dead language? In a case such as this, the voice in that woman's head should be saying something like, *Latin, hmm? Latin, oh dear. Latin, oh, shut up!*

Of course, outside forces are not the only ones at fault for making so many writers feel like inferior posers. Writers are perfectly capable of doing this sort of thing all on their own. In fact, we are the masters of trash-talking our own legitimacy. My friend Lori, who teaches fiction writing to convicted sex felons, told me about a big, scary-looking guy in her class who broke down in tears early in the term, confessing he wasn't a writer. "Why not?" Lori asked him. His reply, "I got bad handwriting."

My heart goes out to this fellow, and yours should too because, except for the sex offender part, this man is no different than you or me or all those other writers out there who harbor misguided notions about what it means to be a Real Writer. You may think, given the man's rap sheet, that the voice in a sex offender's head is a bit more perverse than most. But I can tell you, when it comes to believing in ourselves as writers, this fellow is no more misguided than most of us. I am astounded at the reasons people in my writing workshop, and people I encounter in the world at large, offer for why they are not Real Writers. Here is just a small sample of what the voices in these people's heads are telling them:

You are not a Real Writer because you don't write every day.
You are not a Real Writer because you are eighty-three years old.
You are not a Real Writer because you have never been published.
You are not a Real Writer because you are not Salman Rushdie.
You are not a Real Writer because you had a happy childhood.
You are not a Real Writer because you are a visiting nurse.
You are not a Real Writer because your wife doesn't like the way you write.

What is the voice inside your head telling you? I hope it is not telling any lies like the ones above. Because the truth is, if you are writing you already meet the criteria for a Real Writer. You already belong to The Club. In fact, you are a lifelong member, despite any negative feedback to the contrary. Because The Club of Real Writers is one club where no one—no one with stories they want to tell or a voice longing to be heard—should ever feel like an outsider. As writers, we are all better served not by creating snobby distinctions among ourselves, but by fostering a sense of camaraderie.

So come inside. Make yourself at home. The Club of Real Writers welcomes one and all, and a rejection letter buys you a free drink. Published, nonpublished, literary, commercial, young, and old—there is room for everybody who wants to belong. Just look at all those empty seats between Jonathan Franzen and Oprah's Book Club. Or pull up a stool next to the ghost of Thomas Hardy, he looks like he could use a good joke. Better yet, plop yourself down between Al Franken and Ann Coulter. Someone needs to break those two up.

Exercise: Write down the top ten reasons you are not a Real Writer.

Note: it is very important that you put these reasons down on paper. (Why? Because seeing them in black and white will show you how ridiculous they are.) When you are finished, write something, anything, as long as it is from the heart.

Waiting for Feedback

Wednesday at 10:07 a.m. you send your finished manuscript to your agent, who has agreed to shop it around to publishers. Your immediate reaction is elation. You have done it! You are magnificent! Fame and riches will soon be yours! A celebration is in order; that is, if you can find some friends who are still taking your calls after months of listening to you whine about whether you would ever finish your book.

This sense of elation lasts maybe six minutes, about the time it takes for the glue to fully dry on the back of the overnight express postage you splurged on, given the occasion. Now comes the hard part.

Waiting.

Waiting.

Waiting.

For writers with manuscripts out to agents, editors, or other high-stakes readers, waiting for feedback—whether it represents a publisher's acceptance, or approval from someone whose opinion matters to you—is not only hard, it is also a twenty-four-hour job requiring your undivided attention. When you are waiting, you must concentrate all your energy on not calling the feedback provider to "touch base." You must obsessively check e-mail and voice mail to make sure you have not missed any messages. And if the work is out to potential publishers, you must negotiate constantly with the mercurial gods of acceptance. *If the next song on the radio is a good one, an offer will come through this afternoon . . . If I don't eat this bag of chips, at least two—no, three—publishers will express interest in my work . . . If someone, oh dear God anyone, will just agree to publish me, I will never again tell the student fundraisers from my college that I am not home, or abandon my discarded grocery cart in the middle of the parking lot, or go without showering for eight days in a row.*

Embarrassingly enough, these behaviors reflect my own experience with waiting. I once spent seven months waiting to hear back from an editor about one of my books. I remember hitting bottom near the end of that marathon. Ever vigilant, I had logged on to e-mail for the umpteenth time that day, despite the fact it was a national holiday. The spinning icon on my computer screen indicated my machine was receiving . . . receiving . . . receiving . . . Maybe the editor had come in on his day off! My heart started pounding . . . pounding . . . pounding. *Oh, please be an offer! Please be an offer! Please be an offer!*

Pop! A single message appeared in my inbox.

From: Sue
To: Joni B. Cole
Subject: Complimentary Mortgage Calculator

"Fuck-fuck-fuck-fuck-fuckingness-fuck!!!" What a memorable display *that* was for my six-year-old daughter, who had just happened to come into the room to ask if she could watch another half hour of *SpongeBob*.

I make but one excuse for this behavior: Waiting sucks. It can suck up all our positive energy, our ability to write, and our belief in a benevolent Supreme Being. No one conveys this reality better than Samuel Beckett in his play about two tramps waiting by a tree for a man named Godot, who never arrives. As the tramps' vigil extends to a second day, allowing them time to reflect on the sorry condition of their lives, the theme of Beckett's play becomes excruciatingly clear: life is eternally hopeless and humans are absurdly insignificant. Waiting will do that to a person.

Unfortunately, no panacea exists that can make waiting for feedback from high-stakes readers any easier for writers. But I have learned through my own experience that there is something you can do to make this nerve-racking period bearable, and even enjoyable. You can stop waiting.

Stop waiting.

Stop waiting.

Stop waiting.

Or, to put it another way, you can consciously choose *not* to wait. After all, life is a series of choices about how to behave. So instead of focusing all of your energy on actively waiting to hear back from your agent or a publisher or critique group or writing instructor, why not choose to direct it toward something affirming, something that isn't waiting? For example, you could take up origami, or paint the bedrooms tangerine, or learn how to speak Dutch. The key is to engage in something other than waiting. Change the channel. Do something, anything you like, as long as it isn't waiting.

Of course, telling yourself to stop waiting is a lot easier than actually doing it. One reason is because waiting is an automatic response; it just happens naturally, like entropy. It also feeds on itself. The more you wait, the harder it is to quit, until eventually you become so addicted to waiting that you cannot leave the house for even *one second* because if you do, then that will be when your agent chooses to call with big news. And if you miss that call . . . or don't respond to that e-mail immediately . . . writing career suicide!

Making it even harder to stop waiting is that most of us still engage in magical thinking. Remember when you were a kid and you thought you were the one who caused Uncle Jerome's car accident because the last time he visited your parents you kept wishing he would just go away and leave you and your Barbies the hell alone? Well, all these adult-years later, most of us still believe that if we think about something hard enough—actively wishing for that job offer to come through or that man to call or that publisher to say yes—we can actually *control* the outcome.

Of course, that is not how the Universe works. In fact, my suspicion is that the Universe resents, in particular, writers who think they have a modicum of control over their submissions once they send them out. That is why it holds out on us, purposely refusing to give us what we want, when we want it. But if we concede our powerlessness, if we acknowledge that the future of our manuscript is out of our hands, then that is when the Universe just might drop an acceptance in our laps. Plop. Have a nice day.

During the seven months I drove myself crazy waiting to hear from the editor who was considering my book, my friends gently tried to teach me this lesson. "Move on," they suggested. "Let it go," they counseled. "Give it up to the Universe," they advised. At the time, these friends really got on my nerves. Hell-bent on waiting, I was completely incapable of registering my car, let alone the deeper truths of their metaphoric wisdom. Give it up to the Universe? What was that but a bunch of la-la language, a New Age-y way of saying, "Give up, you loser, that book will never reach publication."

One day when I was on-line, once again waiting for an e-mail from the editor that did not arrive, I happened upon an interview with rock bass pioneer Jack Casady, one of the founders of Jefferson Airplane. Casady was talking about "rests," the spaces between the notes, and how they are as important as the notes themselves. Without rests you don't have music, you have noise. Casady pointed out that a lot of musicians get nervous coming in after rests, so they tend to play a lot of notes to plug in the holes.

Reading this article, it occurred to me that I was doing the same thing, plugging in the holes of my day with waiting simply because I was nervous about what came next. Exhausted from so many months of relentless waiting, this notion of rest, more tangible to me than letting go or giving something up to the Universe, felt like a doable, comforting alternative. I also loved what Casady said about rests helping the artist cultivate groove. It's not just about playing the same lick over and over, he said, the spaces in the music have to groove as well as the notes. Goodness knows, I needed to get my groove back, so I decided to stop filling in the spaces of my day with so much noisy waiting. I decided to give waiting a rest.

Rest.

Rest.

Rest.

For me, resting didn't come as naturally as waiting. I had to struggle to resist the impulse to jump into the empty spaces of the day and check e-mail. I had to stop myself from repeating the same licks over and over—*Oh, please make an offer! Please make an offer! Please make an offer!* I had to work hard to give waiting a rest.

Eventually, however, the more I stopped waiting the better I felt, and in those interludes of rest I discovered something truly worthy of my attention: the present, the here and now. And, my goodness, who should I see there but my two adorable children? My, how they had grown over those past seven months. And look! There, out my window, a tree was sprouting buds and resonating with birdsong. Could it really be springtime already? And halloo! Who belongs to that voice, the one calling out to me in my head? Why it's a creative-type person with an idea for a new book. I think I'll go to the computer and see what she's got to say . . .

And so I began writing again, something I hadn't been able to do for months. Freed from the exhaustion of waiting for a publisher and obsessing about whether someone else thought my work was good enough, I actually remembered why I liked writing in the first place. And the funny thing is, I became so consumed with my new project, writing for the sake of writing rather than for someone else's approval, that when my phone finally did ring a few weeks later, I decided to let the answering machine get it. Because when you are writing instead of waiting, the Universe can just leave a message.

✄ Archer Mayor   *"Emotion is a blinding force."*

I'm on the phone interviewing the acclaimed police novelist Archer Mayor when he gets another call and puts me on hold. After he comes back on the line, Archer offers a quick apology and explains that the caller was one of his medical examiner colleagues. He wanted to give Archer a heads-up that there had been a car accident with multiple fatalities. As back-up medical examiner for the week, Archer might be needed to provide an extra hand.

"So, where were we?" Archer then asks me pleasantly, but I'm still trying to process the shock of the car crash.

"Geez, that's just awful news," I say, needing time to regroup.

"It is for somebody," Archer agrees.

Archer Mayor is many things—warm, funny, gracious—but as he readily admits, "I'm not an emotional guy." In addition to being the author of the long-running series of mystery novels featuring the decent, dependable Lt. Joe Gunther of the Brattleboro, Vermont, police department, Archer also works as a part-time police officer, an EMT, a volunteer firefighter, and—as I was just reminded—an assistant medical examiner. "I do all those things every day," Archer explains. "That's the world I inhabit, so I take things in stride."

It's a pretty safe bet that a man who can keep his cool during emergencies, crimes, and fires probably isn't the type of author who is going to be fazed by negative feedback. "In a real-world context," Archer says, "the recommendations of some editor aren't worth getting all excited about. I think you should take your work seriously," he adds, "but not take people's responses to it equally seriously. I preach this because so many writers get upset about feedback, but I don't see the value of getting yourself all twisted up. You'll only lose the clarity of the creative vision that got you writing in the first place."

Has the popular novelist always been so levelheaded about feedback? How about before he achieved the sanctity of bankable-author status; before his mystery series became a regular on the "ten best" yearly lists of the *New York Times, Washington Post, Los Angeles Times,* and *New Yorker.*

"I've had a lot of interactions with a lot of editors and have never taken their words, which were sometimes harsh in the early days, to heart," says Archer. "I've understood they're just doing their job. And my job is to put aside emotion and apply a rational, thoughtful response," he adds. "Their words of advice are valuable, but I have to filter them through my own discretion because I'm the guy writing the book. I'm the guy from whose gut the book was born. So I see all recommendations as uplifting, even when I think of them as absurd."

Archer published his first Joe Gunther novel in 1988, and has added a new book to the series about once a year. He describes his relationship with his first editor at Putnam: "Roger was terrific because he immersed himself in my manuscript. He covered it in red ink. He wasn't a very good writer, but he would rewrite passages and I'd read them and say, 'Good God, Roger, get a grip!' Then I'd throw the manuscript across the room, but immediately think, *No, this is just how he feels.* So I'd pick up the manuscript and wade through it some more. About 50 percent of his comments were very good."

So good, in fact, that even after Archer left Putnam, he hired Roger as a private editor on the next several Gunther novels—a strategy he recommends for every writer. "If you only rely on one editor," Archer says, "you're shooting yourself in the foot."

Archer clarifies that his manuscript-tossing was about passion, not emotion. "Passion is a creative force," he says, "Emotion is a blinding force." The writer's relationship with an editor is a business relationship, he stresses. It shouldn't be any more emotionally charged than any other business interaction you have during the day. "If it is," he cautions, "you should work on it, because if you get all emotional and lose control, the other guy will be looking at you, wondering why you are foaming at the mouth, and you'll lose the battle."

Archer continues on a more personal note. "I had a complex childhood, and I trained myself rather constructively to ascribe value to every situation I entered, separating the reality from what we sometimes do with it in moments of explosive emotion. But the one thing I didn't want to do was become a cold, aloof person. If you're going to be a writer, you have to be an observer and feel the heat. You need to be cognizant of the emotions of a situation, otherwise you'll write in a way that approximates taking a shower in a raincoat. In my books, I don't do blood and guts, but I sure as hell do loss and pain and bereavement. And to do that you can't turn into a stone. I'm a very passionate guy," Archer says evenly, "but I titrate."

The Value of Toxic Feedback

When I was a teenager, I obsessed about my looks to the point where my mother's refrain became, "Oh for God's sake, get away from that mirror. No one's going to be looking at you anyway." Years later, I recognized this as my first lesson in the value of toxic feedback. Someone can say something that is harsh or even unmotherly, but that doesn't mean there isn't some wisdom or benefit to be gained from the experience.

As writers, it behooves us to develop some survival techniques, or at least a little humor, when it comes to handling derogatory comments about our work. You can't be a writer and not experience toxic feedback. It goes with the territory, whether you present your writing in a critique group or on a store's bookshelf. Everybody's got an opinion.

Part of me thinks, *How sad that every feedback provider can't be sensitive and supportive when talking about a writer's work, especially given the fact that so many of us consider our words to be an extension of our souls.* But another part of me thinks, *Oh well, what the heck.* Feedback providers are only human, and we all make mistakes. I don't mean to make excuses for feedback providers who behave badly, but ultimately it is up to the writer to learn how to deal with toxic feedback—and maybe even get something positive from the experience. Think of it this way. Every day we are surrounded by toxic substances—gasoline, weed killer, nail polish remover—that make our lives better. The same point can be made about toxic feedback. It can kill us or serve us, depending on how we use it.

Some of the people I admire most in life are those who have experienced toxic feedback and didn't let it stop them. There is the graduate student whose advisor prefaced his remarks about her dissertation on feminism in Victorian literature with the words, "I couldn't help but laugh," but she steeled herself against his condescension and completed her doctorate. There is the poet who wanted to try writing prose. "Stick to poetry," advised a member of her writing workshop, but she refused to be confined in that way. Instead she became more attuned to the lyricism in her language and how it helped or hurt each scene. There is the journalist who was once told by an editor, "You can talk, but you can't write," so he made his prose more conversational and stopped trying to sound so intellectual. And there is the timid writer who asked her husband to read a story before she gave it to her creative writing class. "You aren't going to submit *this?*" he asked her on her way out the door. But she did submit her manuscript to the group, and in doing so learned that it is okay to show imperfect drafts—that's when feedback is most valuable—just make sure you show your work to someone who understands the writing process, and who has a better sense of timing.

Then there is my neighbor Pat, who works in social services, making sure housebound people receive medical care. Pat is one of my role models because she is such a good person, and because I envision her as the kind of mother I might have if I lived in a 1950s television show. Always nicely turned out, one time Pat came over to my house with one of those old-fashioned, pink, sponge curlers coiled in her hair. I knew she must have overlooked it, but I didn't tell her because seeing that curler gave me comfort—transporting me back to a safer, more innocent time.

I visited with Pat shortly after she returned from her fortieth reunion at her all-girl, Catholic high school in New Jersey. Pat told me how she and her former schoolmates had reminisced about Sister Mary Martin, a formidable woman who had taught a class on poetry and was clearly a sadist. The nun specialized in ridiculing her students in front of their classmates. "I'll never forget," Pat said, "the class was talking about a poem I'd written and Sister Mary Martin immediately shot it down, saying it was a bad idea for a poem."

Forty years ago being respectful meant never contradicting the teacher, so Pat didn't defend her idea or stand up to Sister Mary Martin, and of course she felt the sting of the nun's public admonishment. At the same time, however, Pat had the sudden realization that this intimidating authority figure was wrong. *To hell with you,* Pat thought, which was no meaningless curse coming from a Catholic schoolgirl to a nun. "Sister Mary Martin's feedback actually got me fired up," she said. "It made me more committed to my own convictions."

One of the reasons I wanted to share Pat's story is because it shows how long hurtful criticism can resonate with a writer. Forty years is nothing in the lifespan of toxic feedback. People forgive, but they don't forget. As a feedback provider, I also see this example as a cautionary tale about the repercussions of humiliating writers. When I am inclined to say something mean to a writer, maybe because I am in a bad mood or feeling jealous, I think about Sister Mary Martin all those decades ago, now damned to an eternity in hell. What a waste of prayer and celibacy. What a reminder to be more careful with my words.

More importantly, Pat's story exemplifies how toxic feedback can benefit us in unexpected ways. I have always been struck by Pat's commitment to what she believes in; this is one of the traits I have respected most about her during our decade-long friendship. The strength of her own convictions, even in the face of formidable opposition, has served her well, particularly given her job in social services, a favorite target for state and federal budget-cutting hawks. When Pat told me the story about Sister Mary Martin, I realized that her fortitude took root forty years ago in the most unassuming of places—a poetry class in an all-girl, Catholic high school. Hearing Pat's story made me understand that the value of toxic feedback isn't limited to how we apply it to writing, but how we apply it to life. Pat could have been diminished by Sister Mary Martin's feedback. Instead she became a stronger person because of it.

As writers and as people, if we have to deal with toxic feedback then let's deal with it in a way that does us some good. Let's not allow other people's disparaging remarks to undermine our faith in our ideas or our potential. Let's use toxic feedback instead as an opportunity to reaffirm our own convictions, to show we are made of sterner stuff, and maybe even to take away a life lesson or two.

I think about my mom's comment when I was a teenager. *"No one's going to be looking at you."* For years, I bristled whenever she made this remark, though you would have thought I'd find some comfort in the notion, given that I hated my looks at the time. Eventually, however, I grew up and was able to gain some wisdom from the experience. Maybe people were looking at me; maybe they weren't. But the value of my mom's feedback came when I realized that I needed to live my life without worrying about it one way or the other.

☞ GIVING FEEDBACK

Preventing Mental Meltdowns

Here is a scientific fact: People can only process small amounts of information at a time before their heads implode (figuratively speaking). This reality was actually quantified in a recent study by cognitive-science researchers at the University of Queensland, who concluded that four is the maximum number of individual variables a person can mentally handle while trying to solve a problem. And that is on a very good day. Add just one more variable and the result is a mental meltdown. The person loses track of the information, his confidence plummets, and the odds of seeing any improvement in performance are no better than chance. This is particularly true in high-stress jobs like air traffic control, where people must juggle multiple factors at once.

Of course, air traffic control is a cakewalk compared to writing, where the writer has to keep track of everything from plot points, to the rules of grammar, to which characters cover their roots and take cream in their coffee. Because writers carry the weight of this responsibility around with them all the time, feedback providers need to restrain themselves when offering constructive criticism. It is so easy to get carried away with all the important things we have to say, while failing to notice that the writer has actually fallen off his chair, eyes wobbling in their sockets from information overload. Underscoring this need for restraint is the fact that when we are giving feedback to writers (as opposed to air traffic controllers or other nonwriters), we have to take into account not only cognitive science, but also abnormal psychology.

Every writer has a split personality—Creator and Editor—and these two sides of the same person have a habit of sabotaging each other's efforts. Good writers understand this, so they strive to keep their Creator and Editor sides apart during the writing process. As a feedback provider, you also need to be aware of these temperamental opposites within every writer. Otherwise, when you present your feedback you are bound to overlook the feelings of one or the needs of the other, hence undermining everybody's efforts.

The Creator is an artistic genius prone to agonizing bouts of self-doubt (when he isn't feeling completely full of himself). His job is to tap the writer's unconscious, allowing all that rich, unfiltered story material within him to flow onto the page. If the Creator thrusts his impassioned scribbling at you and suggests you peruse it on the spot while he just hangs out in the corner, the smartest thing you can do is to read expressively (here, widen your eyes in breathtaking anticipation; there, shed tears of anguish; here, laugh uproariously). This will get your relationship with the Creator off to a good start. What you don't want to do at this point is dwell on the Creator's jarring point-of-view shifts, or impenetrable idiolect, or the fact that he doesn't always spell the main character's name the same way. This will only block the Creator's creative flow and give him the vapors.

The Editor, on the other hand, welcomes constructive criticism because it helps him to do his job, which is to clean up the Creator's mess. (You can see why these two sides of the writer don't get along.) The Editor is capable of achieving miracles in the revision process, but he may not be able to even start rewriting if you confront him with too many problems at once. The best thing you can do for this side of the writer is to help him focus his attention. Give the Editor and yourself permission to let some of the story's faults slide until the next draft, or the next, or the next. In other words, don't worry about dangling participles until the plot hangs together.

Now that I've made it clear how cognitive science and abnormal psychology relate to writers, I'll play out an example of how they apply to the feedback process. Let's say a novelist has asked you to critique what you would call a disaster, but what is more commonly referred to as a typical first draft. Your first impulse might be to say something like, "The main character is cardboard, the plot lags, the flow of thoughts is disorganized, the setting is nondescript, there are too many summaries and not enough scenes, the climax fizzles, the writing is sloppy, I don't get the ending, and, by the way, you're ugly, too!" But that is *exactly* what I'm talking about when I warn feedback providers about how easy it is to get carried away.

A more effective strategy is to concentrate your criticism on just one or two issues. Often characterization is a good place to focus the writer's attention during the early stages of a work, since character drives plot and provides the heart of any good story. But before offering *any* constructive criticism, don't forget about the Creator's need for reassurance. It is no easy feat to sow the seeds of a character on a blank page and this deserves to be recognized. You can also help the Creator gear up for the next draft by asking him thought-provoking questions about the protagonist, whom I'll refer to as Samantha. For example, what does Samantha want? What do her co-workers think of her? Where did she grow up? What's in her grocery cart or the drawer of her bedside table? This type of noncritical feedback helps the Creator because it stirs his creativity, prompts character development, and reminds him that it can be useful to write outside the story. Plus, it is fun for both of you to discuss Samantha as if she is a real person.

Once you have met the Creator's needs, it is time to put forth a measured amount of specific constructive criticism. If character development is your focus, you can highlight places where the protagonist's indifference ("Samantha was never phased by anything her boss threw at her") diminishes your own emotional investment in the story. You can indicate places in the manuscript where you would like to be privy to what she is thinking ("Samantha stared out the window, deep in thought"). You can talk about how abstractions or generalities ("Samantha behaved inappropriately at times") are not nearly as effective as concrete details that enable you to form your own judgments about the character. And you can celebrate examples of successful characterization already evident in the manuscript ("Samantha propped her size ten Easy Striders on her boss's desk"). This last effort will show the Editor that he has already got some momentum, and that you are not asking for the impossible.

In the example I just provided, the feedback focused on the issue of characterization, but in another piece of writing a better focus might be point of view, or structure, or language. Even if the writer attends to just one issue per rewrite, he is likely to improve other aspects of the work in the process. For instance, if the writer clarifies what Samantha wants (a fresh start? power? peace of mind?), this will energize the plot as she strives to obtain her goal. If he develops the details of Samantha's life (she lives in a thin-walled unit of a condominium complex for singles; her father is a retired army colonel who still barks orders at everyone he meets), these enhancements will establish setting and a fictional universe. And when the writer lets Samantha act and talk and think on the page, this will transform dry summaries into powerful scenes.

Generally speaking, the rougher the draft, the fewer the variables you throw at the writer at once. In contrast, if you are critiquing a work that is in fairly good shape (hence the complexity of the challenge has been reduced), you can increase the amount of variables you include in your feedback. At that point, the writer is secure enough about his work, or practiced enough in the feedback process, that he will automatically use his own problem-solving skills to break down the criticism into small, manageable "chunks." For example, the writer may look at your dozens of red pencil marks and instinctively group them all within one variable—line edits—so as not to overtax the limits of his processing capacity.

. . .

As a feedback provider, one of your most important jobs is to size the portion of your constructive criticism according to each writer's ability to digest it. Some writers can choke on a crumb; others are able to handle more feedback at one sitting, although these writers, too, need help setting priorities. I think of an accomplished writer I know working on a novel about Norwegian partisans during World War II. She once spent weeks researching the history of saunas after a feedback provider pointed out a slight inaccuracy in her text. Attention to authenticating detail is crucial in any book, especially historical fiction, but as this writer pointed out herself, perhaps not so much so when you haven't even drafted chapter three. It is remarkably easy for writers to get bogged down or sidetracked by the millions of little things that demand their attention, but will simply have to wait their turn.

How much criticism you put forth, and how much you reserve for the next draft; what matters now and what can be addressed later: these are assessments you will want to make writer by writer and draft by draft, every time you sit down to give someone feedback. It helps to think of giving feedback as an art, but also as a science in which cognitive researchers have proven that less is more. Giving good feedback isn't just about what you have to say, but what *both* sides of the writer can hear.

The Power of Positive Feedback

Dear Mrs. Cole,

I am writing to let you know how much I disagree with you and your sunny-minded colleagues about the power of positive feedback. Today's classrooms and bookshelves are filled with bad writing. Bad, bad, bad. Writing is a discipline. At the end of the day, the job has to be done and done right. Therefore, I fail to see how coddling writers serves to expunge bad writing habits or promote excellence.

    Sincerely,

    Laurence Pierce, Doctoral Candidate (ABD), English Literature

    Chair, Committee for General Excellence

Dear Mr. Pierce,

I appreciate a man of your stature (Chair!) taking the time to write. Your point is well taken. It serves no purpose to coddle writers who need to understand that writing is rewriting and hard work, indeed. Ah, but that is why positive feedback is crucial! To borrow from the wisdom of Lao Tzu, the journey of a thousand rewrites starts with a single step. Consider the acknowledgment in a novel published by one of my former students—"To those of you who said it was good from the start, your comments were invaluable. Without someone saying that, I never would have had the courage to work on it again."

    Sincerely,

    Joni

p.s. Please feel free to address me by my first name. "Mrs. Cole" is better suited for my mother-in-law.

Dear "Joni,"

First, thank you for your nod to my "stature." In truth, all my life I have felt a bit underappreciated; an inevitability, I suppose, as a middle child and now as a devoted scholar of the metaphysical poet William Mauck, whose works have been largely obscured by the looming shadow of Donne. (I'll admit, at times, this goads.) Nevertheless, my views about the so-called power of positive feedback remain unchanged. When it comes to achieving excellence in writing, what practical purpose does it serve?

Sincerely,

"Laurence"

p.s. I don't suppose you have read Mauck by any chance? He is the subject of my dissertation.

APRIL 3

Dear Laurence,

Again, you raise an important issue. The biggest fear among writers is that they have nothing of value to say. Positive feedback is the most *practical* way to overcome this fear. It motivates the writer to keep writing, and in this way he discovers his own voice and connects with his subject matter in a way that is uniquely his. Voice and passion—the heart and soul of powerful writing!

Let me give you an example of our process. Today, my workshop went on a quest—a quest to find the best aspects of a story submission (this being one of the most practical purposes of a writing workshop). You should have been there, Laurence, to witness the collective enthusiasm. "Look here, this is amusing!" "Here, a terrific intensity of feeling!" "There, a lovely example of show, don't tell!" We've never had such a good time in the group, and the writer, an insecure, middle-aged man who brought a teddy bear to the meeting, left the class humming.

Sincerely,

Joni

p.s. I am sorry to say I have never read (or heard of) your poet, Mauck. Are you willing to send along a draft of your dissertation? I hope so!

APRIL 17

Dear Joni,

Enclosed is a draft of my dissertation on Mauck. I must confess, I have not looked at it since receiving my advisor's initial feedback two years ago. Somewhat in my defense, the demands on me as Chair of the Committee on Excellence have consumed much of my time. Still, while I have continued my research on Mauck, I have been floundering over how to address my advisor's multitude of criticisms. I am leaning toward burning this draft, but hesitate since it represents seven years' labor.

As to the issue of positive feedback, while I concede that encouragement has its place (I recall from my research that the more-established Mauck praised the younger Donne's early efforts during their lone recorded encounter in Cambridge in 1609), I remain firm that feedback must focus on a work's deficits.

Sincerely,
Laurence

P.S. Please don't bother remarking on my dissertation. Your positive feedback is lost on me.

MAY 19

Dear Laurence,

Out of respect for your views, I won't offer a peep of positive feedback about your dissertation. But I assume you won't mind if I comment on your subject. Mauck is fascinating! I found your brief mention of his use of extravagant paradox (the secular and the divine; the agony and ecstasy) particularly compelling. How he uses this technique to shock and excite his readers strikes me as the heart of your work. More!

In response to your firm stance on feedback: If the writer is only made aware of the deficits of his text, how is he to know what aspects are succeeding? You might think that writers would assume that the elements of the piece that are *not* criticized are working just fine, but writers being writers, that is rarely the case. Without the feedback provider delineating what works and why, the writer is just as likely to revise the good with the bad. A focus on the positive helps him recognize what to preserve and what to develop—two crucial steps forward *toward excellence!*

Sincerely,
Joni

P.S. Are you a father, Laurence? You seem like a wonderful role model.

AUGUST 6

Dear Joni,

Forgive my long lapse in replying to your last note. Finally, progress on my dissertation! I have enclosed a revised draft (in response to your request for

"More!"). As this draft reflects, I have focused the text more on Mauck's use of extravagant paradox to shock and excite his readers. It struck me recently that this was the core of his genius. Something in my advisor's response from two years ago must have triggered this long-delayed epiphany. I shall thank him when we meet in two weeks to review this latest draft.

Sincerely,
Laurence

P.S. Regrettably, I am neither a father nor married. My former girlfriend ended our relationship two years ago on the eve of my forty-first birthday. She said I was "bringing her down."

AUGUST 18

Dear Laurence,
I was thrilled to read your revised dissertation! What is left, but polishing this diamond?

Happy news on my end, as well. Today the workshop discussed a revision of the teddy bear fellow's story. What an improvement from when we last saw it. As you may recall, our initial discussion of the work focused only on its promising aspects. Yet, with this revision, he has managed to address many of the story's deficits without benefit of our critical remarks. How did this happen, do you suppose? A stroke of luck? Or perhaps the power of positive feedback works in mysterious ways. The writer intends to continue to revise.

Sincerely,
Joni

P.S. I was sorry to read about your girlfriend's rejection (ouch!), but I have confidence that the right woman will come along.

AUGUST 30

Dear Joni,
Alas. I met briefly with my advisor regarding my revised dissertation. I struggle with how to interpret one of his comments in particular ("Laurence, you have a small talent for scholarship"). While only one other contemporary academic has published a brief study of Mauck, I fear his will remain the definitive work, as I seem to be, once again, at a standstill.

Sincerely,
Laurence (Forever ABD)

Dear Laurence,

Don't interpret your advisor's words as a judgment, but as a challenge. Recall your own assertion about Mauck's ostracism from the Catholic church—how it only served to fuel his passion. Your research is formidable. Your focus on Mauck's use of extravagant paradox, inspired. You are connected to your subject in ways that transcend scholarship. Let your advisor's questionable comment fuel your own passion. You know Mauck deserves to be recognized as Donne's equal. Shrug off self-doubt and champion *your* Mauck!

    Sincerely,

    Joni

P.S. "Forever ABD . . ." Puh-leeze!

JANUARY 26

Dear Joni,

Oh happy day! Enclosed is an inscribed copy of my finished dissertation: "The Mark of Mauck: An Expression of Religious Passion through Extravagant Imagery." Despite the steepened pitch of my advisor's eyebrows when he signed off on the text (the man is as intimidating as he is learned), I felt compelled to thank him for his counsel all these many years. I could not have accomplished this work without his critical feedback.

    My oral examination is in three weeks. Perhaps I should bring a teddy bear to my defense? (tee hee)

    Sincerely,

    Larry

P.S. I resigned my position as Chair of the Committee on Excellence. Too much on my plate. I have met a woman named Jasmine, an assistant professor of Romance languages. We see each other every Wednesday evening!

FEBRUARY 8

Dear Larry,

Congratulations on completing your dissertation, and on your budding romance with a professor of Romance. How poetic!

    I truly value my copy of your dissertation, and particularly appreciate the inscription, "Lo, how the weary friends / View excellence through different lens." (Yes, I recognized the wordplay on the first two lines of Mauck's *The Divine*.) You don't need me to wish you luck during your oral exam. The air is already charged with positive energy and that, too, (prepare yourself, Laurence, because here I go again), plays a significant role in achieving excellence.

Sincerely,
Joni

MARCH II

Dear Joni,
I passed! I am free of the stigma of ABD. Now I must dash to an appointment (I am getting my first salon haircut!), but I wanted to make a point to let you know, while it appears we must agree to disagree on the power of positive feedback, I respect your instincts to be gentle with that poor teddy bear fellow in your workshop. Some people are too sensitive to be writers.

Sincerely,
Larry

APRIL I

Dear *Dr.* Pierce!
Congratulations on completing your Ph.D.! I am so happy for you. In celebration of your success, I have enclosed a small graduation gift, which I have named "Workshop Bear." Even as we "agree to disagree," I send this fuzzy fellow along as a reminder of the power of positive feedback. May he inspire your future writing.

Sincerely,
Joni

P.S. No need to be concerned about the "poor teddy bear fellow" in my workshop. He finished his short story and submitted it to the *New Yorker.* You can read it in the upcoming fiction issue.

✒ Grace Paley   *"My nature wasn't ambitious enough to go ahead on my own."*

When Grace Paley and I met in a busy café, I saw firsthand how her trademark mix of candor and affection permeates her conversation as well as her fiction. When the waitress delivered our coffees, Grace told her directly, "I hate the sandwiches here," then she patted the young woman's arm, adding kindly, "but don't take that personally, dear."

Grace started writing short stories in the mid-1950s. At the time, she felt they were probably "trivial, stupid, boring, domestic, and not interesting," especially in a period dominated by masculine literature. Still, these were the stories that were "bugging her"; these were the people she was curious about, mostly Jewish women and mothers living everyday lives in the Bronx. Almost half a century later, Grace's "trivial" stories—animated by the author's inimitable voice and comic vision—continue to resonate with contemporary readers, writers, and teachers of writing.

Doubleday published Grace's first story collection, *The Little Disturbances of Man,* in 1959 to glowing reviews. She followed her successful debut with two more volumes of short stories, but not in any hurry. *Enormous Changes at the Last Minute* (1975) and *Later the Same Day* (1985) were both published by Farrar, Straus & Giroux. Grace has also published books of poetry (as a young woman, she studied with W. H. Auden at the New School for Social Research in New York), and her *Collected Stories* was nominated for the National Book Award in 1994. Then there is the aptly titled *Just as I Thought,* a collection of her articles, reports, and talks representing about thirty years of political and literary activity.

A longtime antiwar and antinuclear protestor, a feminist, and now a doting grandmother (during our conversation, Grace automatically reached for her purse to show me photos, before realizing she had left it in the car), she has always managed to combine the political and the personal in her writing, her activism, and her everyday life. At age eighty-three, she remains an icon of American literature and a likeable "troublemaker," though when I phoned her for this interview she wasn't writing anything. Not because of any waning curiosity or commitment, but because her granddaughter was visiting and her typewriter was in the repair shop.

What is the role of feedback in writing?

It's either encouragement or discouragement. When I first began to write I was working alone. I sent stories out again and again to magazines and they always came back. Many of these are the same stories that have now been anthologized. I was very discouraged. I was very discourage-able. By accident, my first three stories were read by the father of the kids I was babysitting. He was an editor at Doubleday [Kenneth McCormick, editor in chief at Doubleday from 1942 to 1971], and he told me to write seven more. If Ken hadn't said, "I'm going to publish the book," I would have continued to write, but maybe just two or three more stories, or maybe I would have gone back to writing poems, or maybe I would have had more kids. I didn't have the drive. My nature wasn't ambitious enough to go ahead on my own. I'm aware of that encouragement that people like me need.

As a short story writer focused on the lives of "ordinary" women, were you surprised by your book's success?
What I didn't know was that a very big movement was beginning—the women's movement. Every movement requires a literature, so little by little, books like mine and Tillie Olsen's ["Tell Me a Riddle," which won the O'Henry Award in 1961 for best short story] caught on. Philip Roth's first book [*Goodbye, Columbus,* a novella and five stories] also came out the same year as mine. We were all told a lot not to write short stories, to write novels instead. I wasted two or three years trying to do that. Philip, of course, did go on to write great novels, but Tillie and I just screwed around with more short stories.

Is feedback useful in learning to write?
Good literature is the best feedback you can get. You read the great stories, and what you read integrates into your language. It teaches you again and again how to write. There were a lot of short story writers I liked as a teenager. James Joyce was very important to me, not just for his short stories. In my generation we used to walk around reading *Ulysses* aloud. I also learned from reading stories by Stephen Crane. This was pre-Hemingway stuff, but I never liked Hemingway very much anyway.

You taught at Sarah Lawrence for twenty-two years. How do you help students handle criticism in the classroom?
That's a big problem. You get ten or fifteen people in a class, each with a different opinion, so you have to assert yourself as the teacher. And sometimes you get people who are destructive. That's really hard. They have to tell the truth, but it's horrible when they're right. Sometimes they might say something correct, but they're usually not, because the job of criticism is not to say how badly you've written this, but how you can write it better. I always told my students, "The point is not for anybody to kill anybody, but to be truthful, so see if you can get it together."

How do you use feedback when you write?
I take certain people's criticism seriously—my husband's and my daughter's—but I do the revising on my own. You have to learn how to do it on your own because the point of revision is to get closer and closer to what you want to

say. You look at it and say, *It's nice, but that's not what I want to say.* You bring it closer and closer to your truth. So in the end, there is no help with that from anyone in the whole world.

You once wrote, "As far as the artist is concerned, all the critic can ever do is make him or break him." Does feedback from readers influence your writing?

No. Well, that's a lie. You have to fight excessive praise and excessive criticism. I get a lot of nice letters. I have to think, *I'm glad you like it, now leave me alone.* And a lot of people don't agree with me. *Commentary Magazine,* for example [a monthly magazine that takes a special interest in Jewish issues], dislikes my politics and my stories. They hate my position on things, and their literary people go after me. It's good for me, though; good for the soul to get whacked around a few times.

A Right Way and a Wrong Way

Some examples of the wrong way to give feedback are so blatantly wrong they need no explanation. Years ago an advertising executive friend of mine was working at a large insurance company. He took a draft of his first writing project to his boss, the head of creative services. She tore the ten pages in half without even looking at them, then fed the ripped document into the shredder. My friend's jaw dropped. His boss asked, "Did you make a copy?" He hadn't. "Well," she said, "you have just learned two things. One, always make a copy. Two, don't attach your ego to your work."

It's easy to tell feedback providers, "Don't feed someone's work into the shredder," but what about all the other wrong ways to give feedback that have more to do with how you say something, or when you say something, or how many times you repeat the same damn thing over and over again? In giving feedback, style matters almost as much as substance. Think of your relationship with the writer as a marriage. You know if you don't like your partner's tone of voice, you are a lot less inclined to remove your dripping pantyhose from the shower rod or lower the toilet seat, even when asked for the hundredth time. That's exactly the type of resistance you're likely to provoke in a writer if you present your feedback in the wrong way.

One of the most common wrong ways to give feedback is to deliver it in what I would call a "tsk-tsk" tone. This tone of voice sounds like it should come with a starched, white blouse over a big bosom, and a blackboard with squeaky chalk. Listen for the tsk-tsk tone in the following feedback, "Well," (read: *Miss Thinks She Wants to Be a Writer*) "if you expect me to believe that your narrator actually works as a waitress in a casino in Atlantic City, then you really need to do your homework beforehand." Yech. I can't even stand to write that tone because now I hear it in my head—condescending, reproachful, as if the writer should have known better than to misbehave on the page.

Our job as critiquers is to make the writer feel safe sharing works-in-progress, not like some fifth grader who just shot a spitball in class. Consider a few of the more effective ways the feedback provider could have packaged the same point, without resorting to those superior-sounding "need to's" and "should's."

How about gentler phrasing—"Wow, I love the idea of your narrator being a waitress in an Atlantic City casino, but you might consider fleshing her out with more details so I can really see her."

Or how about a supportive approach—"Wow, neat character, that waitress in Atlantic City. I have a cousin who works at a casino. If you want, I can give you her number so you can ask her what it's like."

Or how about a strategy of "genuine ignorance," which encourages the writer to talk about the issue—"Wow! I admire that you're willing to write about a character so far removed from your own experience. How are you planning to research her?" By encouraging the writer to be the educator, this creates a more dynamic interaction and an opportunity for you to gracefully insert some helpful suggestions.

Another common wrong way to give feedback is a tactic I call the "feedback filibuster." This is when the critiquer arrives at the feedback session with an agenda: to hold the floor until he convinces the writer he is right, and to deny anyone else the chance to present an alternative perspective, if this is a workshop or classroom setting. The feedback provider usually starts his filibuster by reciting from a long list of all the things wrong with the draft. "Item one, improbable plot . . . Item two, stilted dialogue . . . Item twenty-seven, split infinitives . . ." As he goes on and on, rambling and riffling, he may even toss in a few positive remarks, but after a certain point it really doesn't matter because nobody is paying any attention anyway.

Rather than resorting to a feedback filibuster, a much more effective tactic is to present your comments one at a time, allowing space between each of your points for the writer to process the information, or for others to follow up with their own insights about the issue. For instance, when the conversation is focused on the story's plot, that is the appropriate time to introduce your feedback about its improbability. When (and if) the story discussion segues to wordsmithing, that is a good opportunity to take issue with split infinitives. By critiquing a manuscript issue by issue, and by linking every comment to specific examples in the manuscript, you will achieve a much more coherent, interactive discussion.

As a feedback provider, you also want to tune in to "teachable moments." These are opportunities that present themselves in the course of a discussion and provide the perfect occasion to educate the writer about something that is relevant in the moment. On a fifth grade field trip to a farm, for example, when Johnny is being chased by a bull, the teacher might take that opportunity to teach the class about safety around animals. In a workshop discussion, teachable moments happen all the time. "Look everybody! See how the writer made this beautiful transition from generalized to specific time. Let's talk about transitions and why this one works so successfully."

Good feedback providers not only respond to the teachable moments, they create them by inviting the writer's thoughts at the most opportune times. "What were you intending to get across with your ending?" "How would you describe your protagonist?" "Tell me where you're heading with your plot." Teachable moments are about reciprocity—the feedback provider and the writer feed off each other in a stimulating way. The flow of the discussion may not adhere precisely to a rigid agenda, but teachable moments allow you to share your insights with the writer, or to explain a fictional technique right when he is most open to hearing the information.

Red-penning every single instance of a recurring weakness in the text is also a wrong way to give feedback. This is likely to leave the writer feeling queasy when he sees the bloodbath you have made of his manuscript, and it makes you come across as overbearing. A better strategy is to point out the weak pattern in the writing, highlight a few examples, and then allow the writer to take care of the rest on his own. Related to this issue is counting how many times a writer repeats a bad habit, as in, "I counted seventy-nine passive verbs in this chapter." And to make matters worse, counters are usually repeaters. "Seventy-nine passive verbs! You used passive verbs in seventy-nine sentences in this chapter alone. That's seventy-nine sentences that didn't have action verbs. I know because I counted them." Taking the time to count the flaws in another writer's manuscript suggests a certain sadistic pleasure on the critiquer's part. It also raises the question, Doesn't the feedback provider have a life?

Let's see . . . What are some other wrong ways to give feedback? It's wrong to be brutally honest when you give feedback because any kind of brutality is just an excuse to take out your own failures on somebody else. It's wrong to criticize the writer instead of the writing, as in, "You stink at writing plots," or "You don't have enough life experience to be a writer." It's wrong to make dismissive pronouncements: "Nobody's going to read a poem about a housewife in Newark." It's wrong to tease the writer: "I read your story, but I'm not going to tell you what I think." It's wrong to bully a writer into rewriting your way; bullying usually backfires, anyway, because the writer is likely to dig in her heels. And here is an example of the wrong way to give feedback that is not only wrong, but stupid. A writer in an advanced fiction-writing class turned in a short story about a hairdresser. Her professor asked, "Have you ever been a hairdresser?" The writer answered no. "Then don't write about hairdressers," he told her.

I am sure there are lots of other wrong ways to give feedback, but this chapter is putting me in a bad mood. So I will close with this final example, which I hope serves as inspiration for all feedback providers to curb any obnoxious tendencies that might undermine their efforts.

A writer submitted a short story for review to my workshop. A new member of the group launched the discussion, reciting from her three pages of carefully prepared notes. Her tone was strident as she ticked off the story's offenses, though she occasionally inserted a token compliment, which only made things worse. The more the feedback provider talked, the more worked up she got, until her voice sounded like Chris Matthews on helium. The other members of the workshop must have been stunned into silence because no one volunteered a supporting or conflicting opinion. As the workshop leader, I knew it was my job to say or do something to stop the barrage, but frankly I was in over my head.

Finally, the story discussion ended and everyone, including Chris Matthews, returned their written critiques to the writer. After the group disbanded and I had taken three Advils, I thought about how well the writer had held up under the attack. She had listened attentively, a receptive expression molded on her face. Because she had been in several of my previous workshops, I knew she was thick-skinned and good at processing feedback. Once, she had even told the group that she saves her rejections from literary magazines—which I realize can be useful, but for wimps like me this seems like a form of self-flagellation.

This writer will know what to do with Chris Matthew's feedback, I reassured myself, tossing the used coffee filter into the trash. And that's when I saw it—the discarded critique—three stapled pages of strident handwriting, dumped in the garbage, and now dripping with grinds.

Can You Please Be More Specific!

Beth Rider is an assistant professor of pediatrics and codirector of the Communication Skills Teaching Program at Harvard Medical School. Part of Beth's job is to provide feedback workshops for faculty and medical students, who seem to have no issues with peering into open chest cavities or sewing up gaping wounds, but often react squeamishly to the idea of giving each other feedback.

Beth told me a story from her own student days as a pediatric resident treating inpatients at a Boston hospital. When the time came for her formal evaluation by the attending physician, the two met at the elevator en route to the sixth floor. "You're doing a great job," Beth's boss told her on the ride up. She looked forward to their conference and hearing more. Then the elevator doors opened and he took off. End of evaluation. "It was great I got my *A*," Beth said, "but how did I get it? What did I do right?"

In her workshops for the medical school faculty, Beth emphasizes that good feedback is more than a grade or an evaluation. Feedback should be descriptive. The teacher should include examples that illuminate what the medical students are doing right or wrong so that they can improve performance. For instance, instead of calling an intern "lazy," which is a criticism of the student, the more useful feedback would be to direct the criticism to the behavior—"In your last workups, I noticed you took shortcuts that saved time and energy, but caused you to miss the giant growth on the patient's forehead." Now that is specific feedback the student can act on.

Beth adds that the same principles of good feedback apply to the four-year-olds she sees in her practice. Saying to young Damian, "I don't like your behavior," is certainly better than telling the child he is possessed. But it is not as effective as giving him a specific example of what he is doing wrong so that he knows which behavior to change—"Damian! No squeezing your new baby brother until he turns purple."

Medical students, four-year-olds, writers—we are all alike. When it comes to feedback, we need specifics. In the writing realm, if you are critiquing an early draft, specific feedback might focus on such bigger issues as point of view, structure, or characterization. With a more polished draft, specific feedback might hone in on scene details or the mechanics of writing. In either extreme of the drafting process, the value of specific feedback is the same. It directs the writer's attention to potential problem areas or opportunities in the text, while offering insights into why something is working or not working for you, as a reader. Specific feedback may even go so far as to include "solutions" to the problem or concrete suggestions, which can be useful to the writer as long as you don't present them as mandates. To avoid this, it helps to couch your suggestions in language that reminds the writer whose story it is—"You may want to think about limiting point of view to just one character because this would make me feel more emotionally vested in the story; but of course it's completely your call."

As a feedback provider, you might feel reluctant to offer *any* criticism for fear of hurting the writer's feelings, or driving him into a funk. Writers, however, can handle specifics. It's the generalities that bring them to their knees. "Your story didn't work for me." "I don't get it." "This isn't my thing." Those are the kinds of demoralizing conclusions that only serve to leave writers feeling more at a loss than usual. After all, how does a writer revise so that a reader "gets it"? In contrast, writers appreciate detailed responses to their work, which they can use to inform the choices they make during the rewriting process.

In fact, most writers are dependent on feedback providers. After prolonged exposure to their manuscripts, writers often suffer the editorial equivalent of snow blindness. The pages become reduced to a white blur too painful to look at any longer, and without some outside perspective helping to guide them toward the next draft, they can only stagger around blindly, hoping the direction they are heading with revision is the right one. With time and distance, writers may regain their vision and return to the terrain of their own manuscripts with more acuity, but it is always much safer and more expedient to have someone by their side, pointing and shouting out when necessary, "Look out for that crevasse!"

Here is an example of how you, as a feedback provider, can turn a generalization into useful, specific feedback:

"Your narrator doesn't work for me." (Now be more specific.)

"Your narrator doesn't work for me because she is mean and I don't like mean people." (Now be even more specific.)

"Your character doesn't work for me because she purposely ran over her husband with the car on page six, but until that point in the story she seemed genuinely to love him. So I don't understand her motivation. I'm not convinced by this sudden personality change."

Now that is valuable feedback, alerting the writer to the fact that she omitted something crucial in the text. Enlightened by the specifics of your response, the writer will react to this feedback not with frustration, but with a sense of direction and purpose, knowing that she will spend her next writing session happily developing a scene in which her narrator discovers her husband smooching with the attractive new neighbor lady shortly before she turns him into a speed bump.

As this example shows, giving writers specific feedback requires more effort on your part as a critiquer. It is much easier to make generalized assessments—"I was so terribly bored"—than it is to figure out where the piece lost your attention, or why. Some readers fail to offer specific feedback because they are shiftless and their mothers still make their beds. Also, I suspect a few feedback providers secretly enjoy the ego boost that goes along with making autocratic judgments—"I now pronounce this story stultifying!"

Those readers aside, I think most people hesitate to give specific feedback because they lack confidence in their "legitimacy" as a feedback provider, or because they lack the vocabulary of criticism. Certainly, the more experience you have providing feedback, the easier it becomes to analyze and articulate the reasons why you think some aspect of a story needs work. "Here, Mr. Writer, the text disruptively shifts from the third-person, limited-omniscient point of view to an objective voice. Here, the protagonist's emotional crisis wasn't manifested in an externalized action. Here, the lyrical prose rhythm is at odds with the tension of the scene." Whoa! That's good stuff, very impressive, and if you can critique in those terms, help yourself to burnt coffee in the faculty lounge.

Even if you lack the vocabulary of criticism, however, you can still provide valuable feedback, and the bonus is that your comments won't be cloaked in any literary jargon. For example, you may not know that the traditional features of the short story form are conflict, crisis, and resolution, but you do know that you were restless while reading the story until chapter four when the upstanding main character got that phone call from his old drinking buddy, fresh out of jail. That's specific, useful feedback. You may not know how James Joyce's use of the term *epiphany* applies to literature, but you do know that you felt cheated when the mother in the story didn't seem to be phased one bit after the browbeaten daughter she had depended on for years finally got her own apartment six hundred miles away. That's specific, useful feedback.

Experienced or not in the art of literary analysis, if you simply pay attention to your reactions as you read, you will be able to provide the writer with thoughtful input. What's more, you can take comfort in the fact that your feedback doesn't even have to be right—it just has to be sincere. It is up to the writer to weigh your opinions and observations against her own writerly instincts and intentions for the story.

One last point. Most of this chapter focuses on the need for specificity when offering critical feedback. But specificity is also important when it comes to providing positive feedback. "Good job!" "This story is perfect!" "Can I have your autograph?" Of course, secretly, that is *exactly* the kind of feedback all writers think they want to hear when they hand over a manuscript to a critiquer. In reality, though, sweeping affirmations empower the writer only until he begins a new story. Tomorrow, faced with a blank page, with no specific understanding of how he achieved his former success, the writer will be much more inclined to see that last story as a fluke rather than as a cumulative achievement of masterful plotting, vivid characterization, powerful language, and appropriate comma placement.

What's more, sweeping affirmations often backfire. Maybe it is the way humans are hardwired, or because a lot of us still believe in the Evil Eye, but most people are loathe to accept compliments of a general nature. You see proof of this all the time. Tell your best friend she looks nice, and she immediately points out the stain on her blouse. Applaud your child on his beautiful painting, and he angrily rips it in half—"Couldn't you see how the bunny's ears don't match!" Say to a writer, "Great story!" and she automatically thinks, *Oh, you're just saying that. This is probably the worst thing I've ever written.*

But if you offer specifics, then people will actually believe you.

"That blue blouse really brings out the color in your eyes."

"I love how the bunny sunning himself on the hill looks so cute."

"Your main character's journey through adolescence reminded me exactly of the restlessness and insecurity of my own childhood."

Positive feedback is more convincing and easier to accept when it is specific. As pediatrician and Harvard professor Beth Rider emphasizes in her workshops, "If you want good behaviors repeated, you need to be descriptive." Whether you are providing positive feedback to medical students, four-year-olds, or writers, you can help them continue to succeed or just feel terrific by letting them know *exactly* what they did right. And for that reason alone it is worth more than the time it takes to ride six floors up in an elevator.

✒ Khaled Hosseini   *"Even if the book is good, no one is going to want to publish it."*

Much of Khaled Hosseini's blockbuster first novel, *The Kite Runner,* is set in his native Afghanistan, a country many Westerners would have had trouble finding on a map before the tragedy of September 11, 2001. The story evolves from the doomed friendship of two Afghani boys—one upper class and one outcast—and spans thirty years of the country's recent history, from the end of the monarchy, to the Soviet invasion, to the Taliban's reign of terror. Khaled was about halfway through writing the novel when Afghanistan drew the eyes of the world.

Khaled began shopping his novel around to agents in June 2002, less than a year after the United States had bombed Afghanistan in search of Al-Qaeda members. He sent the manuscript to agents six to eight at a time, collecting an early string of rejections. In the midst of this lackluster beginning, he received a particularly crushing letter. One agent reported, "The book is good, but the public doesn't want to hear any more about Afghanistan," Khaled recalls. Afghanistan is passé. That was the agent's implication.

Despite the fact that only two tenuous months had passed since the Afghanistan Grand Council had established an interim government to replace Taliban rule, Khaled was convinced the agent was right. After all, by the summer of 2002 much of the world's focus had shifted to Iraq, with headlines of a possible United States–led invasion bumping any news of Afghanistan to an occasional copy line on the CNN ticker bar. "It felt like a no-win situation," Khaled said. The agent had suggested he should think about writing a book about something else, and he was inclined to agree. "Even if the book is good, no one is going to want to publish it," he recalls thinking. "There was no fix for that. After that feedback, I was in the doldrums."

He stopped sending the book out for a brief period, until his wife, Roya, intervened. Khaled had been relying on Roya's editorial advice as he drafted the novel, but now she sounded in with moral support. "She kept pestering me to keep sending the manuscript out to more agents," he laughs. Reluctantly, he followed through, sending the manuscript to six more agents. One of those six was Elaine Koster, who had no doubts about the book's timely appeal. Elaine quickly sold *The Kite Runner* to Riverhead Books, who rushed it into publication in 2003.

In an earlier draft of the book, Khaled's protagonist, Amir, was married to an American woman from Ohio. For some time, Khaled's editor had been suggesting that the wife's character was problematic, and that the second half of the book lost much of its cultural flavor. Three weeks before the final manuscript was due, Khaled was still trying to address these issues— tweaking here, tweaking there—when the solution suddenly dawned on him. "I called my editor and said, 'I figured it out! The wife isn't American; she's Afghan!'" Khaled says. His editor agreed; in fact, she had been thinking the same thing, but had hoped he would come to this realization on his own.

Amazingly, Khaled met his deadline less than a month later. Because he was working full-time as a physician, he would write from five p.m. until two in the morning, then fax the pages to Roya, who was pregnant with their second child and staying with her parents for a few weeks. Roya would fax her suggestions back to Khaled, who would revise accordingly, then e-mail the new work to his editor. "I felt like I was standing in front of a mountain," Khaled says, "The idea of reinventing, reimagining the whole middle of the book seemed like such a Herculean task. But it's an act of faith. You do what your gut tells you and hope it's right."

And what about that one agent's prediction that a novel about Afghanistan was passé—feedback that almost stopped Khaled from pursuing publication? When *The Kite Runner* first came out, *Publishers Weekly* stated, "It is rare that a book is at once so timely and of such high literary quality." This sentiment was reiterated when Borders announced *The Kite Runner* as the winner of its 2003 Original Voices Award, describing its themes as "timeless." Even more compelling, Khaled consistently hears from readers who tell him that the book came out at just the right time.

Now in paperback, *The Kite Runner* remains on the *New York Times* bestseller list years after its original release, and has been optioned by Dream-Works. For the author, the enormous success of his first novel is exciting, but nothing means more to him than the feedback he receives regularly from people wanting to donate money, resources, or goods to Afghans, particularly donations for the children. Khaled tells of one moving note from a couple that had started the process of adopting an Afghan child after reading the book. "I appreciate the reviews and accolades, but this was the real world," Khaled says. "Real people affecting real lives. It goes to show you what a subjective business publishing is."

The Moment of Truth

If you know anything about the University of Iowa Writers' Workshop, you have probably heard stories about the late, great Frank Conroy, who served as the director of the program for eighteen years and loved his job of helping emerging writers. I never went to this prestigious program, and I never met the man, but every article I have read about Conroy makes some mention of his blunt, curmudgeonly approach to teaching creative writing, including his admission to making one student cry and another one faint with his classroom criticism. In a 2004 Associated Press interview, Conroy said with a laugh that it was lucky one of the other students in the fainter's class was a doctor; who realized what was happening and caught her before she hit the ground.

I am not so sure I see the humor in making writers faint, but I do understand that you can't be a good feedback provider if you are not honest about a work's faults, or the writer's bad writing habits ("personal tics," as Conroy referred to these unintended glitches that show up in the prose). That is why, in almost every feedback session, there needs to come a Moment of Truth. Criticism, in combination with kindness, is part of your job description. So if you avoid the Moment of Truth, then you and the writer might just as well go roller-skating, or get matching tattoos, or indulge in some other pleasant diversion that isn't intended to enable good writing.

When I was just starting to write this book, I gave one of my first completed chapters to my friend Cathee for feedback. Cathee and I had met when she took one of my fiction-writing workshops a few years earlier. Sometimes, secretly, I use the workshop as a recruiting ground for new friends. When Cathee showed up at the first class, two things spoke to her potential to improve my social life: from the first story discussion it was obvious she was gifted at providing feedback (a prerequisite for friendship in my world); and her youngest daughters are the same ages as my two girls. Right away, I started pursuing Cathee for lunch dates and play dates; and how could she say no when she still had to face me every Thursday night in the workshop?

After I had given Cathee my chapter for review, three long weeks passed without hearing a response from her. Suffice it to say that three weeks is *way* past the statute of limitations for giving feedback to friends, so I knew that this delay didn't bode well. Instead of being passive and paranoid about the situation, however, I decided to act like an adult. I picked up the phone and called Cathee to arrange another play date, knowing this would corner her into giving me feedback.

The next day, Cathee and I were visiting in her living room while our four girls played downstairs in her romper-room basement. The subject of my book happened to come up in the conversation. Actually, I brought it up, partly because of my agenda to force Cathee's feedback, and partly because I talk incessantly about a book when I am working on it, even though my husband has repeatedly mentioned that this gets old, fast. "Did you have a chance yet to read the chapter I gave you a few weeks ago?" I asked casually.

"Another cup of tea?" Cathee answered, and that's when I knew she was stalling for time and that she hadn't liked my chapter at all. I also knew that she knew that I knew that she was stalling for time and hadn't liked my chapter at all, because girlfriends always know when something awkward is unspoken between them. We don't let on directly that anything is amiss, but we do get weirdly polite and start pushing the tea.

Cathee retrieved her copy of my chapter from a nearby desk and took the seat beside me on the couch. Right away, I noticed that the top page didn't bear any line edits or notations. Maybe I had misinterpreted the situation. Maybe Cathee thought my chapter was perfect! Then she asked me again if I wanted a refill of tea, and at that point all hope faded.

Cathee's first few comments about the piece were positive. She pointed out a handful of well-written passages and a few lines she particularly liked; but then she hesitated, and we both knew what had to come next—the Moment of Truth. To her credit, Cathee didn't mince words. "I think you need to start over," she said. She went on to explain in the gentlest manner possible how she felt the chapter was disjointed, like a mishmash of thoughts pasted together. She wasn't sure what point I was trying to make. The chapter, in short, didn't have a structure or a message; at least not any that she could discern.

To my credit, I got through the Moment of Truth without doing any of the things I felt like doing—crying, hitting, kicking a bunch of stuffed animals across the room. As usual, one part of my brain started thrashing my ego—*Bad writer! Idiot! You'll never be able to write a book about feedback!* Yet, even while I was silently catastrophizing, another part of my brain was registering Cathee's insights. Just as every good feedback provider has a responsibility to arrive at the Moment of Truth, every feedback receiver, too, has a responsibility to keep it together enough to face the Truth, and use it to become a stronger writer.

I know it was hard for Cathee as a feedback provider, and especially as a friend, to speak honestly about my chapter. The best feedback providers are well aware of the emotional impact of their words. Sometimes, no matter how kindly you package your criticism, you can never eliminate the wince factor completely.

I spoke about this issue with a writing workshop instructor and author in Chicago named Enid Powell, who has been teaching for over twenty years. In her former life as a writer for a soap opera, Enid experienced plenty of toxic feedback in a working environment where favored writers received gold stars on their scripts, while others were reduced to a "puddle of shame." Now, with her adult students, Enid says, "If I find myself frustrated or upset when I'm giving feedback, I stop, because if I don't critique with love, they won't understand what I'm trying to say."

Enid came upon this sudden insight in the middle of editing a manuscript, and it was a shock. "I had to stop and do something else, to remind myself of my affection for the writer and for her work in the past," she explains. "The time-out seemed to give my brain time to think of solutions to the problem, instead of the blind *No, No, No* that comes when frustration makes me blank out."

The need to curb any impatience with the writer also applies during story discussions, Enid adds. "Recently, I found myself about to interrupt three times during the lengthy reading of a manuscript, and not with a kindly 'Excuse me, I think we've heard enough.' Thank God I stopped myself," she says. "It would have been disastrous. I would have lost the trust this person places in me to even have the courage to tackle a difficult topic. By staying silent, I gained time to remind myself of the vulnerability of all my writers; then I could think more clearly about what was salvageable in her work, so that the discussion ended on a positive note." Continues Enid, "My goal is to keep people writing, and to prove to them that when they say, 'Nobody will be interested in this,' they're wrong."

Enid also told me about the time she was critiquing a novel and realized that the writer needed to switch the point of view from third person to first person for a variety of convincing reasons (one being that, with three female protagonists, the third-person perspective created a confusion of "she's"). Enid felt so bad, yet certain, about the need for this significant change that she offered to retype the writer's entire manuscript for her.

For all of you feedback providers who are softies like Enid, here is a comforting thought. The Moment of Truth is just that—a moment, relatively speaking. Once you put forth your constructive criticism you can then move on to happier discussion topics, like the remarkable power of revision, and where the writer might go from here.

After Cathee told me I needed to start my chapter over, she began asking me questions, the first one being, "What exactly are you trying to communicate in this piece?" Our subsequent conversation not only distracted me from my misery, but also enabled me to clarify my thinking and regroup. Eventually, I understood why the chapter failed. One reason was because the introduction was a leftover from an earlier draft in which I had focused the chapter differently. I had been too lazy and enamored with the writing to let it go, so I had revised the lead to death, hoping to save it and avoid extra work. With the realization that I needed to abandon the opening entirely, the rewriting process had already begun, and the wince factor had already started to diminish.

Thanks to the Moment of Truth, I saw that my point—and I did have one—could rise from the ashes and be reborn as a new chapter, but only if I got a fresh start, didn't cut corners, and scheduled a few more play dates.

Common Human Decency

Every year, Houghton Mifflin publishes *The Best American Short Stories,* an anthology of twenty stories culled from thousands that were published in magazines in the United States and Canada the previous year. The series editor also chooses an additional hundred short stories of distinction, and lists them by title and author in the back of the book.

One year, my friend Catherine discovered that a short story of hers was listed among the honored one hundred in the back pages. She learned this happy news when she was skimming through the anthology in a bookstore, debating whether she could afford to shell out the $11.95 to buy her own copy. Suddenly, amid the usual autonyms—Alice Munro, Lorrie Moore, John Updike—she spied her own name and story title bouncing off the page like a bright dot from one of those inadvisable laser pointers. This came as quite a surprise. Until then, Catherine hadn't even been aware that her story, originally published in a small literary journal, was in the running for this lofty collection. Given the circumstances, she decided to spring for the book.

I still find it hard to believe that this—this happenstance—is how my friend learned that a story of hers had been chosen as one of America's most distinguished for that year. Every time I think about it, I just can't get past the "what if's." What if Catherine hadn't bothered to browse through the back of the book? What if she had *never* learned about this honor? What if she had spent her whole life assuming that her name and the name of Alice Munro had never graced the same list of distinguished authors, and this assumption had eventually led her to stop writing and degenerate into someone sad and pathetic, say an HGTV addict, reeking of handcrafted pomander balls, surrounded by wicker trash baskets converted into kitschy side tables, and surviving on stale-but-still-edible picture frames? This didn't happen to my friend Catherine, but I'm sure it has happened to some writer, somewhere, who didn't know her work was appreciated.

Which begs the question, Why *didn't* the editor at Houghton Mifflin simply pick up the telephone to tell Catherine the good news? Even a perky, short note would have sufficed. "Dear Writer, Congratulations! We loved your story and selected it as one of this year's most distinguished. XOXO, the Editor." Such a simple gesture, but think of the difference it could make to a writer. So why-oh-why didn't the editor take the time to do this?

I can tell you why, though if you have had any experience querying editors or sending submissions out to magazines or publishing houses, you probably know the answer. Editors have no common human decency. This is not a statement on their character. (Having once been an editor of a regional magazine, I can attest to the fact that at least some editors are actually quite nice in real life.) No, a lack of common human decency is simply a requirement of the job, as delineated in *The Professional Editor's Handbook,* Rule No. 7,849: "Editors must refrain from exhibiting any form of compassion, enthusiasm, interest, or basic manners toward writers at large."

The reason for this rule is perfectly obvious. Editors who exhibit even the slightest sign of common human decency run the risk of desperate, aspiring authors (of which there are legions) inundating them with phone calls and e-mails about their latest scintillating story ideas, their passion for the written word, and their unpaid cable bills, all under the misguided notion that one innocent, supportive gesture constituted an "in." No busy editor— routinely beleaguered by time, budget, and page constraints—can afford to take this risk. Hence Rule No. 7,849. And hence the necessity for the biggest indecency of them all: the form rejection letter ("Doesn't meet our needs"), used even for cases where the story may be good, but the fit isn't.

Here, gentle reader, I am going to presume that you are not a professional editor at a magazine or publishing house. As such, you are not required to curb your enthusiasm around writers at large, and your behavior should conform to an entirely different set of rules, with Rule No. 1 being, "If you like a writer's story, tell her!" Otherwise, your silence becomes a form of toxic feedback, forcing the writer to make assumptions about how you feel about her work. And allowing writers to assume anything is never a good idea because they will always assume the worst.

You would think that a feedback provider who actually enjoyed a writer's efforts would jump at the opportunity to tell her so. After all, how often is it that we get to spread a little good news for a change? Yet, remarkably, readers often fail to show enthusiasm, or even respond, to writers whose work they enjoyed. Making this silent treatment all the more peculiar is that oftentimes these very same readers had invited, sometimes even nagged, the writer to share her work with them. Once the manuscript is received, however, some trait in these readers (perhaps cluelessness, laziness, or a tad bit of jealousy) prevents them from extending their congratulations on a job well done.

Equally perplexing is when a reader/feedback provider volunteers only a stingy or cryptic response to a submission, which sometimes can be worse for the writer than no response at all. Here is one example of this (which happened to me), but I have heard dozens of similar tales. Recently, I asked a writer friend to look over a finished essay, before I submitted it to a publisher. In the cover note, I also asked him to verify the spelling of his name because he was referenced in the piece. A few days later, I received his feedback: "My name is spelled correctly." For days, I fumed about this pathetic excuse for a response. Finally, unable to let it go, I e-mailed this person back. "Just curious . . ." I wrote. "What did you think about the essay?" His response: "I thought it was EXCELLENT!" All caps.

So why didn't he say so in the first place?

Writers work hard, often without pay. They also spend way too much time thinking and inferring. For these reasons and many more, writers need and deserve some honest gushing over their successes. Yes, once a story or a book is accepted, editors are often effusive in their praise, but during the writer's long and arduous journey toward publication (if that is the writer's goal), external validation, compliments, or even just a supportive thumbs-up can be ridiculously hard to come by. This is not right. Not right at all. Praise nourishes the ego, and writers—to be able to continue doing what they do—need all the ego they can get.

So here is an entreaty to readers and feedback providers everywhere, including workshop participants, writing instructors, friends, spouses, colleagues, parents, and anyone else who doesn't work as a professional editor at a magazine or a publishing house. Show a little common human decency. When you read someone's work and like it, make a point to say so. Don't make the writer ask twice. Don't hold back. Don't worry about looking like a crazed fan. Chase the writer down an alley if you have to, waving her manuscript over your head and shouting at her retreating form, "I loved your story! I loved your story!" At the very least, drop her a form affirmation letter: "Dear Writer, Your work really met my needs!!! XOXO, [your name here]."

Small addendum: Gentle reader, on the off chance that you actually do work as an editor at a magazine or publishing house, I would like to say for the record that when I made that statement about editors having no common human decency, I meant that in a *good* way. And because you are a professional editor who has clearly taken a personal interest in my work (why else would you be reading this book?), I am sure you wouldn't mind sending me your contact information so that I can tell you all about my latest scintillating book idea, and my passion for the written word, and my unpaid cable bills. Better yet, I am free for lunch tomorrow and every day in the foreseeable future. Just let me know what works best for you!

✤ Don (D. B.) Johnson *"My best advice is to marry well."*

I was going to meet Don (D. B.) Johnson at an upscale coffee bar to talk about his award-winning picture-book series that conceptualizes Henry David Thoreau in the form of a cubist-style bear. But the coffee bar wasn't open when we arrived, so we moved our meeting outside to a picnic table under a tree. This turned out to be a much more fitting setting for a conversation with a writer and illustrator who grew up in rural New Hampshire, loves nature, and has spent much of his adult life trying to reconcile the desire to be an artist with the reality of needing to earn a living. "If you live in the country with three kids, you do a lot of justifying," Don smiles.

For more than twenty years, Don worked as a freelance illustrator, first doing editorial cartoons for newspapers around the country, and then taking more lucrative, corporate assignments. About once a year, he picked up his copy of *Walden* and reread it, inspired by Thoreau's defense of living the creative life. In one passage, Thoreau recounted the story of how a friend suggested he travel to Fitchburg by train, to which Thoreau countered that it would be faster to walk the thirty miles than to earn the ninety cents to pay for the ticket. In 1991, Don noted this passage in his "idea file," thinking it might make a good story.

Seven years later, having just returned from a trip to Russia to visit his son, Don found himself back in his studio without any work. Rummaging through his idea file, he saw the reference he had made to Thoreau. "It was serendipity," Don recalls. His trip to Russia had reminded him of his own childhood, seeing clothes on the line and experiencing life without so many modern conveniences. While there, he had even taken a train ride to the Russian countryside. "Everything came together," Don says, and he knew it was time to act on his idea. He would create a picture book—a series of picture books, actually—embodying Thoreau's beliefs, starting with a story centered around Thoreau's passage on why it was faster to walk to Fitchburg.

Because Don thought of himself as an illustrator, not a writer, he asked his wife to write the text that would accompany his illustrations. She declined, saying Thoreau was his passion and that he should write the story. "She was right," Don acknowledges, and two months later he had finished the manuscript and a sample illustration. Two weeks after he sent the work off to Houghton Mifflin, they called with an offer. Published in 2000, *Henry Hikes to Fitchburg* became a *New York Times* best seller, and won the Ezra Jack Keats New Writer Award and *Publishers Weekly* Best Book of the Year. Since then, Don has written three more Thoreau-inspired picture books, as well as an unrelated children's story called *Eddie's Kingdom,* about a boy who lives in an apartment.

During the writing process, Don finds his most useful feedback close to home. "My best advice is to marry well," he says, referring to the fact his wife, Linda Michelin, is a writer who often serves as his editor. "I think all my ideas are good, but they probably aren't. Having a spouse or friend who can evaluate your work gives you clarity of reason. It's impossible to judge your own writing."

Don also values the feedback he receives from his young readers, whom he describes as "the best audience ever because they are so open. It doesn't matter if they haven't heard of Thoreau, or pick up on the social issues in the books, as long as they like the story." After a reading in Boston of *Henry Hikes to Fitchburg* (which makes the point that you don't need money to get somewhere; you can just put on your boots and go), one little girl in the audience recommended he write another book—Henry Goes Shopping. "She thought I should do a story about Henry going to the mall," Don laughs. "It just goes to show, you can't get to kids soon enough."

But if young readers don't always recognize Thoreau's influence in Don's books, most of their parents do. Feedback from adults about the series and its meditations on materialism, nature, and individualism has been overwhelmingly positive, not surprising given the fact that a recent *Newsweek* poll listed Thoreau among the top ten most respected American figures.

For some parents, however, Henry the bear's affinity with his independent-thinking namesake makes him suspect as a character in a children's book. At one public appearance a mother said to Don, "I hope you're not planning to do any Henry books about civil disobedience," a reference to Thoreau's 1849 essay on the right and obligation to follow your conscience, even if it means breaking the law. At the time, Don hadn't been planning to do a story around this issue, but the woman's comment inspired his next book, *Henry Climbs a Mountain.* In that story, Henry is sent to jail for refusing to pay a poll tax as a matter of principle. While in prison, he draws a picture on his cell wall of a mountain, which he then escapes into and climbs, demonstrating that you can lock up a person's body, but not his mind. "I owe that mother a lot," Don smiles.

From the inception of Henry the bear, Don had planned to write just three books in the series. He had a change of heart, however, after several parents commented on Henry's friend in the first book, who works all day at odd jobs in order to earn his train fare to Fitchburg. "Some of the parents thought I was trying to undermine the idea of work," Don says, "when what I was trying to do was to expand readers' ideas about what work could be." To address this issue, Don decided to write a fourth book, *Henry Works,* which shows that writing, too, is a form of labor, even if its value isn't always measured by income.

"As a writer, you are taking a chance on yourself whenever you write a proposal or take months or years to write something," Don points out. "Writers take risks, and part of that risk is being seen as that lame person who doesn't have a job." Like Thoreau and his eponymous bear, Don believes that people should spend less time working to earn money and more time doing the things that interest them. He knows from personal experience that it isn't always easy to put that philosophy into practice. "I respect people," Don adds, "who buck the system in that way."

Editorial Biases

I can't stand it when pets die in stories. In fact, I like to think that if I had been Steinbeck's editor when he wrote *The Red Pony*, I could have saved generations of kids a lot of wasted heartache. This is one of my editorial biases, and so whenever I am critiquing a story in which a pet is killed or even injured, I try my hardest to make the writer change it. My longtime workshop participants know this about me. One of them, a family doctor who has produced a terrific and growing collection of short fiction, once tried to get away with having his main character throw a cat against the wall. The protagonist was drunk; his behavior in keeping with his character. The scene fed into the climax of the story beautifully. As if I cared.

"Change it," I demanded.

Every feedback provider comes with editorial biases. These are predispositions or conditioned responses we have picked up along the way that can adversely affect the quality of our feedback. For instance, maybe you are biased against a certain genre of fiction or toward a particular poetic paradigm. Or maybe you hate freckle-faced characters, or love *New Yorker*–type stories (or at least you *say* you love *New Yorker*–type stories). Unlike your editorial instincts, which shape your feedback according to what you believe is best for the work, your editorial biases shape your feedback in a way that often says more about *you* than about the writing.

As feedback providers, it is important we set aside our editorial biases in order to provide impartial feedback. Of course, there really is no such thing as impartial feedback (after all, we are humans, not robots), but the notion—similar to the concept of absolute zero—still provides a useful baseline, however theoretical. For example, if I weren't so biased against animal cruelty in fiction, what *would* I have said to the workshop participant who had his protagonist throw the cat against the wall? The answer to that question moves me closer to impartial feedback by several degrees. It also showcases the gap that can exist between your editorial instincts and your editorial biases, and how the latter can easily compromise the former.

So how do you learn to recognize your editorial biases in order to set them aside when critiquing a work? The first place to look is genetics. Some people are born liking science fiction while other people's DNA makes it impossible for them to understand why anyone would attend a Star Trek convention, even to people-watch. To figure out your genetic editorial biases, just picture the kinds of books you buy when no one is looking. Now picture the kinds of books you wouldn't be caught dead buying unless required to for a class or a book group. There you go. These are your genetic editorial biases, all lined up for you on your mental bookshelf.

If you were just reading for pleasure, these biases wouldn't matter so much because the only person you need to please is yourself (though it wouldn't hurt to branch out once in a while). As a feedback provider, however, your purpose is to serve the writer, which means your tastes are not only irrelevant, but could get in the way if they predispose you to liking or hating a piece before you have even read it.

Your first inclination might be to disqualify yourself from critiquing a piece written in a genre or style you don't normally read. Of course, you can't do that in a workshop, where your commitment is to help every writer in the group, not just the ones who write to your sensibilities. So when you do sit down to critique something in good faith, you must try your hardest not to railroad the writer. Otherwise, if you are into neosurrealism poetry, for example, you may find yourself challenging the poet-submitter to break the boundaries of syntax, and shoot for a little less intellectual authority and a lot more edge, despite the fact that what he has presented for critique is a Petrachan sonnet. Similarly, if your taste in novels runs to traditional happy endings, you may push the writer to have the boy get the girl in the end, despite the writer's clear intent to have the boy get the boy. In situations like these, it is important to remind yourself, *This isn't my work. This isn't about me. It's about helping the writer achieve his intent.*

The fact is, even if you are reviewing a work that falls outside the realm of your usual reading habits, you can still provide the writer with useful information. After all, much of the criteria of good writing applies across the board. Did the work create an emotional response? Is it memorable? Are the characters' actions believable? Is the fictional universe well established? Do any scenes feel underdeveloped? Is the language clear or confusing? Plus, here is a bonus. By having to thoughtfully critique a work in a genre or style you don't normally read, you are likely to discover its unique qualities and strengths, and maybe even expand your own reading tastes.

In addition to our genetic editorial biases, we also acquire biases from external sources. And the weird thing about a lot of these acquired biases is that they often have less to do with how we actually feel about a piece of writing, and more to do with how we *think* we should feel about the work.

Say you go to a writing program that proselytizes minimalist fiction, or "K-Mart Realism," as novelist Thomas Wolfe negatively referred to the proliferation of Raymond Carveresque stories, with spare prose and a focus on small (but meaningful) moments in the main character's limited life. Before you know it, you may be introjecting the program's editorial biases into your own feedback—discouraging stylistic variation or alternative forms of narrative—without even being aware that you are doing this. If everyone else in the class follows suit, you can see why some MFA programs are accused of promulgating homogeneous writing, and are branded as "cookie cutter." A similar phenomenon can happen in critique groups, especially if one of the members has Rasputinlike powers that sway everybody else's feedback and writing style.

The media and publishing industry also serve to shape our editorial biases, influencing our feedback by telling us what is in or out of vogue. In addition, social or cultural expectations affect feedback. My friend Bindi is a short story writer who immigrated to America with her Sikh parents when she was five years old. Bindi can't write about an Indian woman protagonist without at least one critiquer suggesting she focus the story around an arranged marriage, or the issue of being caught between two cultures. "It's as if every Indian story has to contain those particular thematic landmarks in order to be legitimate," she says. Bringing these kinds of expectations to your feedback sends the wrong messages to the writer–"Stick to the standards." "Don't veer from popular themes." "Don't innovate."

In addition, biases can creep into our feedback because of how we feel about a writer personally. There is no denying that when we sit down to critique a manuscript, we all have a tendency to go easier on someone we like and be more dismissive of someone who gets on our nerves. Some classes attempt to sidestep the issue of personal biases by making the writers anonymous, but to me this tactic feels like a charade. When I was giving feedback in a class that did this, I couldn't concentrate on the story discussion because I was so obsessed with trying to figure out who wrote it. And when my own story was on the table, the only thing I could think about was not giving myself away. *Don't look nervous! Don't jot down any notes! Should I make comments to throw people off, or say nothing?* Given all these distractions, it seems to me the better solution to overcoming personal biases is simply to rise above them. React to the work, not the writer. Let's all critique like grown-ups.

For better or worse, we would not be who we are if it weren't for how nature and nurture have shaped our tastes, proclivities, and idiosyncrasies, literary and otherwise. Regardless, having editorial biases doesn't mean you can't be an excellent feedback provider on all kinds of writing by all kinds of writers. I have seen proof of this over and over—how a group member who abhorred horror novels learned to critique one skillfully and without judgment; how a critiquer who only read action adventure came to appreciate the equally intense firepower of women's fiction; and how two group members who disliked each other in real life still managed to provide one another with supportive and thoughtful critiques.

As for me, I am getting better at overcoming my own editorial biases, though I still have a lot of room for improvement. I see an introductory clause and my knee-jerk reaction is to slash it out, without even considering whether it is in keeping with the authorial voice. I read certain kinds of foreshadowing ("Young Sarah didn't know it at the time, but this was to be the last day of her childhood innocence") and the manuscript is flying out of my hands before I even stop to consider whether this is my issue or the writer's. I see a confusion of characters and my first recommendation is to simplify—"Give the couple two children instead of four"; "Send the visiting relatives back to the their own flea-infested apartment." But is my bias toward simplicity in keeping with the writer's intent, or my own need for peace and quiet?

As a feedback provider, my goal is not only to give the writer my honest response to his work, but also to understand where that response is coming from, just in case it is coming from some crotchety old windbag inside me. If I recognize any editorial biases creeping into my feedback, I need to revise my comments accordingly, or at least present my feedback with a warning, "Heads up, writer! I despise foreshadowing with the white-hot intensity of a thousand suns, so you might want to think twice before following my advice to cut it all out." That said, even if you are uncertain whether your feedback is biased or not, I do think it is better to speak up than remain silent. Otherwise, you are not giving the writer the benefit of the doubt that he can determine for himself whether to ignore or act on your feedback. My personal credo is simply to do my best to give feedback that serves the story and not just my own tastes . . . with one glaring exception.

Remember that family doctor in my workshop who had his protagonist throw the cat against the wall? Well, he refused to follow my demand to change this. In the story the cat dies of a broken neck (it pains me to write about it even now). But the good news is, I still see this writer on a regular basis, and I am still pushing hard for a miracle cure for the cat. Because, bias or not, pets should *never* be killed or even injured in stories.

Get That Look Off Your Face

When I was growing up, my parents had no tolerance for whining or self-absorption, which I think was the main reason I felt put out much of the time. How could I appreciate an otherwise happy childhood when the world did not always revolve around me? As a result, I spent much of my youth moping and preoccupied with my own sorry circumstances, though I knew better than to voice my bad attitude aloud. My mother wasn't fooled by my stoic silence. "Get that look off your face," she would always be telling me.

Fast-forward to a few months ago. I received a phone call from a retired surgeon in his early seventies, who invited me to lunch at a swanky, historical inn. He had just finished writing a memoir, and his wife had heard from someone in their senior housing community that I taught writing workshops and had recently had a book published. This gentleman wanted my advice about getting published, a subject I am asked about on a regular basis—which seems strange to me because I still see myself as a desperate wannabe. *My* advice on how to get published? Get a New York City phone book; get a copy of *Writer's Market;* and prepare to feel like Joan Crawford's adopted daughter in *Mommy Dearest* every time you check the mailbox—"No more wire hangers! No more wire hangers!"

The gentleman and I met at the swanky, historical inn, wonderfully genteel with its sun-faded, floral wallpaper, white tablecloths laden with delicate china, and a preponderance of diners of a certain age sporting tweed jackets and pocketbooks with clasps. My host, whose handsome, surgeon hands still looked capable of massaging a human heart back to life, invited me to start the meal with a glass of wine. Who was I to argue? Here was an alternate universe, far removed from my own reality at home all day, writing in my holey jeans, lunching on Lean Pockets, just me and my beloved seventeen-year-old dog, her bony back curled against the roller of my office chair. Looking at the elegantly etched faces all around me in this lovely dining room, it occurred to me that I needed to get out more, or at least make more money so I could save up for a facelift.

Over crab cakes, the gentleman asked me about my writing and my life. As usual when I am talking about myself, the time passed quickly and pleasantly. Late in the meal, however, the conversation turned to his memoir, which he told me he had been urged to write by his wife and several of his friends. I have noticed that memoirists do this a lot; they bring up the fact that someone else was behind their decision to write their personal story, as if they need second-party validation to justify a book about their lives.

"I think everyone should write a memoir," I reassured him sincerely. "Lots of them in fact." That last remark might have been the wine talking, but I really do believe that every person has memories worth chronicling and sharing. Memoirs only disappoint because of how they are rendered, not because the writer isn't a worthy subject. "No, I'm sorry, your life doesn't qualify for a memoir. Now, if you had been a geisha or a super-hero . . . Next!"

I asked the gentleman if he had started looking for an agent, remembering that the purpose of this lunch was to talk about publishing.

"I've done a bit of research," he said, dismissing his efforts with a shrug.

"The ideal agent is a compassionate barracuda," I announced, borrowing this phrase from one of my successful novelist friends. I wasn't sure this observation qualified as useful advice, but I have always liked saying it and pretending it was my own.

"Actually, I'm not really interested in agents or publishers at the moment," the gentleman confessed, after the waitress had removed our empty plates and refilled our coffee. "I've been toiling alone on this memoir for two years now, and what I really want is an outside perspective. I was wondering," he paused to take a sip of his decaf, and I thought I noted a slight tremor in his steady, surgeon's hands, "if you might possibly consider reading the book and offering me some feedback?"

Oh my. This was a different situation entirely, one that required more than committing myself to a leisurely, free lunch. The gentleman hastened to add that he would pay me for my services, but by this time I was feeling more than a little cornered and guilty about having hogged most of the conversation. Plus, I had made a point of ordering dessert because I wasn't the one picking up the tab. So I told him I would read his memoir, and that lunch was payment enough; though that last part might have been the wine talking, too.

Three weeks later, I was driving to the gentleman's house at 7:45 a.m. with a bad attitude, a travel mug of espresso, and my copy of his 238-page manuscript that I had earmarked with suggestions and edits. I had scheduled the feedback session as early as possible because I wanted to keep the rest of the day free, or at least free until 2:30 that afternoon, when I needed to pick up the damn kids. I had my own writing to do, which wasn't going well, deadlines were looming, and I felt fat. At stoplights, I drummed my fingers on the steering wheel and glared at the manuscript on the passenger

seat, reminding me of all the hours I had lost in the past few weeks reviewing somebody else's work, when I needed somehow to salvage my own.

When the gentleman opened his front door, I was greeted by the smell
of freshly baked cranberry muffins. He offered me one and apologized for
Snowball, the cat, who was circling my legs and fuzzing up my black tights.
I noticed that the writer had set out on the breakfast table a clean copy of
his memoir with two sharpened pencils beside it. From a room in the back
of the apartment, his wife appeared. "Be merciful," she said by way of greet-
ing, then quickly retreated, followed by Snowball, either to escape or to give
us some privacy.

Thank goodness for the little things that jar us out of our own snits. Maybe
it was the travel mug of espresso I had downed on the ride over, or maybe it
was the wife's "be merciful" before she backed out of the room, but I think
it was seeing those two sharpened pencils poised for note-taking on whatever I had to say that made me suddenly aware that I needed an attitude ad-
justment. Here I was, standing in a writer's kitchen, exuding negativity and
impatience. The fact that I wasn't complaining or whining aloud meant
nothing. I had, as my mother used to point out, that look on my face, plain
enough for even Snowball to realize he had better leave me the hell alone.

You cannot be a good feedback provider if you have a bad attitude. Attitude is huge in affecting outcomes; this is true in any realm of life, from
overcoming disease to landing that promotion. As a feedback provider,
attitude affects the way you approach a critique; are you focused on the
writer's needs or your own? Attitude affects the way you frame your comments; is your language encouraging or disdainful? Attitude also affects
how the writer reacts to your input; will he be receptive to your suggestions
and gain confidence, or will he feel smote from the black energy emoting
from your ears and never want to share his work again?

For me, the crazy thing is that I love giving writers feedback, but that
still doesn't stop me from falling into snits. This has nothing to do with the
quality of a manuscript, and everything to do with my recurring, childish
tendency to feel put out when the world does not revolve around me.
When the gentleman had delivered the draft of his memoir to me, I had
felt the heft of those 238 pages, and all I could think about was how much
work I had ahead of me. I didn't have time for this. I wasn't even getting
paid. What the heck did this old person want from me?

Later, standing in the writer's kitchen, confronted by those two sharpened pencils, I was reminded in the nick of time that the real effort was on

the gentleman's part. Two years of work had gone into drafting this memoir. Not just work, but heart. This situation wasn't about me. It was all about the writer—his issues, his needs. I had no right to undermine his effort by projecting negativity. I also wasn't doing myself any favors. By focusing so narrowly on my own dark thoughts, I was bound to miss out on the real enjoyment that comes from helping a writer improve his work.

And so, I got that look off my face. I consciously shook off my bad attitude and replaced it with a positive one. I did this not by changing my personality (*as if*), but by shifting my focus to the writer. Giving feedback is an opportunity to relate to another person in a truly meaningful way; an opportunity that will be squandered if we do not make a point to engage wholeheartedly in the process. We owe it to the writer to be "up," even if that means manufacturing our enthusiasm at first. But here is the nice thing: by our simply making the effort, real positivism usually follows.

For two hours, the gentleman and I bent our heads together over manuscript pages and cranberry muffin crumbs. Here it is important to note that while I changed my attitude, I did not change the main message of my feedback. The memoir needed work. The writer had captured key events in his life vibrantly through scenes, yet the scenes needed to be more thematically connected, shaped into a central narrative with an end point. The difference, however, was that now my message had a much better context. My attitude made it clear—I valued the gentleman's writing. I was on his side. And I knew, with additional effort and one or two more drafts, he *would* shape his memoir into a very fine book. Of that, I was truly positive.

☞ Ted Kooser   *"We all serve communities."*

The same week Ted Kooser found out he had been appointed to serve a second term as America's poet laureate, he also received the 2005 Pulitzer Prize for Poetry for his book *Delights and Shadows.* Pretty extraordinary events for a man whose verse focuses on the ordinary—spring plowing, walking to work, laundry, a grandfather's cap. The first U.S. laureate from the Plains States, the Nebraska writer has published ten collections of poetry that have earned him numerous prizes and honors over the years, including two National Endowment for the Arts fellowships and the Pushcart Prize. He is also a professor at the University of Nebraska.

Ted has been described as sharing the perspective of the "average American," yet it is his ability to illuminate in a flash the beauty and significance of everyday moments that sets him apart. His poems are short; his style accessible. "I never want to be thought of as pandering to a broad audience," he once told an interviewer, "but you can tweak a poem just slightly and broaden the audience very much. If you have a literary allusion, you limit the audience. Every choice requires a cost-benefit analysis." Spoken like a true insurance executive, which he was for thirty-five years before retiring in 1999.

In his poem "Selecting a Reader," Ted describes a woman in a dirty raincoat thumbing through one of his poetry collections then returning it to the shelf. "For that kind of money, I can get my raincoat cleaned," the woman says in the poem. "And she will," Ted concludes in the last line. "Writers need to remember that readers have priorities," he says. "Sometimes it's a lot more important to have a clean raincoat than a new book."

He also understands readers' impatience with poetry that is hard to understand. When Ted worked at the insurance company he would sometimes run poems-in-progress by his secretary to test them for clarity. In the end, a verse that appears straightforward may have taken forty or fifty drafts, demonstrating the truth that the art is to hide the art. As a poet and now a promoter of poetry, it is Ted's blend of accessibility and artistry that has helped academics and mainstream readers find—and appreciate—common ground.

How do you use feedback when you write?
I have several writer friends with whom I correspond about my poetry. In exchange, I look at their poems on request. Right now I am using three of these people almost exclusively, Leonard Nathan, Dan Gerber, and Jim Harrison. When I have a fairly satisfactory draft of a poem I send it to one or more of these people, either by e-mail or regular post, and they generously offer comments. They might point to an awkward usage, or a clumsy grammatical construction, or even a misspelled word. It is understood that they wouldn't criticize the general thrust of the poem, only the mechanics.

When you teach and do workshops, how do you use feedback to help students?
I treat my students in pretty much the same way that I described my friends treating me. I go for specifics: problems of usage, clumsiness, and so forth.

How would you recommend writers use the feedback process?
It's good to find a reader for your work who will be specific with his or her comments. It doesn't help to have somebody say, "I like this," or "This is

interesting." You need to have specific suggestions, like, "There's an apostrophe in line five that confuses me."

What's the biggest danger when it comes to writing poetry and feedback?
One must be careful not to make use of the suggestions of others unless they have made a really persuasive argument. You don't want them writing your poem, and sometimes you have to refuse to let go of your own way of writing. There have been times when I've tried to follow suggestions and wound up ruining the poem.

Do you have a "best" feedback story?
When I was a very young writer, Robert Bly read a poem of mine and said, simply, You're making it up. He meant that I was using my imagination to furnish the poem, and he wanted me to actually observe the subject, carefully, and write from the real experience. I found that very helpful. I made a number of changes in the poem before it was published, but it has been too long ago for me to remember them precisely. But it was Robert's helpful comment that set me on the right track for a successful revision.

As poet laureate, how do you encourage people to read more poetry?
I think the best sell is to show them poems that I think they will be able to relate to. That's really the purpose of my newspaper column, to provide examples of poems that can move people, but still be relatively easy to understand. Teaching by example is the preferred method here. [Note: Ted provides newspapers and on-line publications with a free weekly column, "American Life in Poetry."]

When you give readings, what is the general tenor of the feedback?
I have been deeply gratified by the responses I've had. Many people have come up to me after a reading and told me that they appreciated it that I seemed to be writing for them, or that I was taking their lives into consideration.

Any final thoughts about feedback?
We all serve communities, and because of this it is important to think about the community into which you direct your writing. You should choose your outside readers from the community you wish to reach with your work. For example, if your intended audience is a broad segment of the population, people who don't have Ph.D.'s in English, you should choose an outside reader from that community.

Small Miracles

Maybe because I am a writer, and the opposite of intimidating to anyone who meets me, people are always asking me for feedback on their stories, book proposals, articles, even cover letters for job applications, though I haven't had a real job in years. Usually I say yes, partly because I have run up so much karmic debt that I am afraid to say no. What if I bring on some cosmic curse by selfishly refusing to help others, especially after all the help I have been given with my own writing? But the other reason I am willing to give people feedback is because it makes me feel really, really powerful.

Writers care what you think about their writing. They care more than you can sometimes fathom, unless you are a writer yourself, of course. Here is what I mean. Tell a person she is a bad driver and she doesn't start agonizing over whether she should turn in her license. She just keeps on recklessly and merrily driving, sideswiping mailboxes and going forty in the passing lane. But tell the same person she's a bad writer and she's apt to go to pieces, or maybe even quit writing forever—which is strange when you think about it, since bad writing, as opposed to bad driving, doesn't endanger innocent lives.

It's heady having that kind of power.

As I was working on this book, I invited every writer I encountered to tell me his or her experiences with feedback. Even I was surprised by how much emotion this subject evoked; how big a role feedback plays in writers' lives, whether they are new to the craft or have been publishing for years. Non-writers, too, have their own share of defining feedback moments. A few months ago, I met a ninety-one-year-old man at a book party. He had spent his entire adult life working for the railroad, yet the first thing he told me after we were introduced was how he had won a high school play-writing contest back in 1931. "The prize money was twenty-five dollars," he tapped his cane for emphasis. "You'd better believe, that was a lot of money during the Depression."

In the introduction to this book, I wrote that almost every writer has a toxic feedback story; how somebody's ill-considered, insensitive, or just plain wrongheaded feedback undermined their writing or their confidence. Here, I would like to add that the opposite is equally true; just as many writers have stories about a particular someone whose feedback encouraged or sustained them along the way.

One of these stories belongs to Teresa Lust, the author of *Pass the Polenta and Other Writings from the Kitchen,* a memoir and cookbook inspired by her childhood family meals and her experiences as a professional cook. When Teresa was getting her master's degree in liberal studies at Dartmouth College, she was too intimidated to sign up for any of the writing courses offered in the program. "I thought, *If I can't do it, I'll be crushed,*" she said. Teresa did, however, enroll in an environmental studies class taught by Noel Perrin, an English professor who drove a solar car and was the author of numerous essays and books about his experiences with rural life. Teresa's first assignment in the class was to write a paper on anything that pertained to the journey of Lewis and Clark. She wrote about the endangered salmon habitat at the mouth of the Columbia River, where Lewis and Clark spent the winter of 1805, and where Teresa had worked her first kitchen job. When Noel returned Teresa's paper to her, his feedback took her by surprise. "You're a writer," he told her, which she automatically denied. "Well," Noel countered in his amiable way, "if you don't think of yourself as one, then you won't be."

From this brief bit of feedback came a "small miracle," as Teresa put it. To be a writer, she realized, you have to stop worrying about whether other people are more qualified than you, or whether you will be any good. You just have to write. Noel's feedback motivated Teresa to enroll in her first writing course, a Dartmouth class in creative nonfiction. The echo of Noel's encouragement also gave her the courage to write about what mattered to her—food and family.

The first essay Teresa submitted to the class for review described how her German grandmother had taught her to make pie dough. Witnessing the quality and content of the pieces the class discussed before hers, Teresa grew increasingly nervous about her own submission. "I thought I should be writing about world history, or synapses, or something more sophisticated," Teresa explains, "but at the same time I felt I expressed my heart." To her relief, the feedback process was "very positive," she said. "It wasn't that they told me, 'Don't change a word,' but they liked what I was writing, and they gave me feedback that helped crystallize what I wanted to say."

Teresa's essay, "Easy as Pie," marked the start of a collection of food-related anecdotes and recipes that evolved into her master's thesis, and ultimately earned her a publishing contract before she had even finished her graduate program. After Teresa's book came out by Steerforth Press in 1998, Terry Teachout of the *Washington Post* wrote, "Of the many cookbooksas-memoirs to appear in recent years, the one I like best is Teresa Lust's *Pass the Polenta and Other Writings from the Kitchen,* a beautiful collection of essays by a one-time professional chef who cooks not for money but for love." Teresa happened upon this review, which was part of a longer article about several books within the same genre, when the piece ran in her local newspaper. When she read the reference to *Pass the Polenta* her immediate response was, *Oh no, someone else wrote a book with my same title!* Then it registered—the praise was for her.

Noel Perrin wasn't the only feedback provider who helped Teresa on her progression from insecure graduate student to published writer. In the acknowledgments of her book, Teresa also thanks her thesis advisor and her writing group, which evolved from the class where she timidly submitted her first essay. But Teresa's story exemplifies a lovely truth. Sometimes it only takes one person to help a writer on her way; to change the course of a writing life. For Teresa, that person was Noel Perrin.

For another writer, it could be you.

I once read an article on leadership that stated that we all influence 250 people in our lifetime. That number strikes me as conservative, especially if one of your roles in life is that of a feedback provider for writers. A few words of honest encouragement, a thoughtful response to a manuscript, a few hours of your time . . . What may seem like a small effort on your part may resonate with the writer more than you know. Think about this the next time someone asks you to comment on her writing. Think about your own feedback stories, and the particular someones who have been instrumental in your writing life. As a feedback provider, you have the opportunity to replenish the good karma. It is in your power to make a positive difference. You could be a writer's small miracle.

IN THE COMPANY OF WRITERS

Hey, Let's Put On a Workshop!

You tried a writing workshop advertised on a flyer on the wall of the health food store, but it turned out to be more of a support group for aging hippies. You took a community college course on fiction writing, but now that you've passed with a *B*-plus you feel it's time to move on. You even asked your wife to critique your work, but for the last story you gave her the only feedback she offered was, "Do you really think I'm fat like the wife in the story?"

So where can you turn to for the kind of insights, camaraderie, and deadlines you crave during the writing process? How about putting on your own workshop? That's what I did over a decade ago, when I moved from Minneapolis to small-town New England, where legend had it the woods were filled with writers—but none of them seemed to congregate except at the feed store.

The move from big city to small town left me with a bad case of workshop withdrawal, particularly because Minneapolis is the home of the Loft Literary Center. Founded in 1974 above a bookstore, the Loft offers a cornucopia of workshops and programs for whatever genre or aspect of writing you are into. When I lived in Minneapolis, I took back-to-back, fiction-writing workshops, most of them from an instructor who came from England and used to play rugby. I didn't know much about his teaching credentials, but I loved his accent and my writing improved. After our weekly meetings, the whole class would go out drinking and flirt and bitch about how hard it was to be a writer. Those were the good old days, at least from what I can remember.

Except for the drinking, flirting, and bitching part, my fiction workshop is modeled on those classes I took at the Loft. On average, I offer three workshops per year, which means I have had the pleasure of witnessing hundreds of writers find their voices, strengthen their writing skills, and start and finish powerful stories and novels. At some point, participants dubbed my class the "Back Room Workshop" because we meet in an extra room in the back of my house, furnished with little more than green plastic chairs and a Foosball table. During our meetings, my husband does his best to contain the kids and the dog to the rest of the house.

If you would like to start a workshop or critique group, all you really need is a back room of your own, if not in your house, then maybe in a private room in the public library, or a corner of a bookstore café. The logistics are simple. You will want to allow two to three hours per meeting, enough time to accommodate both a meaningful agenda and the attention span of adults who have to be up at six the next morning to face their nonwriting lives. I recommend holding your workshop on Thursday evenings, since everyone seems to be doing something else on Wednesdays.

My workshop runs its course in ten weeks, though I almost always tag on an extra meeting at the end because it's fun, and hard to stop the momentum. Having an end-date to the workshop strengthens the commitment among members because they know from the outset that their participation is time-limited. It also allows for a more graceful disbanding—no lingering demise as members drift away. Writers who are interested in continuing can always sign up for the next session, and the next, and the next . . . In my group, several writers have been in the workshop off and on since its inception.

When I first started advertising my workshop, I was lucky if three people were willing to sign up for a class at the house of a strange woman, who may be a close talker or a flake. Nevertheless, even with a small group, we did good work and had fun. That said, I think the ideal size for a workshop is anywhere from six to twelve participants. In either extreme, the group is large enough to offer a range of opinions and maybe even a consensus, but small enough to feel close-knit. Some workshops qualify members through writing samples, but I love the idea of a true community workshop that gives everyone permission to try creative writing. So many times a novice who arrives at class with no immediate display of talent ends up being one of the workshop gems. I also find value in diversity. It gives me hope for all of humanity when I see advanced writers and neophytes, and writers of genre and literary fiction, intermingling in the same workshop, breaking down barriers as they learn how to critique and appreciate each other's work.

One of the biggest challenges of a writing workshop is to help people overcome their nervousness about sharing their work. To alleviate this fear as quickly as possible, I start the workshop (and most meetings) with a timed writing exercise. You can find dozens of books full of terrific writing exercises, or just make up your own, but it is always a good idea to keep the first one light, even silly. Launching the workshop with an in-class assignment to write a scene that evokes DOOM, for example, just isn't going to help people loosen up, or set the right tone for the workshop.

One of my favorite starter exercises is to have each participant choose an item from an odd assortment I have amassed in a basket: a potato peeler, a feather boa, a pack of Juicy Fruit gum, etc. We write for about fifteen minutes, with only these expectations: keep your hand moving, and write down whatever comes to mind. No second-guessing or fretting. After the allotted time, willing members read their exercise aloud. No one is more surprised than the writer herself to see what has emerged on the page— images, characters, entire scenes she had no idea were tucked inside her. Do this in your own group, and you will be equally amazed at what flows from your unconscious to the page, given a fifteen-minute deadline and a pack of sickly-sweet gum.

Most of the meeting time is spent reviewing participants' manuscripts, with each writer getting at least two opportunities to submit something for formal review. Here is how we organize the feedback process in my workshop. Evening one, I pass around a sign-up sheet that lists the dates of the upcoming meetings. Each writer puts his name next to two of these meeting dates. These are the evenings he is committed to distributing copies of his manuscript to the other participants. Submissions range from short, exploratory scenes to chapters that have been through multiple revisions. The only parameters are that the writer submits something she genuinely wants to develop or polish, and a ceiling limit of thirty or so pages.

Participants use the week between meetings to read the manuscripts and critique them. I suggest everyone read each submission at least two times, with the first read preferably done in the bathtub, without a red pen. This perusal is for pleasure and first impressions; the second read is to scrutinize the text as an editor, which is likely to cause you to be hypercritical. That's okay, though, because you can always weigh your harsher judgments against your first impressions. Are you simply looking for problems? Or is something truly problematic? Use your feedback notes on the manuscript to guide your comments during the discussion, and be sure to return them to the writer. That way, she can just listen during the meeting, and sift through your written comments later.

A good discussion of a manuscript takes about forty minutes. Less time means the group probably isn't giving the work its full due. More time means the group is likely rehashing the same points to death. The manuscript dictates what aspects of the piece deserve the most attention— characterization, plot, voice, detail, pacing, dialogue, prose rhythm, language, even punctuation in some cases, if the story only needs polishing. A common misconception among workshop members is that the story discussion only benefits the writer. No way! Every story discussion illuminates valuable lessons about craft and art that apply to every writer in the room.

Another element of my workshop is an assignment I call a "surge," which I use to motivate all the participants to write between meetings. A surge may be a single page or an entire chapter, the only criteria being that it represents fresh progress. I invite participants to read their surges at the start of the next meeting, and am always surprised by the quality of the writing. I think the magic of a surge has to do with the combination of the relatively short deadline (one week) and the collective challenge (everyone must produce something), which pushes participants to get out of their own way. A member of the workshop once told his wife he was writing a surge for class, but she misheard him and thought he said, "splurge." Actually, I think that is a more apt description because these assignments often do lead to sudden extravagances of scenes, breakthroughs, and profluence.

Story discussions. In-class writing exercises. Surges. That's about all there is to putting on a workshop; though of course I am being simplistic. A successful workshop takes continual effort, but the rewards far outweigh the challenges. A good workshop gives you access to a diversity of reading talents, since some members will be good at critiquing plot; others, good copy editors; and others, confidence-boosters. Plus, a writing workshop not only teaches you how to write, but how to be a writer. This communal experience helps you see the world through a writer's eyes, to notice and listen as a writer, and to read as a writer.

How will you know if your workshop is successful? In my case, I think of something Carole, a participant who has taken the workshop several times, told me the week after a chapter from her young-adult novel was critiqued. On the drive home that cold autumn night, Carole felt compelled to roll down all the car windows, let the wind stream through her long, brown hair, and put the pedal to the metal. That was how charged up she felt to get back to her writing desk, and go at it again. And that is how you will know if your workshop is successful.

Back Room Workshop Itinerary

6:50–7:00 p.m. Gather, gossip, grab some coffee or tea. As the group organizer, make sure to serve cheap, store-bought cookies to provide a sense of hominess and a sugar high, without creating the expectation that you will be baking every week.

7:00 p.m. Writers claim their seats. Important! Once a writer stakes out a chair at the first meeting, he "owns" that seat for the rest of the workshop. Writers hate disruption of their personal habits, so even if you are the first to arrive at subsequent meetings, do not try to move in on someone else's space.

7:00–7:15 p.m. Share writing news. Who faced what writing challenges that week? Who triumphed? Did anyone learn or read or hear anything relevant to writing?

7:15–7:45 p.m. Group writing exercise. Inevitably, certain members will gripe about this and claim they can't write anything good under this kind of time pressure. Ignore their whining and make sure to congratulate them later when they do, indeed, write something good, which will always be the case; if not that evening, then the next. (Some weeks, read surges aloud instead of doing a writing exercise.)

7:45–8:30 p.m. Discussion of the first story submitted for formal review. Make a conscious effort to create a balanced, upbeat discussion.

8:30–8:45 p.m. Rest-room, coffee, and chat break. Chatting is a must; it's fun and part of the bonding experience.

8:45–9:30 p.m. Discussion of the second story submitted for formal review. Make a point to maintain the energy level for the entire discussion. You don't want to give this writer short shrift.

9:30–9:45 p.m. End the meeting ten to fifteen minutes late. I have no idea how to avoid this, so perhaps you could let me know if your group manages to finish on time.

How to Have a Good Group Discussion

Have you ever been in a workshop when a submission comes up for review and a silence falls over the group? Not the kind of silence that feels like people are gathering their thoughts, or reliving the sex they wish they'd had last night, but the kind of silence that implies no one can think of anything remotely useful or good to say about the work. At least that is how it feels to the writer, who is sitting there wishing she could disappear between the floorboards. Meanwhile, the other group members are avoiding eye contact by staring at the toes of their damp, wool socks peeking out from their Birkenstock sandals (if it is winter in Vermont). Some of them really can't think of anything good to say. Others aren't sure what they are supposed to say. And some members just don't want to be the first one to say anything because what if they say something foolish?

Why wouldn't this happen in a writing group? Group dynamics can be weird under any circumstances, but when a group has the emotionally charged agenda of helping writers improve their writing, that is bound to make things even weirder, especially since the whole workshop scenario is a bit of a setup. A writer submits his work for criticism, which can make everyone else in the group feel pressured into criticizing it, which can make the writer feel lousy. And to make matters worse, you personally could be the culprit! You could be the villain in someone else's toxic feedback story, even though you are only there to be helpful.

The good news is, it is possible to alleviate the tentativeness, awkwardness, and negativity that place a pall over so many group discussions (and one-on-one feedback interactions). What follows are some suggestions on how your group can foster a feedback session that is both productive and positive. I promise you, there is always something good to talk about in every submission. I know this for a fact, having participated in hundreds of workshop discussions. What I don't know, after all these years, is why anyone in their right mind would wear socks with sandals, *especially* if it is winter in Vermont.

Take every submission seriously: Writers don't submit anything frivolously; too much is at stake, emotionally speaking. What may look to you like a dashed-off piece or a scant few pages may represent a world of effort on the writer's part. As workshop participants, it is not our place to judge the worthiness of someone else's submission. If it matters to the writer, it matters.

Meet the story where it's at: Is the submission a first or fifth draft? Is the writer looking for a general response or line edits? This kind of information can help you tailor your feedback appropriately. Think of it this way: You don't fault a baby for not being an adult. If the writer's submission is in the early stages of development, you will want to focus your feedback on the piece's potential, rather than its lack of sophistication. Conversely, if a mature work is presented, you will be doing the writer a favor by pointing out any lingering traces of babbling or self-indulgence that undermine the story's refinement.

Invite the writer to do a mini-reading: Before launching into the discussion, invite the writer to read a few pages aloud. This lends dignity to the submission. It also magnifies a work's strengths and glitches, and allows you to pick up on nuances of voice or other aspects of the writing that you may have missed when you read it silently. If you think a piece works better read aloud, it probably means the inflections, pacing, and emotions the writer is bringing to the read need to be reinforced on the page.

Be up: It's important to create as much positive energy as commentary because the latter without the former can leave the writer nonplussed. *Geez,* the writer leaves the meeting thinking, *They told me they liked my story, but then why didn't anyone act like it?* As every writer knows, showing can be a lot more effective than telling, especially when it comes to enthusiasm.

Start with praise: Why make things harder than they have to be? Start the session by talking about what you like in the piece and why. Here is an example: "I like how the character of the grandma swats flies while she is canning, and her sweat drips into the preserves. Those details really showed the heat of the kitchen and the old woman's perseverance." Starting with praise makes the writer feel good (for good reason) and gives her the perspective she needs to counterbalance any critical remarks that follow. It's a lot easier on you, too.

What do you notice? Telling the writer what you noticed in the text is another terrific way to launch the discussion, especially if you are having trouble coming up with something you liked about the piece. "I noticed the alliteration in the first stanza." "I noticed the father was absent for most of the story." "I noticed that the part of the story from the aunt's perspective was written in the past tense, and the part of the story from the niece's perspective was written in the present tense." These observations may seem small, but they are useful because they tell the writer what aspects of the writing are drawing your attention.

Emphasize what's there, not what's not there: It's time to let go of the deficit model of teaching that has been ingrained in most of us since birth (or at least let's loosen our grip). Instead of focusing the discussion primarily on what a submission lacks so the writer can fix it, focus instead on what the piece offers so the writer can enhance it. What characters pique your interest? Where is the language powerful? What themes are emerging? Emphasizing what's working in a draft helps the writer know what to keep, and where to build.

Critique in a continuum: Good dog! Bad dog! Maybe you need to be that definitive when training Trixie the Wonder Dog, but writers respond better when feedback is part of a continuum (not working, almost working) rather than categories (good, bad). After all, which would you rather hear, "I don't think your plot is working yet," or "I think your plot is bad." Incremental feedback softens the blow. More importantly, it helps the writer gauge how close he is to achieving his intent. It tells him whether he needs to rethink or refine.

Burst into reading: Think of your writing group as a movie musical. Just as the characters in a musical burst into song at opportune moments, you, too, can burst into the discussion reading aloud your favorite sections. What better way to display your appreciation for a particular passage of writing, and pump up the energy of the workshop?

Turn suggestions into what ifs . . . : Half the time writers resent suggestions, and half the time they glom on to them; which means you probably shouldn't make any, except it is so much fun (and useful at times). If the writer is open to suggestions, be sure yours have more to do with the writer's story than your own version of the writer's story. It is also helpful to phrase your suggestions as "what if's" rather than declarations. Consider the difference between "Cut the opening!" and "The opening about the character's marital history didn't hook me. What if you filter all this background info into the story later?"

Go beyond yes-or-no questions: Say you ask your best friend, "Does this dress make me look fat?" If she says yes, you're crushed, and if she says no, you're happy; but what you don't know is that the fringe on the bodice makes you look like an aging Dallas Cowboys Cheerleader, and the back of your hem is bunched up in your pantyhose. This speaks to the importance of asking open-ended questions in a story discussion—"What does everyone think about the ending?" "Why are you confused?" "How does the language affect the pacing?" Open-ended questions help stimulate the discussion and deliver useful insights that give the writer the whole story.

Take yourself out of it: Most How-to-Give-Feedback worksheets tell us to "own" our opinions by expressing them in terms of "I feel" or "I think." This makes sense, but you may want to ban the use of the "I" construct (at least temporarily) if it is limiting the depth of the constructive criticism. Notice the difference between "I think the diner waitress is really greedy" (the "I" construct makes it easy to stop after giving your opinion) and "The waitress in the diner comes across as greedy because she steals the other waitress's tips." Another example: "I don't like the long flashback starting on page two" versus "The long flashback starting on page two stopped the action right when it seemed to be picking up momentum."

Try different formats: Even if your group's existing format works just fine, it can be fun to experiment with new ones. Here are four options:

1. Allow each feedback provider three minutes for his critique (yes, use a timer), then move on to an open discussion.
2. Organize the discussion around four areas of critique: What is the piece about? What did you like about it? What didn't you like about it? How would you improve it?
3. Only put forth positive feedback, not a word of constructive criticism.
4. No written submissions; participants simply read aloud and follow up with verbal comments.

Show your appreciation: I still remember the first time a feedback provider thanked me for allowing her to read my submission. Somehow, this unexpected show of appreciation made me feel more like a "real" writer. It reminded me that even though my piece wasn't finished, my work already had value for the reader. I think the nicest way to close a group discussion is to say to the writer, "Thank you."

☞ Gregory Maguire *"I don't revise in an architectural way."*

Envision yourself as an imaginative, high-energy boy growing up in a restrictive, Irish Catholic household. Money is tight and television is forbidden, with the exception of the one movie your parents allow you and your six siblings to watch once a year— *The Wizard of Oz*. How do you overcome your feelings of boredom and confinement without getting yourself into trouble? If you're Gregory Maguire, who grew up to become the author of over a dozen children's novels and five novels for adults (including the bestseller *Wicked: The Life and Times of the Wicked Witch of the West),* you read, read, read, and you teach yourself how to write stories.

As a kid, Gregory wrote hundreds of stories, but rewriting, says the author, wasn't part of the process. "My method was to keep working, keep spewing, not go back and fix things up. I rarely crossed out a word or changed a paragraph. If I reread something and didn't like it, I figured I'd just do it better the next time." In fact, the only thing Gregory was less interested in than rewriting was getting feedback on his stories. "I only cared about my own satisfaction," he says. "I wrote and illustrated for an audience of one."

Gregory was twenty-three when he first received feedback, after submitting a fantasy novel for children to Farrar, Straus & Giroux. He was encouraged when the editor asked him to meet with her, until he saw his novel on her desk. "The pages were edged with so many Post-it notes it looked like a hedgehog in epileptic shock." Page by page, the editor walked him through her comments on pacing, character inconsistencies, errors in grammar, etc. "This terrified me," Gregory says, "but I sat through three and a half hours of this exercise because I figured she was going to offer me a contract."

Instead, the editor closed the meeting by handing him back his heavily edited manuscript. She told him that if he made the effort to revise, he could resubmit the novel. Otherwise, try another publisher. "This was in the days before personal computers, and that marked-up manuscript was my only copy," Gregory says with a laugh. "I had no choice but to redo it." Four months later, he turned in a significantly revised version of *The Lightning Time,* which Farrar published in 1978.

"It's taken me twenty-five years to get used to the feedback process," Gregory says, "and I'm still not always a gracious receiver of critical comment."

In his early twenties, he did join a writer's group, but only lasted for two sessions. He was turned off by the group's "micromanaging syllables," and uncomfortable with any discussions about the moral reasons for a story to exist. "I knew myself well enough to know that if I let anyone question a particular phrase or turn of events in my story, I could become paralyzed. I was only interested in productivity." A writer who describes himself as "colossally self-motivated," he still prefers to hang on to his work until he thinks it is finished. "But for all I say I've taught myself to write without feedback," Gregory adds, "I do need it."

Over the years, Gregory has "cobbled together" a band of three or four feedback providers, including his editor at HarperCollins, his artist spouse, and his brother Joe, a mathematician whom Gregory often turns to when he is in a narrative pinch. For example, when Gregory was writing his fourth novel, *Mirror, Mirror* (2003), a revision of *Snow White,* he decided a change of focus would help stimulate his thinking about the dwarves. So he asked his brother to explain the different properties of the numbers seven and eight. After hearing Joe talk about eight being a complex number (divisible in many ways) as opposed to the prime number seven, the author found the narrative structure he had been seeking. In the book, the dwarves start out as a "stable constellation" of eight, but when one goes on a journey, everything changes.

Asked if he is more willing to revise now than in the early days, Gregory answers with a conditional yes. When he was completing his newest novel, *Son of a Witch* (2005), for example, he wasn't confident about one of his female characters, so he asked for feedback from two men and two women. The male readers thought the character worked fine, but one of the women found her inconsistent, and didn't believe her actions at the end. "Since that was my sneaking suspicion anyway, that's the reader I listened to," he says.

"I don't revise in an architectural way," Gregory adds, "because I don't start something until I feel confident in the framework, and I devise the structure as a larger metaphor for the theme of the book. People have never said to me, 'Make the ending the beginning,' or 'Bring in the dancing girls in chapter four.' I couldn't do that," he explains. "If I have to bulldoze, I'm not interested in doing it again. The structure is what it is. It's concrete," the author asserts, "but I will move the furniture around the room."

Who's in Charge?

The worst writing group I was ever in consisted of six friends, all fiction-writing instructors and workshop leaders. You should have seen us, posturing and pontificating just to show how smart we were, feuding and fuming over each other's personality defects ("She always interrupts me when I'm talking" "He never spends as much time on my stories as I spend on his"), and defending our own stories to the bitter, bitter end ("I *meant* to leave the reader confused"). The six of us exhibited every bad behavior imaginable in a critique group short of hair pulling, and don't think it didn't cross my mind.

Thankfully, we disbanded after a few months, and eventually most of us were restored to kinder, gentler relationships with each other, though I still avoid one member when I spot her at the grocery store. I often wondered why this effort was such a disaster, until one day the answer hit me—here we were, a writing group of teachers and workshop leaders, yet nobody was leading the group.

Every writing group, without exception, needs someone to be in charge. This may be just my opinion, but on the other hand I know I am right, and not just from my own track record. I bet you have experienced your own share of failed groups; or heard stories, as I have, of writers who banded together to support each other's efforts, only to suffer unhappy consequences. Likely these were good writers, and nice people, too—the kind of people who bring warm banana bread covered in gingham cloth to the meetings for everyone to share. Regardless, with no one at the helm, they quickly turned into the Jets and the Sharks, or fizzled out, or worst of all became a coffee klatsch, an unpleasant-sounding term derived from the German word for "gossip." No wonder so many writers are suspicious of joining a group.

Here let me clarify an important point. When I refer to a group leader, I am not talking about a group tyrant. In fact, one of the first duties of the leader is to make sure the group runs like a democracy. As a whole, the group should decide, by consensus or majority vote, its goals, its structure, and the norms of behavior for participants. For example, your group may decide to meet once a month, with the host for that evening being responsible for bringing the munchies. Or your group may commit to providing written feedback for every submission. By establishing these things collaboratively, every member will feel more vested in a successful outcome. Plus, it makes it a lot easier for the leader, or any member of the group, to nail someone nicely if he doesn't follow the established protocol—"Oh, Curtis, when can I expect your written comments about my story?"

Which brings us to the question, Who should be in charge of your group? The answer isn't always obvious because, unlike a class or a workshop where participants pay for a teacher or senior writer's expertise, a critique group is made up of peers. You all serve as teachers and learners, and the last thing you want to do is to distinguish the leader as the *best* writer in the bunch, or the best anything for that matter. It is bad enough when writers are ranked in MFA programs and pitted against each other like gladiators, but it is the kiss of death in a critique group. Yes, I know there are some writers who thrive on competition. An editor once told me about a now-famous mystery writer who confided to her that his writing group fueled him on because he realized he was so much more talented than all the other members. Unlike this fellow, though, most of us do better in groups that foster a sense of community rather than competition.

So if a good writing group functions as a community, then the leader can be thought of as heading up the Neighborhood Watch. While every member contributes to the group's safe, nurturing learning environment, it is the leader's responsibility to keep a watchful eye on the whole. This is a particularly important duty during the story discussions, where most of the crimes are committed. You may want to assign the moderator role to one of the more assertive members of the group, the person naturally gifted at saying things like, "Hey! Excuse me! You two in the corner making out, can we please get back to the scene on page fourteen?"

On the other hand, you may want to rotate leadership, which encourages every member to become more attuned to what constitutes a good (or bad) story discussion. After all, moderating a group discussion isn't rocket science, it is about *paying attention,* a skill every writer should be cultivating anyway.

Let's say you are the group leader for the evening. With you at the meeting, as always, is a room full of separate agendas, biases, needs, insecurities, egos, and personalities. Because of this, many things are likely to require your attention; here is just one possibility. During the discussion one member disses the story on the table with such authority and vehemence that his negativity sucks in the other group members. As a result, this first negative comment is followed by another, then another, then another, until, before you know it, what you have on your hands is a full-blown *discussion vortex,* a whirling mass of negativity spiraling out of control.

Discussion vortexes happen all the time in groups (and not just writing groups). People's own insecurities and free-floating energy make them susceptible to being swept away by other people's convictions, which is how negativity begets negativity and how an otherwise civilized group of individuals can work themselves up into a collective frenzy. As the moderator, this is where you step in. If you sense a discussion vortex gathering momentum, rechannel the energy. Direct the group's attention to a positive aspect of the story. With a single, sincere, positive comment, you can dispel the gathering dark force.

One additional point about discussion vortexes. Groups also can fall into *positive* discussion vortexes, where one paean starts a swirl of hyperbole, until, by the end of the forty-minute discussion, members are carrying the writer around the room on their shoulders, chanting his name. This is fine, great in fact, if the story is flawless. But if not, you will want to encourage the group to put forth some constructive criticism.

Positive or negative discussion vortexes, or any kind of groupthink in which members conform their opinions to what they believe to be the consensus of the group, eat up a lot of time and energy, and can seriously mislead the writer.

Clearly, a big part of your job as moderator is to pay attention to *what* is being said during the story discussion. But you also need to pay attention to *who* is doing the talking. A writing group is not *Jeopardy,* where only the fastest people on the buzzer earn the right to speak. Some group members are good at jumping into the conversation, others are not. If you are paying attention, you can see these more reserved members leaning forward in their chairs, hands half raised, wishing they would be called on. So call on them. Create a space in the discussion in which they can comfortably insert themselves. "Banana Bread Lady, did you want to say something? We'd love to hear your opinion."

As group leader, you must never grow lax about fostering inclusion. I have led a writing group out of my home for years, enjoying such a familiarity with most of the members that I don't even bother to vacuum anymore before they come over. Recently, another member invited a new writer to join our group. This new person had just moved to Vermont from Indiana. She brought her knitting to our meetings. For the first few sessions she didn't contribute any feedback and I paid her no mind, other than the fleeting thought that she might be a bit slow. Then one meeting, she took me aside and softly asked if I ever organized the discussion by going around the room? She thought it might be a more inviting format for some of the quieter members of the group, including herself.

Go around the room! What was she talking about? Was that how they did it in Indiana? And who were these other quiet members she was referring to? Our group wasn't quiet. If anything we were raucous. Exuberant! One big, happy family! My first reaction to her suggestion was to react defensively, at least in my head. What's more, I don't like going around the room. It makes me feel antsy. I much prefer the spontaneity of "popcorn" discussions where people can just burst into the conversation at will. I come from a big, loud family with Romanian bloodlines. We've never waited for anyone to finish a sentence in our lives.

Then I remembered that our group was a democracy, and that it wasn't all about me and my preferences. I also recalled that, before I had gotten lazy about my role as moderator, I used to intersperse rounds into the discussion on a regular basis. Rounds are indeed a great way to make sure every voice in the group is heard. They also alleviate the noise and chaos of a free-form discussion, replacing it with a different kind of energy. Rounds raise the anxiety of the group, but in a good way: every member knows they are going to be called on to speak. With rounds, there is no place for slackers to hide and they know it, so readers take extra care to be prepared.

And so, I launched the next story discussion by suggesting we go around the room to present our feedback. As I antsily waited my own turn to speak, I realized that we actually had not heard from some of the more reserved members of the group for quite a while. It also occurred to me that certain other group members (who shall remain nameless) had been dominating the discussion a bit too much with their loud-mouthed, Romanian ways. And when the group's newest member, the quiet one from Indiana, offered her insights, I could see that she wasn't slow at all. In fact, she was really quite smart, and not just because she could knit and provide feedback at the same time.

I could make a list pages long of all the things that could go wrong in a discussion, and that merit the moderator's attention. Groups are so easily sidetracked. We launch the meeting with characters and plot points, but somehow end up talking about those evil Republicans who want to drill for oil in the Arctic, or the stain-removing power of the Magic Eraser. We repeat ourselves endlessly and get lost in minutiae—"On page 572, the comma should go outside the quotation marks. Oh, the plot? Yes, whatever,

Ten Tips for Moderating a Group Discussion

The key to moderating a discussion effectively is to be restrained, but always in control. Here are some suggestions and convenient phrases you can use to assert your authority gently, and keep the discussion running smoothly.

If you don't want to come off as the group Gestapo: Use humor (even if it's pathetic) to keep everyone in line. For example, if two members start fighting over a point like dogs over a bone, merrily sing out, "Ding! Ding! Ding! End of round one."

If it's too hard to say something directly: Some groups rely on code phrases to alert members when they step outside the established norms of behavior. For example, instead of telling a defensive writer to zip it, the leader (or anyone in the group) can just invoke the code phrase, "Alan Dershowitz!"

If the discussion is lackluster: Ask an open-ended question. "Why?" "How?" "Tell me more about . . . "

If people are carrying on distracting side conversations: Slam down your clipboard to get everyone's attention (while smiling), and suggest, "One person at a time, please." This serves the dual purpose of waking everyone up.

If someone launches into a feedback filibuster: Politely interrupt, "Hold that thought. Let's hear how the other members feel about some of the issues you've already raised."

If members are rehashing the same point: Tap your watch and suggest, "Moving on . . ."

If the discussion is becoming a free-for-all: "Time out!" Go around the room so that members can make their points and be heard. You can also direct questions at some of the quieter members of the group, as a way to include them in the discussion.

> **If the discussion gets off topic:** "But we digress. Let's save that con-versation for the coffee break."
>
> **If a writer complains to you privately about another participant:** Resist the temptation to gossip. Don't take sides. Advise the person to speak directly to the other participant. Your role is moderator, not mediator.
>
> **If someone says something downright mean:** Say something nice and mean it.

but that comma on page 572 . . ." We get defensive and monopolize the conversation and ask improper questions—"Was your father really a serial killer like the one in the story?" We mismanage the time, and let the en-ergy level drop, and say mean things about the writer behind her back, even though she is right there in the room with us. We try our best, but we need a leader because somebody, anybody—and that includes you and the Banana Bread Lady—has to be paying attention to all of this stuff. Other-wise, things can get pretty awkward at the grocery store.

The Top Ten Rules of a Successful Writing Group

W. Somerset Maugham reportedly once said, "There are three rules for writing the novel. Unfortunately no one knows what they are." I'd like to add here that there are also rules for writing groups . . . and I think I've figured them out.

We come together in a workshop to do important work, but little things can get in the way, like misconceptions about what to expect or what is expected of us. That is why successful writing groups establish parameters up front, from how frequently participants can submit their work to how many pages for each submission. Successful groups also abide by a set of rules, a code of conduct, if you will, that helps keep everybody honest and raises the quality of the discussion. Below are my personal top ten rules of a successful workshop. You can bend them, but don't break them, and I promise your group will thrive.

1. **Make a point to show up.** Absenteeism is demoralizing to the writer whose work is being discussed, and it undermines the energy and collective commitment of the group. Plus, if you don't show up, how can you learn from the story discussions?
2. **Be prepared.** Read the manuscripts and prepare your critiques *before* the meeting. Otherwise you will be playing catch-up in class, reading when you should be listening, or scribbling down comments when you should be contributing to the discussion.
3. **No whining about the in-class writing exercises.** It doesn't matter if they make you nervous or you think they are dumb; do them anyway. It is only ten or fifteen minutes of your time, and one of these days you are bound to get something out of them, like maybe a plot breakthrough or the start of a great story.
4. **Don't submit anything that is non-negotiable.** If you have no intention of changing a word of your manuscript, then perhaps you would be better served by a copy of *Writer's Market* than a writing group.
5. **No bystanders allowed.** It is important that every group member submits something for critique on a regular basis. If you don't, it is too easy to sit in judgment when critiquing the other writers' efforts. Plus, you're missing the heart of the experience.

6. **Put yourself in the writer's place.** When providing feedback, your best guide is to remember what it feels like to have your own work critiqued.

7. **Avoid comparisons.** Maybe the novelist next to you can't write like Tolstoy, but then again Dostoevsky couldn't write like Tolstoy. Comparisons within the group only get in the way of helping writers hone their own voices.

8. **Don't assume the characters and events in a story are true.** Writers are more likely to be guarded if the other members of the group have a habit of asking intrusive questions like, "Was that really true?" "Did that really happen?" Accept and discuss each work as fiction, not personal history.

9. **Don't plagiarize.** No matter how much you love someone else's plotline or concept or language, don't lift it for your next work. And especially don't lift it and then present it to the group for critique.

10. **Respect each other's privacy.** Don't show a comember's submission to anyone outside of the group, unless the writer has given you permission.

✍ Julia Alvarez *"My dream of becoming a writer was a fool's dream."*

When she was a little girl living in the Dominican Republic, Julia Alvarez loved to make up stories, but her "lying" wasn't always appreciated by her family. When she came to America at age ten, she faced language barriers and name-calling, but she knew by the time she was in high school that she wanted to be a writer. When she finished a graduate program in creative writing, mainstream America showed little interest in Latino literature, but still she was determined to tell her stories. To make a living, Julia taught writing in schools around the country, eventually earning a tenured position at Middlebury College in 1991, the same year she published her award-winning first novel, *How the García Girls Lost Their Accents.* At the time of her debut success, she'd been writing for twenty-plus years.

A genre-defying author, Julia has published poetry and children's books, short stories, essays, and novels for adults, including *In the Time of the Butterflies,* which was made into a movie in 2001. I contacted Julia for her thoughts about feedback at her office at Middlebury College, where she still keeps her hand in teaching, which she loves. She wrote me the following response.

· · ·

I thought I could tell you my worst feedback story. I wrote about it in a poem called "First Muse" from *The Woman I Kept To Myself.* A famous writer whom I greatly admired stated during a talk he gave that no poet could write a poem in a language he hadn't first said "Mama" in. I was a passionate young poet, sitting in the first row and sinking into my seat. Spanish was my "mother tongue." With his statement, I felt the door of American literature bang shut, leaving me out. My dream of becoming a writer was a fool's dream.

What I learned from that: never to make pronouncements. You will always be surprised. The halting, awkward young poet in one of my workshops might step out of the confines of my judgment and make that quantum leap into her own unique, powerful voice. As a result of this experience, I won't read someone's work "cold." Often, a "stranger" sends me some poems or stories and wants me to tell her what I think. Really, what he or she is asking is: am I going to make it as a writer? I don't want the power to decide that! I don't want to make those kinds of judgments, pronouncements. Besides, it strikes me that the young writer is focusing on the wrong thing when he or she asks a more established writer that question. I love what I heard Spike Lee say about making movies, "The only way to be flashproof is to keep doing the work." Fame and fortune—we all get sucked in by them! I want to return the young writer to the poem or story. I can only do that consistently and effectively in an ongoing workshop, so it seems to me.

So I'd much rather have a relationship with young writers in which I'm invested in their growth, travel a stretch of their apprenticeship with them. It's a big investment, but it's the only thing that works, or, that worked for me as a young writer, those muses and mentors who accompanied me, not all of them living, I should add. I went a long stretch with Whitman. One still ongoing with Emily Dickinson.

The best feedback, again for me, is "invisible" feedback. A gentle touch, a nod, a question, a quiet observation that really leaves me to solve the problem, doesn't tell me how to do it. Some editors (myself included!) give too much response. What happens to me when I get a heavily marked-up manuscript is that it crowds out my story or poem. I can't hear it anymore and can't tell how it is going wrong and how I might fix it. I loved Lore Segal's "response" to my manuscript at Bread Loaf. She wrote a concluding general remark, brief but to the point, with some page numbers where I might go back and revise. But mostly, throughout the manuscript there were little pencil checkmarks in the margins. I thought she was pointing out typos or grammatical errors. So, I asked her, what do the little checkmarks mean? They mean, she told me, that I'm having a good time.

Only years later did I realize how helpful and affirming those checkmarks were. Lore Segal was marking the places where my writing was working well. By going back and revisiting those places, I was learning intuitively where my writing was getting off the ground. I was focused on the work, not on her response. (A checkmark!) I was learning to listen to myself, which is really what the best editors do: get you to peel back the layers to where your own voice is fresh and true.

Meet the World's Worst Workshop

Any workshop instructor can tell you, there are certain types of participants who show up in their classes on a regular basis and irritate the bejesus out of everybody else. It is easy to recognize these types when they are sitting next to you, ruining the group dynamic, but it isn't so easy to recognize when you are one of them. For example, when I was working on this chapter, I asked other writing teachers what types of participants they would include in the world's worst workshop. My list overlapped with theirs with one exception—the Nervous Talker. Eventually, I figured out why this personality type had never occurred to me. *I* am the Nervous Talker. I am that participant who fills in every quiet interlude with my own white noise. Once I start talking, I can't seem to shut myself up.

We all have aspects of our personality that could use some work.

What follows is a class roster for the world's worst workshop. If you recognize yourself in any of these types, take credit for being honest. Then take a few moments to think about how you might modify your behavior the next time you participate in a workshop discussion. Meanwhile, I'll just be sitting here quietly, not saying a word, giving you a chance to read in peace, though you might catch me wringing my hands if the silence goes on for too long.

The Shadow: You show up at every meeting, but never volunteer any comments. What if you said something wrong! Unlike some members of the group who could use some lessons in manners (oh yes, you have your opinions, you're just not wont to air them in public), you never exhibit bad behavior or annoy the other workshop participants, mostly because they've forgotten you exist.

The Star: It's remarkable how you always manage to be the first person in the group to have your work critiqued. Yes, some of the members have dissenting opinions about your gifts, but those people didn't have an essay published in *Reader's Digest* when they were just sixteen. Besides, you're only here to see if the instructor has any polishing advice before you ask him to introduce you to his agent. Sometimes you feel guilty that you never bother to read anyone else's submissions, but writers have to be selfish. Faulkner didn't even attend his own son's birthday party.

The Grammarian: Of course you'd love to join in all the fun talking about a story's themes or the feelings a poem evokes, but someone has to put first things first. If you don't drive home the fact that a participial phrase at the beginning of a sentence must refer to the grammatical subject, then who else is going to do it? You're well aware of what others whisper behind your back—"obsessive," "nitpicky," "weirdo"—but they'll never find fault with your punctuation. If you've told the group once, you've told them a thousand times, "Using an exclamation point is like laughing at your own jokes!"

The Devil's Advocate: If someone says black, you say white; not because you give a crap about white, but because it's fun to stir up trouble. After all, isn't that what your old man did whenever he made it to the supper table? "Dad, my soup is cold." "Like hell it is." "Dad, I want to be a writer." "Like hell you do." That's what you call character building. That's how you learned to be a man, and fend for yourself after your dad got sent to the big house. A social worker once described you as oppositional. Like hell you are. Anyway, writing isn't for sissies.

The Interrupter: You're impulsive and yes, you'll admit it, patience isn't your strong suit. Other people start talking and you just have to run with their ideas, or cut them off if they're saying something stupid. Some people call you rude. Then again some people take forever to say what they have to say. Besides, the other group members are just as bad, always interrupting you to ask, "Will you *please* let me finish?" Then half the time when you do let them finish, they can't even remember what they were going to say. Now what does that tell you?

The Outpatient: You figure a writing group is cheaper than therapy so you come to the meetings to work through your issues and connect with other emerging souls. You know your weeping is a distraction, but in that last story, the way the husband took out the trash, it just brought it all back how you and your last lover shared so many domestic routines during the two months you were together. He left without taking the self-portrait you wove him for his birthday. He left without providing a forwarding address. Oh God, it felt good to let those feelings out.

The Social Conscience: Your hybrid car is smothered in bumper stickers. You once spent a night in jail for verbally assaulting a smoker. *Everything* you write is a political act. Wake up, people! Writing workshops have a moral imperative to change the world one poem, one short story at a time. The rainforest is being destroyed at a rate of 2.4 acres per second. Now that's conflict! Third World countries are struggling under a $523 billion debt burden. Now that's crisis! And in the United States alone, per capita meat consumption has risen dramatically in the past twenty years. Now that's just gross!

The Bibliophile: From the ancient classics to the masterpieces of the twentieth century, you've read them all, and doesn't everybody know it. You've got a recommended reading list to accompany every submission. "Have you read the *Iliad?* Now that's how you do battle scenes!" "Be sure to check out Conrad. His sea novels address your themes brilliantly." You also make a point to keep everybody current, like when you let one of the other workshop participants know that Margaret Atwood had just come out with a brilliant new book with a plot identical to hers, and it was already a *New York Times* best seller!

The Voice of Experience: What a lucky coincidence—the writer's main character is a competitive kickboxer and so are you. And that poem you discussed last week about whooping cranes—you know all about whooping cranes, thanks to an uncle who used to rehabilitate them. Oh, and in that story where the narrator drives a Winnebago cross-country—you once drove a Winnebago from St. Louis to Seattle, but never again. No way! In fact, it's hard to believe any character would drive all that way when flying is so much faster. One thing you know for certain, if something in a story doesn't mirror your personal experience, then readers are not going to believe it.

The Lark: You're in the group because you love being around writers (they're so *intense*), and because the swing-dance class you had hoped to take on Thursday evenings was already filled. You can't help it that you're always late to the meetings; it's just the way you are. You usually arrive in the middle of a writing exercise, which is perfect timing since you always bring energy food. "Dim sum, anyone?!" It's a shame you haven't had time to get your own story idea down on paper, but you told the other writers all about it, and they thought it was really good!

Those Who Can't Do . . . : It's demoralizing having to teach housewives and retirees who think writing "might be fun." Plus, it's *their* fault you haven't been able to write anything new, not since your debut novel came out over a decade ago ("astonishingly complex," wrote the *Providence Journal;* "a ripening talent" declared the *Denver Post*). You know your comments in class come across as harsh—"Nobody's going to give a damn about your childhood!"; "A nun could write better sex scenes!"—but you're only doing these people a favor. Why feed their hopes? Besides, it hurts when your students go on to get published.

Publishing 101

The first time I went to a panel discussion on how to get published, it took me months to recover. The independent publisher who sat on the panel spent much of his time prophesizing the demise of his financially strapped company. The representative from one of the big publishing houses lectured on the need for writers to do more market research. The agent warned, Be prepared to get your heart broken because publishers are in the business of making money, so the literary merits of a work won't be enough to make it sell. And the successful author on the panel actually did a role-play to demonstrate how, as she put it, "editors aren't going to give a shit about your writing." The panel concluded with a string of dire warnings: "Don't quit your day job." "Don't expect writing to feed your goldfish, let alone your family." "Don't think getting published will make you happy." *Obviously.*

Now that I have seen a few of my own books in print, I can understand why insiders feel the need to give aspiring authors a reality check about the business of publishing. Like the author who did the role-play, I also find myself feeling compelled to warn the uninitiated about the challenges that lie ahead. The other day a woman told me that she had a great idea for a book about her now-healthy seven-year-old son. The mother's emotions were palpable as she described the boy's struggle to overcome a rare disease, and how he had defied his doctor's bleak prediction that he wouldn't survive past infancy. Meanwhile, the whole time this woman is talking I'm thinking, *Yeah, yeah, everybody's got a great book idea. So what makes your kid's story any better than all the rest?*

That's when I knew it was time for another reality check. Not the kind you get from publishing panels and insiders, but the kind you can only get from being around writers who are engaged in the act of writing. Writers benefit from the company of other writers for all sorts of reasons, one of the most important being to serve as a reminder that our work matters outside the publishing realm, separate from its marketing or income-earning potential. With this kind of feedback—an affirmation of the writing process itself—writers learn one of the first and most important lessons about publishing. If you write what truly interests you, if you write from the heart, you are much more likely to produce the kind of books that editors will ultimately buy.

Yes, finding a publisher can be challenging, and the word most of us are likely to hear a lot is "pass." On the other hand, writers are offered publishing contracts every day—so why not you? Why not me? One of the things I've learned in my own efforts to get published is that it helps to go to panel discussions to understand the business of publishing, but it also helps to be part of a community of writers who know how to mix business with pleasure. Here are ten good reasons why writers should stick together before, during, and after the publishing process.

Who else can relate? You know how mothers love to swap childbirth stories, even if their children are now in their fifties? Writers enjoy the same kind of bonding experience when talking about creating their books. "How long did it take?" "Was it painful?" "Did you opt for drugs or go without?" Who else but another writer can fully appreciate the gory details and rewards of this labor of love we call writing?

Perspective: I used to feel sorry for myself because I often have to get up at four a.m. to find enough quality time to write. Then I kept meeting or reading about other writers who do the exact same thing. Writers get up at four a.m. That's just what we do, whether you're a working mom like me, or a retired insurance executive like Ted Kooser, the poet laureate of the United States. Understanding this fact of a writer's life has not only given me perspective, but also the names of people I can call if I need someone to talk to at that ridiculous hour.

Deadlines: Some of the most prolific members of my workshop can't seem to write between sessions. This actually works to my advantage since most of these writers have advanced well beyond my teaching abilities, yet they still need me for my deadlines. Yes, setting a deadline with no real consequences is a bit of a contrivance. (What are you going to do if the writer fails to deliver—fine him?) Nevertheless it works. Most writers are motivated to produce when they know someone, anyone, is expecting to read their work by a certain time.

Persistence: The writing process has two components. There is the *fun* part when you are captivated with the newness of your idea and the words just flow. And then there is the *Are we having fun, yet?* part when you realize you've got another couple hundred pages to go before you complete a first draft. The echo of encouragement from your last meeting with your writing group can make all the difference when deciding whether to sit down and write for the next three hours, or plant some more beans in the garden.

Preparing for your big debut: Why-oh-why do some of the contestants on *American Idol* make their singing debut on national television? Wasn't there anyone who cared enough to tell them to practice a few more years in front of a full-length mirror? As a writer, you don't want to submit your work to a discriminating audience of agents or publishers before you've honed your talents. By getting feedback throughout the writing process, you will improve your work, and with it your chances for making a good first impression.

Confidence: Related to the previous point, an editor of a literary magazine told me she knows after reading just the first few paragraphs of a submission whether the piece is publishable. "There is an authority in the writing," she explained, "a sense that the writer has reached a point of confidence appropriate for publication." Among the two hundred submissions this editor receives weekly, those that exude confidence on page one are the only stories she bothers reading to completion. Other writers can help you test your own authority *before* you submit a piece. Ask them if your opening paragraphs inspire them to keep reading.

Contacts: An acclaimed psychiatrist sent his self-help book to two agents. They both rejected it for the same reason: too academic. So he rewrote it in a "trade voice," but worried that it wasn't any good. A writer friend finally bullied him into letting her read it, and she loved the new draft so much she insisted on giving it to her agent. Now the psychiatrist is the author of an "entertaining and literate" best-seller, underscoring the fact that when you are trying to get published, a good "trade voice" is important, but so are pushy writer friends with contacts in the business.

Illegitimi Non Carborundum **("Don't let the bastards grind you down"):** Intellectually, you know when a publisher rejects your work it might not have anything to do with whether it's good or bad. Getting published is as much about fit as quality—hitting up the right publisher at the right time. Understanding this, however, still doesn't stop you from feeling deflated when you recognize that SASE in your mailbox. One thing that does help, however, is commiserating with other talented writers who are amassing their own paper logs of rejections, some of them even bigger than yours.

Editing: You've got a book deal. Hurray! But if you are assuming your editor is actually going to edit your book, you may be in for a surprise. An increasing number of editors at publishing houses are focused more on making deals than modifying manuscripts. This is potentially bad news for both you and your reading public. One solution is to hire a book doctor or freelance editor (check references and do a test chapter), but a more affordable alternative is to find a qualified critique partner willing to pinch hit as your editor, with the promise, of course, that you will return the favor when her book is accepted by a publisher.

The Book Party: You're a published author! It's time for a celebration. Who better to invite to your book party than all the other writers who helped you along the way by affirming the writing process, giving you perspective and deadlines, sharing their publishing contacts, commiserating with you when the manuscript was rejected, and lending you their editorial expertise before and after your work was accepted. This is a party commemorating the publication of your book, but it is also a celebration of what can be achieved when writers connect with other writers.

✒ Jodi Picoult *"I call our relationship my second marriage."*

When Jodi Picoult graduated from Princeton with a degree in English and creative writing, several literary agents came knocking, eager for a look at her thesis/novel. "There weren't a lot of creative writing programs at the time, so anyone writing a thesis got solicited by the big agencies," Jodi says. "It was exciting, flattering." Among the first to approach her was a woman from mega-agency ICM. A few weeks later, this same woman also earned the distinction of being the first agent to reject Jodi's manuscript. "Something about it not being what she was looking for, standard rejection stuff," Jodi remembers.

In her quest for an agent, Jodi amassed hundreds of rejections, the kind of collective negative feedback that might have deterred a less determined writer, particularly given the fact that agents speak with the authority vested in them as gatekeepers to the publishing world. Jodi persevered, however, and two years after her first rejection, she heard from Laura Gross, an agent just starting out in the business. "Laura loved the book's character development and the voice I seemed to have, apparently even back then," Jodi says. "I think it's rare for a twenty-one-year-old to turn out a well-crafted novel. It bodes of better things to come, and I think Laura saw this."

At that point, Laura hadn't yet sold anything to any publisher, but Jodi trusted her. "I think what I responded to was the way she presented selling my book as something *we* would do together, instead of her doing *for* me. It made me feel like I had a partner in what would prove to be a long, continuous minefield of publishing, and I never forgot that."

Laura spent a year trying to sell Jodi's Princeton novel, to no avail. ("Thankfully," Jodi admits, "that manuscript will never be published.") Meanwhile, Jodi completed a master's in education at Harvard and worked several jobs, including teaching creative writing to middle and high school students. In 1991, the same year Jodi was pregnant with her first child, she finished a new novel, *Songs of the Humpback Whale.* Laura sold the book to Faber and Faber within three months, and the novel was published the next year. Since those salad days, author and agent have enjoyed a tight friendship and professional partnership, recently celebrating their fifteen-year anniversary. "I call our relationship my second marriage," Jodi says.

Fast forward to 2003. Jodi's tenth novel, *Second Glance,* had just made the *New York Times* best-seller list. That same year, Jodi received the New England Bookseller Award for Fiction, recognizing her body of work as a significant contribution to New England's culture. Out of the blue, Jodi's publicist received a call from a high-powered agent at ICM. The woman wanted to fly her to New York City for lunch and talk about representing her work. As Jodi was listening to her publicist relay this news, it hit her. The woman's name . . . ICM . . . this was the same agent who first rejected Jodi's Princeton manuscript. "Everyone wants to back a winner," she laughs.

Even as an author long lauded for writing fictional page-turners, Jodi still feels flattered to be wooed. Nevertheless, she told her publicist to decline the woman's invitation to lunch. She was completely happy with her current agent. "I didn't trust myself to have any contact with her," says Jodi, who doubts if the ICM agent even remembers rejecting her manuscript all those years ago. "It would have been nice to rub it in her face, but I don't live my life like that."

Jodi did tell her agent about the unexpected phone call. The next day, in appreciation for her loyalty, Laura sent Jodi flowers. "But honestly," Jodi acknowledges, "usually I'm the one sending them to her after she's negotiated a particularly good deal!"

Can Creative Writing Be Taught?

A creative-writing instructor once informed me, "You know, you can't really teach creative writing. People come to my class and they're writers or they're not." *Says who?* I thought. And how can you tell the difference—from their GPAs? Their ability to pronounce the word *anathema?* Their third drafts?

I think this instructor has it all wrong, not to mention a sad-sack attitude. I think creative writing can be taught, and if it can't then why are thousands of creative-writing teachers at universities and community colleges and MFA programs still on the payroll? For proof creative writing can be taught, just hold up any sincere student's first draft and fourth draft, then drive a truck through the gap in narrative quality.

Still, the issue persists; and with it a lingering whiff of academic elitism—"You are either born a writer, or forget it." I blame this elitism on Thomas Jefferson, a man who promoted education as "the equalizer of all children," but clarified that for the "laboring" class, the basic level of elementary education would suffice. I also blame it on Prince Charles (or more likely, that damn Camilla) who recently wrote in a memo to a senior staff member of his household, "What is wrong with everyone nowadays? Why do they all seem to think they are qualified to do things far beyond their technical capabilities?"

What is wrong with everyone, indeed?! Who are all these students who march into classrooms with the hope of learning the aspects of creative writing—characterization, plot, setting, point of view, syntax, sentence length, and the like? And even if they can be taught craft, good creative writing requires more than mastery of a certain skill set. It requires inspiration! Perhaps one or two "ordinary" students might be struck by the proverbial bolt of lightning, if they are lucky, but we all know that it is much more likely to hit the long, lanky fellow with the wire rims, two desks over. The "gifted" student, as he is often referred to by the instructors in the faculty lounge.

From first grade on, teachers have tried to tag the writers in their classrooms, but it is never as easy as it seems. "Oh, Darryl, he's the *writer* in the class." Then twelve years later, Darryl goes on to be a NASCAR driver and never writes another word beyond his autograph. The same thing happens in MFA programs. "Shh! Don't tell anybody, but we've ranked Virginia the least likely student to succeed as a writer. No funding for her, I'm afraid!" Then, after graduation, the low-ranked Virginia manages to defy the program's expectations and write five best-selling novels, allowing her to eventually pay off her enormous student debt.

The funny thing about writers is, you can't always distinguish them from the flunkies or science majors or loggers of the world. At least not right away. For years, a student's talent may remain dormant, but then suddenly (after years of scribbling) she discovers her own voice, or a bit of encouragement, or a fictional technique that finally solves that niggling problem she's been having with transitions—and bloom! the person everyone assumed was "unteachable" emerges as a wonderful writer.

Can creative writing be taught? In the classroom, everything we do is a form of feedback that contributes to the answer to that question, from our attitudes about writing and teaching, to the students we single out for praise and attention, to the unspoken signals we project. Even when we know enough not to say something outright dismissive or negative, it is so easy to inadvertently send a discouraging message. One evening when I was teaching my writing workshop, I realized something startling. I was sitting with my chair angled a certain direction in our circle, my back literally turned away from one of the members of the group; the member who happened to show the least promise.

Yes, creative writing can be taught, but to succeed teachers need to take it on faith that every student that comes to them can learn, from the undergrad who is trying too hard to be Salinger, to the executive who writes so tidily her sentences have hospital corners, to the octogenarian who can't use a computer, but wants to preserve the family stories for her grandchildren. There is a reason these students found their way to those chairs in the circle. They must have some affinity for writing or they wouldn't have had the gumption to show up in the first place. As creative-writing teachers, one of the most important parts of our job is to honor *every* student with the distinction of being the writer in the class, because just that feedback alone can make a remarkable difference.

Below are a few tips for teaching creative writing.

Create a nurturing learning environment: By your fostering a sense of community rather than competition, students will be more willing to put forth their own voices and story material, not imitative prose that simply reflects the style of a famous author, or the class darling, or whatever type of writing happens to be in vogue in contemporary literary culture.

Push students to write, write, write: The first hurdle to creative writing is intimidation. The second is procrastination. The only way to help students overcome both is to immerse them in the writing process. Doing is the fastest route to learning.

Give them an "in": Some students aren't sure what to write about or where to start. That's where writing exercises and short assignments come in handy, helping students overcome the intimidation of the blank page and connect to the ideas and stories that are percolating just beneath their consciousness.

Encourage the play: A lot of students who have the ability to write, can't, because they have internal editors nagging them all the time. "What would your mother think?" "How dare you use that word!" "That's a horrible sentence." Encourage students to silence these voices and just go for it during the outpouring stage; to write like they did in first grade when making up stories was fun. The craft part can be added in good time.

Build up their skills: Urge students to let their protagonists act, not just be acted upon. Encourage them to use active verbs to energize the language, and not to confuse dialogue with conversation. The more tricks of the trade you share about craft through minilessons, readings, story discussions, and constructive criticism, the more you empower your students.

Bring literature down to earth: Creative-writing students need to learn to read as writers, not as English majors. To that end, it helps to analyze Hemingway's signature terse prose, or his use of objective correlatives, rather than his literary themes. It also helps to mention that the author rewrote the ending of *A Farewell to Arms* thirty-nine times.

Don't just referee story discussions, set the lead: If you take the writer and his work seriously, if you provide specific constructive feedback, and if you make a point to keep the discussion upbeat, then students will model your behavior when critiquing each other's work. What you don't want them to model, however, are all your opinions, so be sure to invite different points of view.

Reiterate key points: In a lively story discussion the comments come fast and furious, and not every feedback provider is perfectly articulate. Help the group process all the information by making a point to reiterate, translate, elaborate, summarize, or adjudicate throughout the discussion.

Personalize the process: Insecure students benefit from relentless encouragement and gentle guidance; other students may be able to handle bigger doses of constructive criticism; and all students improve when you show them you believe in their abilities, and honor their work. When giving feedback, tailor your teaching to each student's needs and sensibilities.

✍ Crystal Wilkinson *"Processing feedback has to be a meditation."*

In the good old days, before Crystal Wilkinson had published her first short story collection, *Blackberries, Blackberries,* named Best Debut Fiction by *Today's Librarian* magazine, and before her second collection of linked stories, *Water Street,* was nominated for two prestigious writing prizes, she could take creative writing classes and workshops anytime she wanted. Now, as an established author and assistant professor of creative writing at Indiana University, it's not so easy. "I love being in workshops and being a student," Crystal says, "but now if I try to take a class with one of my friends teaching it, they feel I'm infringing because they know I'm published; it's not a true student kind of thing. I miss not having more feedback," she adds, "that's how I thrived and got my first two books written."

Crystal, who grew up in rural Kentucky and describes herself as "country," is currently working on her first novel. "This sounds crazy," she says, "but the next time, I don't want a book contract up front. I've missed five million deadlines already, but I can't write at my best when I feel the breath on my neck. My agent checks in and says, 'How's it going?' and I say, 'Yep, I'm still going.' Something about being published ruins everything," she laughs.

A writer who claims "an affinity for the blank page," she finds the process of writing a novel—of always having to move forward—unsettling. "Writing has always been easy for me," Crystal says, "but having your head around a novel, staying committed to this larger thing, the density of the work and all the situations, it's like holding up a world. Being in the middle of it is still play," she says, "but getting to it is daunting. Every time I pull it up on the screen, I think, *Ugh, there you all are, ready to get on my nerves.*"

For help along the way, Crystal relies on a few steady friends, including Nikky Finney, a writer and teacher whom she met years ago through the Affrilachian Poets, a Kentucky-based writing group whose members identify as both African American and Appalachian. Given the women's busy schedules and the fact that they now live three hours apart, the situation has required some improvising. For a while, the two met Sunday afternoons to read aloud new work and swap verbal feedback (neither had the time nor energy to critique one more written manuscript). "Now we check in and motivate each other in other ways." Crystal describes a recent phone call from Nikky—"'Okay, Crissy, get up. It's four a.m. Put some water on your face. Here we go.'"

When asked about how she processes feedback, Crystal explains, "I don't take suggestions literally. I go in and try to figure out, why is it unclear? Is there a missed opportunity here where this needs to be opened up? Do I need to get rid of it all? Do I need a bulldozer or a brushstroke?" Crystal's method is to revise surrounded by pages marked up with other people's comments. "Feedback takes me someplace different altogether," she says. "It makes me really think about the work."

As a teacher, Crystal recognizes the danger of workshops if students don't process feedback appropriately. She describes an "amazing" writer in her class who takes every suggestion from the other students and goes down the list, revising her story. "She ruins it. Totally ruins it," Crystal says. "As writers, we're looking for that validation and approval of others, so we get caught in thinking, *If I do all these fixes, everyone will like it.* You have to practice that ability to stand back and do a meditation on the whole piece."

From her own graduate student days at Spalding University, Crystal recalls workshopping one of her stories that later appeared in *Water Street*. "I was one of those rare birds in grad school that already had a book contract so I had that breath-on-my-neck thing going already, and was anxious to get feedback." The piece, entitled "My Girl Mona," was about a woman talking to her psychiatrist about her memories of a childhood friend who turned out to not be a good friend at all. Early in the discussion, a few readers, including the professor, decided that the story was about a woman with a split personality. This had never been Crystal's intent. "During the feedback, you're not supposed to talk," Crystal says, "so I kept silent, trying to be the good girl, but what I should have done is stopped them because once the professor got on board with that idea, all the students followed suit. All the feedback was about the 'Sybil' factor, and I got nothing out of it."

Now, when Crystal senses this kind of snowball effect building among her own students, she tries to stop it by inviting dissenting opinions. A similar danger occurs when students "preworkshop" a story, arriving at class with a collective opinion. Recalling her own story, "My Girl Mona," which became one of the pivotal pieces in her linked collection, she worried right through the galley stage of her book that the story didn't work; that maybe she should have "fixed" the main character whom the class had assigned a split personality. Her worries were unfounded. "My Girl Mona" won the Indiana Review Fiction Prize, and the collection was a finalist for both the Orange Prize and a Zora Neal Hurston/Richard Wright Foundation Legacy Award in fiction. The main character in "My Girl Mona" also started her down the path of her current novel.

"Processing feedback has to be a meditation," Crystal reiterates. "Otherwise, you'll slaughter your story."

In Appreciation of Bad Writing

I often get asked (privately) by members of my writing workshop, "How can you always find something positive to say about every submission?" Sometimes I suspect that they think I am a Pollyanna or just faking my enthusiasm; but the truth is, I really do get excited about every story, with or without narrative occasion.

My workshop has only one prerequisite: you have to want to write fiction. Given this open-door policy, we have seen writers who struggle to eke out a two-page submission alongside writers who gush on and on for an eternity. We have seen short stories without any story, endings that ought to be beginnings, and flashbacks piled on flashbacks. We have waded through deep purple prose, dodged countless eyes roaming around the room, and tried to envision a character who looks just like Clark Gable and Errol Flynn (at the same time). If adverbs alone were currency, some of the writing in my workshop could save Social Security.

It's not that I don't recognize all this bad writing when I read it. But part of the reason it doesn't dampen my enthusiasm is because I don't see bad writing as bad. I see it as part of the creative process. In fact, I think it is pretty safe to say that if it weren't for bad writing, there wouldn't be much good writing because literature doesn't just burst forth fully armed, like Athena from Zeus's head. As writers, we are the accumulation of all the writing we have done in our lives. We learn from writing things that work, and we learn just as much from writing things that don't work. So in this sense, even bad writing is good.

Yet, most of us tend to forget this, especially when we are providing feedback. We look at a writer's murky, messy draft and make snap judgments about her abilities, and think snooty comments— *Why did she even bother to submit something so bad?* We see bad writing as a strike against the writer and a waste of our reading time as feedback providers, when in fact it is exactly the opposite. Bad writing is what germinates good writing. As feedback providers and writers, we need to remember that it is from four hundred pages of bad writing that the best two-hundred-page books emerge.

A while back, two new participants joined my workshop at the same time. One had wanted to write fiction for years, but even though she was bold enough to serve as chair of her community's school board, she couldn't muster the courage to give creative writing a try. Then she turned forty and realized that she was even more afraid of going through her whole life *without* trying to write stories because that wasn't the kind of person she wanted to be. The other new participant came to the workshop with an MFA and had written a novel way back when, which didn't get published (not enough plot, apparently). So he took a respectable job, got married, had kids, and didn't write another word of fiction for fifteen years, until a mutual friend gently bullied him into taking my class.

When the workshop started, the chair of the school board signed up to be our first submitter just so she wouldn't chicken out. And the MFA fellow with the respectable job set himself a goal of two thousand words a week. Do you think when I read her first four pages of fiction writing full of honest emotion that I saw her sporadic point-of-view shifts as reason for discouragement? Do you think when I read the opening chapters of his long-delayed second novel that his occasional authorial intrusions really mattered in writing that hinted at phenomenal talent? Just look at what these two people had already achieved! They were writing! They were writing! They were on their way! What's not to appreciate, except a blank page?

But seeing someone try fiction writing for the first time, or come back to it after a defeat, isn't the only reason I appreciate all the writing in my workshop. Let me tell you about my "regulars." Some of these writers have been in my classes off and on for over ten years, before I had children and crow's-feet, and when I had even fewer insights into the publishing business than I do now. After all these years together, my regulars know all about my tendency to overedit, my narrative pet peeves, and my pet peeves in general. And I know all about this one's bad habit of run-on sentences, and that one's difficultly fictionalizing her childhood, and how this fellow writes beautifully but struggles with recurring bouts of self-doubt.

I credit my regulars for helping me truly understand the creative process. Draft after draft, story after story, year after year, they have shown me how you have to start *somewhere* or you will never start, how order emerges from chaos, and how powerful stories come from humble beginnings. Just a few weeks ago, we critiqued one of the last chapters of a novel that had started from a fifteen-minute, in-class writing exercise we did in the workshop about two years ago. Witnessing this writer's progress every step of the way—the trials and errors as she developed her characters and discovered her plot and revised or tweaked everything from the structure to the dialogue tags—taught me as much about writing as a hundred books on craft. Now the novel is almost complete and shows such promise it recently earned the writer a generous grant from a writing foundation.

I love this privilege I have been given through the workshop of seeing stories and novels in the making. I love this opportunity I have every Thursday evening to talk about the craft of fiction writing, and then to see our discussions put into practice. And I love every writer in my workshop. Even if I don't love them in real life, I love them for those forty or so minutes when their stories are being discussed. Here they are, taking emotional risks and exposing their work to criticism when they could be home safe, reading a good book. They have entrusted me and the other members of the workshop to read their bad writing in the hopes we can help them make it better.

This isn't just an act of courage, but generosity. Writers need to see other writers in the thick of it. We need to see the creative process at work. Otherwise—just like the school-board chair who was afraid to try fiction writing—we too could find ourselves avoiding the blank page for fear that what might come out is *bad writing!* We could find ourselves feeling discouraged about our own disastrous drafts to the point of quitting. When I feel this way (about once a day), I remember all the bad writing in my workshops and it cheers me up. Not because these writers failed, but because, ultimately, they succeeded. And if they can succeed by persevering then maybe, just maybe, so can I. And so I keep writing.

In exchange for the writer's generosity, feedback providers need to make a point of putting bad writing in perspective. Bad writing is what it is—here today, likely gone in another few drafts, and likely to return at the start of a new story or chapter. By acknowledging—even appreciating—the role of bad writing in the creative process, we can stop using it as a judgment against the writer, or treating it as the eight-hundred-pound elephant in the room that everyone sees, but no one dares to mention. And once you put bad writing in perspective, it is easy to see past the problems in any piece of writing to its potential.

In a previous chapter, I mentioned that my writing workshop meets in a back room of my house that my family seldom uses. Sometimes when I am home alone, struggling in the midst of my own bad writing, I will wander back to that room in the quiet of mid-week. There is our haphazard circle of vacant, green plastic chairs, and the stain on the pink rug where my dog had a long-ago accident, and a column of dust particles illuminated in a sunbeam. I see all of these imperfections, but I also see so much more.

This room is alive with twelve years' worth of characters telling their stories. I see a fisherman's wife who left her husband after he gambled away their life savings; and a fiddle-playing Houston detective who solved a grisly crime; and a zombie who just wanted to be loved. I see a Vietnam veteran who found peace in the classroom; and buglike aliens that took over the earth; and a soccer mom who learned to appreciate the daily routines of her ordinary existence. I see an engineer at Los Alamos who rewrote history by stopping the development of the A-Bomb; and an old-time logger who searched a lifetime for a mythical tree; and a little girl rocking back and forth against the wall outside her parent's bedroom, as she waited for her cancer-stricken mother to die.

This is what comes from bad writing. This is potential fulfilled, scenes that transport me; writing so good I feel humbled to know the writer; finished stories and novels rich in life, drama, entertainment, and meaning. And I was there! I got to witness their creation and watch them develop from nothing to really something. Somebody asks, "How can you always find something good to say about every submission?" My answer—"How can you not? Just step into my back room and see what I see."

Epilogue: Feedback and the Real World

The other day I hurried out the front door, late for meeting a friend for coffee at the bookstore. I stepped outside to find that the car was gone, or at least the only car I can drive because our other rust-bucket is a standard, and I never was able to learn how to shift and accelerate at the same time, not with so many important things on my mind. My husband must have used my car to drive our daughters to the movies. Who knew when he would be back, given that the man never runs out of errands.

Naturally, I was put out by this inconvenience, especially since I'd let him know that morning that I was going out later to meet my friend. When my husband eventually moseyed on home, I reminded him of our conversation. "We even talked about my meeting," I said. "Remember, I told you I'd stop by the bank because I'd be right next door, *meeting my friend* at the bookstore."

"We didn't talk about it," my husband replied. "You told me you were going out, and I didn't pay attention."

Breakdowns in communication happen all the time. Here, I am not talking about within the writing realm, but in the real world at large. Just pick up any newspaper and read the headlines, or look at the evidence closer to home: town meetings that dissolve into shouting matches between neighbors; church groups and PTA committees that suffer under the tyranny of one or two members; couples that break up because one partner is miserable while the other one thinks everything is happily ever after. The workplace, too, is fraught with bad communication. A publicist once told me that her boss had written on her employee evaluation that she was "stupid." *Stupid.* How does that improve job performance? And why is this boss working in the field of communications?

This book focuses on feedback and writing, but most of the issues addressed in these pages are just as applicable to *any* kind of communication between people. After all, feedback is just that—a form of communication—one that permeates our daily lives. Whether you are helping your child with his homework, or brainstorming a new product idea at a business meeting, or asking the waiter to take back your overcooked steak, you are giving or receiving feedback.

Consider the tiff I had with my husband after he left me stranded at home without a car. "You told me you were going out, and I didn't pay attention." It is tempting to leave you with the impression that I was completely blameless in this situation, but that would mean omitting a few key details. For example, when I told my husband I was going out later that day, I was heading up the kitchen stairs at the time, too busy to wait for his response. I also was feeling guilty for assuming he would be available to watch the kids, and I know my tone reflected my defensiveness. In one of the previous chapters, I emphasize that it is not just what you say, but how you say it and when you say it that can make all the difference between being heard and being obnoxious. From this, you can draw your own conclusions.

My hope with this book is that you and I both use these insights about feedback to enrich not only our writing, but our everyday lives as well. When we are aware of the emotional factors underlying our interactions with family, friends, and coworkers, we can communicate with more sensitivity and clarity. When we are open to other people's perspectives, we will discover new opportunities to learn and to grow. When we remain true to our own instincts, we can change for the better and never feel compromised. When we show faith in people and treat them with respect, we are much more likely to gain the ear and the respect of others. When we are positive in our words and in our attitude, life will be easier, even when it is hard. And when we make a conscious effort to connect with others, even at the risk of exposing ourselves to criticism, we will be contributing to a collective goodwill that can change the world.

Acknowledgments

Six years ago, I started jotting down notes for a book about feedback, but then children, a few other book ideas, and a wee bit of procrastination intervened. All that time, however, my enthusiasm for the idea never waned. I knew just what I wanted to say about feedback, if I only had the chance to put these thoughts and feelings into a book. Then I got the chance. My friend and editor, John Landrigan, invited me to submit a proposal for *Toxic Feedback* to University Press of New England. For this small gesture of encouragement—which made a huge difference—I am truly appreciative, as I am for his unwavering support, editorial expertise, and preternatural vocabulary.

After the book contract, but early in the writing process, I confessed to John something that had only recently occurred to me in a moment of panic. I wasn't any authority on feedback! His response was reassuring: "No author knows everything about their subject matter before they start writing. They learn as they go."

Toxic Feedback is derived from my own experiences as a feedback receiver and provider, and from my educational conversations with dozens of aspiring and published authors, writing group participants, creative-writing teachers, professional editors, and friends. So many people were willing to share with me their knowledge and stories related to this subject. Without their generosity—and especially their feedback—this book would not have been possible.

For saying "yes" to an interview and making my day, many thanks to: Samina Ali, Julia Alvarez, Jennifer Crusie, Ernest Hebert, Khaled Hosseini, Don Johnson, Ted Kooser, Archer Mayor, Gregory Maguire, Grace Paley, Jodi Picoult, Sarah Stewart Taylor, and Crystal Wilkinson.

For their insights, support, and various other, important contributions to this book, I would like to express my appreciation to: Jenefer Angell, Meredith Angwin, Patty Baldwin, Anne Belden, Lori Ladd Brown, Lisa Burke, Steve Cahill, Dave Callaway, Mary Childers, Chris Collins, Tracy Comeau,

Craig Czury, Ed Doughtie, Vicky Fish, Judi Forman, Vicki Forman, Beth Garland, Sarah Ginestet, Mary Hays, Janet Hutchings, Kathy Kimball, Marv Klassen-Landis, Paige Kempner, Don Kollisch, Teresa Lust, Pat Martin, Doug Merrill, Stephanie Montgomery, Enid Powell, Elizabeth Rider, Jennifer Satterwhite, Jim Schley, Pam Sexton, Hannah Silverstein, Carrie Thornton, Marilyn Weigel, Rob Welsch, Sarah Welsch, Margaret Wiley, and Sel Yackley.

For their abiding friendship and encouragement, I am grateful to: Cathee Clement, Nancy Fontaine, Melissa Gray, Judy Janoo, Becky Joffrey, Deborah McKew, Frances McManus, Bindi Rakhra, and Catherine Tudish.

And for my parents, Joan and Myles Hyman: I love you both very much.

About the Author

A professional writer and editor, Joni B. Cole is the creator of the *This Day in the Life* books, including *This Day: Diaries from American Women* (2003) and *This Day in the Life: Diaries from Women across America* (2005). She has led fiction-writing workshops for twelve years, and has developed a workshop based on the concepts covered in *Toxic Feedback*. Joni lives in Vermont with her husband, Stephen, and daughters Esme and Thea.

For more information about *Toxic Feedback* or its author, visit www.toxicfeedback.com, or e-mail joni.beth.cole.adv95@alum.dartmouth.org

Responsive Professional Education:
Balancing Outcomes and Opportunities

by Joan S. Stark, Malcolm A. Lowther, and
Bonnie M.K. Hagerty

ASHE-ERIC Higher Education Report No. 3, 1986

Prepared by

®   *Clearinghouse on Higher Education*
The George Washington University

Published by

Association for the Study of Higher Education

Jonathan D. Fife,
Series Editor

Cite as
Stark, Joan S.; Lowther, Malcolm A.; and Hagerty, Bonnie M.K. *Responsive Professional Education: Balancing Outcomes and Opportunities*. ASHE-ERIC Higher Education Report No. 3. Washington, D.C.: Association for the Study of Higher Education, 1986.

Cover design by Michael David Brown, Inc., Rockville, MD.

The ERIC Clearinghouse on Higher Education invites individuals to submit proposals for writing monographs for the Higher Education Report series. Proposals must include:
1. A detailed manuscript proposal of not more than five pages.
2. A 75-word summary to be used by several review committees for the initial screening and rating of each proposal.
3. A vita.
4. A writing sample.

Library of Congress Catalog Card Number 86-82077
ISSN 0884-0040
ISBN 0-913317-30-6

ERIC® **Clearinghouse on Higher Education**
The George Washington University
One Dupont Circle, Suite 630
Washington, D.C. 20036

ASHE **Association for the Study of Higher Education**
One Dupont Circle, Suite 630
Washington, D.C. 20036

This publication was partially prepared with funding from the Office of Educational Research and Improvement, U.S. Department of Education, under contract no. 400-86-0017. The opinions expressed in this report do not necessarily reflect the positions or policies of OERI or the Department.

EXECUTIVE SUMMARY

Enrollments in college programs that prepare students for professional occupations remain strong. At the undergraduate level, they now have surpassed enrollments in liberal studies programs. It seems clear that students will continue to select collegiate programs with promise of professional employment, yet many educators believe such programs are inappropriately narrow and specialized. In truth, few attempts have been made to examine the intended outcomes of professional preparation programs to determine whether these beliefs are justified. An initial step in bringing educational philosophies and curricular outcomes into better alignment is to clarify the goals and dilemmas of educators in professional programs. Is it true that professional educators concentrate on technical skills and devalue broader aspects of their students' education? If so, is this posture more characteristic of some fields than of others? What commonalities and distinctions of professional preparation programs are most important for faculty members and administrators to understand? Can better understanding of common issues faced by professional educators help identify ways in which faculty and administrators can foster educationally effective interprogram collaboration? What research models, with appropriate modifications, can be used to explore the achievement of outcomes in diverse professional programs?

While this report does not answer all of these important questions, it takes a first step toward improving understanding of intended outcomes in various fields of professional preparation by identifying several competences and attitudes that are generic outcomes of professional study, by exploring the emphasis professional educators believe should be placed on these outcomes, by summarizing outcome-related issues and trends common to professional education in diverse fields, and by providing some recommendations for the future.

The generic outcomes described in the report were derived from existing literature about professional education. They include six aspects of professional competence—conceptual competence, technical competence, contextual competence, interpersonal communication competence, integrative competence, and adaptive competence—and five attitudinal outcomes—career marketability, professional identity, professional ethics, scholarly concern for improvement of the profession, and motivation for continued learning.

The issues and trends concerning these outcomes identified in the report are drawn primarily from recent articles in the educational journals of 12 professional fields: architecture, business administration, dentistry, education, engineering, journalism, law, library science, medicine, nursing, pharmacy, and social work.

The synthesis of the literature should be helpful to three audiences: (1) college and university administrators seeking better comparative understanding of professional preparation programs; (2) professional program and liberal arts faculty members desiring to facilitate interprogram collaboration; and (3) researchers seeking to address a variety of related issues, particularly documentation of the outcomes of professional study.

What Aspects of Professional Competence Are Educators Discussing?
Professional educators devote considerable attention to field-specific aspects of professional competence, such as foundational knowledge and technical skills. Yet, within these two areas, educators in diverse fields are addressing some common issues. All fields are reviewing program purposes, curricular validity, the role of foundational courses, and the volume of conceptual and technical material students must learn. Such reviews have common origins in the rapid growth of specialized knowledge, changing practice roles, including application of new technologies and response to new socioeconomic conditions, and increasing responsiveness to a broader range of clients. Across fields, concern also is apparent for better ways to cultivate cognitive problem-solving skills.

Although literature in the educational journals more heavily emphasizes the development of technical competence, faculty members in professional fields judge technical competence of graduates to be slightly less, rather than more, deserving of emphasis than conceptual competence. Additionally, faculty strongly believe that students should understand the social, cultural, and economic context within which professional practice occurs. While such a contextual emphasis is more widely espoused in "helping" and "informing" professional programs than in "enterprising'' programs (like business, architecture, and engineering), all fields are questioning whether traditional liberal arts is the best curricular vehicle for its achievement. Particularly as they attempt to serve diverse client populations, the helping and informing programs are rapidly infusing social science content into their professional courses to ensure its relevance to professional concerns. Although traditional written and oral communication remains important, communication skills required of new professionals now are conceived more broadly to include interpersonal relations with colleagues and relationships with clients. In four-year undergraduate fields where expansion of the knowledge base has already crowded the curriculum, this desire for broad education is difficult to implement.

In all fields, the nature and function of simulated or real experiences that assist students to integrate concepts, skills, contextual knowledge, and interpersonal skills into competent professional judgments are being actively debated. Fields with formal field experiences are grappling with similar problems of supplying appropriate field supervision, ensuring adequate role modeling, providing feedback to students, and maintaining good relationships with practitioners. Discussion of these curricular management issues appears to overshadow the need to define more clearly the outcomes of field and clinical placements. Perhaps because little is known about the learning process through which integration takes place, professional educators seem to link quite loosely the processes and intended outcomes of integrative field experiences.

Professional educators recognize rapid technological change that affects classroom teaching as well as practice settings. Nonetheless, discussions about integrating various components of professional education have not yet fully focused on the need to help students understand that they will be responsible for adapting professional practice to future societal changes. As technology develops, simulations increasingly may help bridge the gap between classroom and real world settings and the gap between current and future practice.

What Aspects of Professional Socialization Are Educators Discussing?

Development of accepted professional attitudes and commitment, that is, professional socialization, is of greatest concern to educators in health and in human and information service fields and of less importance to educators in fields like architecture, business, engineering, and law. Even when professional educators express strong interest in fostering attitudes like long-term career awareness, professional identity, and ethical standards, discussions primarily focus on providing opportunities for these attitudes to develop. Articulating and measuring such attitudes are discussed very little. Nonetheless, some professional fields can provide useful examples for other educators. To illustrate, educators in dentistry, accounting, and social work are developing new models of career guidance; nursing educators pay particular attention to making preservice students aware of needs for continuing education and research to improve professional practice.

Writers in professional education journals exhort their colleagues concerning the need for students to internalize accepted ethical standards. Despite such rhetoric, little consensus is apparent in most fields about what these standards are and how best to teach them. Social work, nursing, and law educators feel they have incorporated professional ethics in their curricula, but at the same time, law educators as well as journalism and business administration educators believe agreed-upon standards or codes do not exist.

Recommendations for the Future
This literature review and survey of professional education faculty found little evidence to support the view that educational outcomes are narrow in intent. To the contrary, professional education faculty are struggling to maintain, and even to initiate, curricular breadth that is relevant to developing professionals. Strong concerns about continually increasing curricular volume and related time constraints are coupled with a sense of unrest regarding the contribution of both traditional liberal arts courses and traditional professional foundations courses. Thus, opportunities are excellent for interprogram collaboration, particularly in courses that convey to students the importance of the social context in which the professions are practiced, the anticipated effect of technology on professional practice, and the need for broader interpersonal communication skills. College administrators should encourage such dis-

cussions of collaboration, as well as frank exchanges among liberal and professional education faculty about mutual needs and services. Joint problem solving among professional educators and between liberal arts and professional faculty may be productive in devising solutions to mutual problems of integrating theory and practice and in articulating more effectively the outcomes and processes generally thought of as professional socialization.

Several outcomes of professional education seem amenable to measurement. Yet because measurement largely has been restricted to field-specific conceptual and technical competence, professional educators seem to have foregone opportunities to demonstrate successful achievement of broad educational goals. The generic outcome framework used in this synthesis of the literature provides one vehicle that groups of professional educators might use for badly needed comparative research.

ADVISORY BOARD

CONSULTING EDITORS

Richard Alfred
Associate Professor and Chair
Graduate Program in Higher and Adult Continuing Education
University of Michigan

G. Lester Anderson
Professor Emeritus
Pennsylvania State University

Robert C. Andringa
President
Creative Solutions

Robert Barak
Deputy Executive Secretary
Director of Academic Affairs and Research
Iowa State Board of Regents

John B. Bennett
Director
Office on Self-Regulation
American Council on Education

Carole J. Bland
Associate Professor
Department of Family Practice and Community Health
University of Minnesota

Larry Braskamp
Assistant to the Vice Chancellor for Academic Affairs
University of Illinois

Mark H. Curtis
President Emeritus
Association of American Colleges

Martin Finkelstein
Associate Professor of Higher Education Administration
Seton Hall University

Andrew T. Ford
Provost and Dean of College
Allegheny College

Mary Frank Fox
Assistant Research Scientist
Center for Research on Social Organization
University of Michigan

Timothy Gallineau
Vice President for Student Development
Saint Bonaventure University

G. Manuel Gunne
Adjunct Associate Professor
College of Nursing
University of Utah

Richard M. Millard
President
Council on Postsecondary Accreditation

L. Jackson Newell
Professor and Dean
University of Utah

Steven G. Olswang
Assistant Provost for Academic Affairs
University of Washington

Patricia Rueckel
Executive Director
National Association for Women Deans,
    Administrators, and Counselors

Richard F. Stevens
Executive Director
National Association of Student Personnel Administrators

Thomas R. Wolanin
Staff Director
Subcommittee on Postsecondary Education
United States House of Representatives

CONTENTS

FOREWORD

Recent blue ribbon commission reports have criticized higher education, especially the curriculum. What is the curriculum? Is the curriculum "a set of independent courses taught by independent professors held together only by a central heating system and a common complaint about parking," as has been alleged? Perhaps a more accurate definition is "a reflection of the needs of society?" A more honest attempt is to define the curriculum simply as "the faculty." It has also been described more broadly as the total educational experience of attending an institution of higher education and more narrowly as the combination of courses taken in fulfillment of a particular degree. Which definition is most accurate? Probably none; possibly all. Like the four blind men with the elephant, there are as many definitions as points of view. Frederick Rudolph described the higher education curriculum as well as anyone when he said:

"Values change and so does the curriculum, as the more than 300 years since the founding of Harvard College clearly say. Since that time long ago, when a peculiarly self-demanding band of alienated Englishmen got themselves a college almost before they had built themselves a privy, change in the course of study has been constant, conscious and unconscious, gradual and sudden, accidental and intentional, uneven and diverse, imaginative and pedestrian."

Regardless of how we define the curriculum of higher education, the undeniable fact is that over the last decade, students have dramatically shifted their educational preference from liberal arts to the professions, as shown by the table on the following page.

Whether the students are choosing professional fields over liberal arts as a reflection of the rising cost of higher education and therefore the increasing dependence on bank loans to finance it, or simply as a reflection of the increasingly rigorous requirements for entry-level positions in our computerized, technological society is not an issue here. What is important is that this shift has occurred. And shows no signs of abating.

It is therefore important to have an understanding of the curriculum of the professions in order to make informed

---

Bachelor's Degrees Conferred by Institutions of Higher Education			
Program Areas	*1973–74*	*1983–84*	*% Change*
Business and Management	131,766	230,031	75%
Communications	16,250	38,586	131
Computer and Info Science	4,756	32,172	576
Education	185,225	92,382	− 50*
Engineering	42,840	75,732	77
Foreign Languages	18,840	9,479	− 50
Health Sciences	41,394	64,338	55
English	55,469	33,739	− 39
Library and Archival Sciences	1,164	255	− 78
Life Sciences	48,340	38,640	− 20
Mathematics	21,635	13,211	− 39
Philosophy and Religion	9,444	6,435	− 32
Physical Scienes	21,178	23,671	12
Psychology	51,821	39,872	− 23
Social Sciences	150,298	93,212	− 38

*Minus sign indicates decline
Source: U.S. Dept. of Education, 1985

judgments about the quality of specific programs and higher education in general. This report, written by Jaon Stark, professor of higher and adult continuing education at the University of Michigan and director of the National Center for Research to Improve Postsecondary Teaching and Learning (NCRIPTAL), Malcolm Lowther, professor of higher and adult continuing education at the University of Michigan and research associate at NCRIPTAL, and Bonnie Hagerty, a doctoral candidate in higher education and nursing at the University of Michigan, reviews the similarities and differences of the curricula for twelve professional fields. After reviewing well over 300 publications, the authors divide their study into professional competences and professional attitudes.

In this analysis of six professional competences and five attitudinal outcomes, the authors not only examine the purposes for and successes or failures of professional education programs, but raise the larger issue of evaluating competence and measuring outcomes for other curricula. This monograph provides administrators with an understanding of the frustration felt by faculty members trying to fit all the necessary requirements for a professional degree into the allotted time-frame. It also gives faculty a clear understanding of the major issues and relative importance paid

to each one in similar professional programs nationwide.
Effective professional education is important because of
the impact professionals have on our society. And as the
educational preference chart shows, professional education
programs are becoming the foundation of more and more
institutions of higher education.

Jonathan D. Fife
Series Editor
Professor and Director
ERIC Clearinghouse on Higher Education
The George Washington University

ACKNOWLEDGMENTS

This report was prepared over a three-year period as part of a broader study of preservice professional preparation programs in colleges and universities. During that period, many individuals provided assistance, particularly with time-consuming tasks of locating, classifying, and reviewing nearly 3,000 journal articles. Our thanks go to current and former graduate students Ann Austin, Dennis Dieckman, Carol Freedman-Doan, Pamela Lokken, Cynthia Orczyk, Mark Ralph, Peter Rush, Jan Starr, and Karen Swift, all of whom assisted at some time with the project conceptualization and literature review. Daniel Alvarez and Natalie Fisher helped to compile the bibliography. Special thanks go to Mrs. Helen Candiotti for tireless and dedicated typing and retyping.

Numerous colleagues and faculty members at The University of Michigan and elsewhere provided ideas and suggestions. We appreciate financial support for the project from a Spencer Foundation Seed Grant, and we are grateful to Dean Carl F. Berger of The University of Michigan School of Education and to University of Michigan Vice Presidents Bill E. Frye and Alfred S. Sussman.

The Diversity of Professional Study

A focus on outcomes of professional preparation is particularly timely. Enrollments in programs that prepare students for professional occupations have remained strong for years. At the undergraduate level, they now have surpassed enrollments in liberal studies programs, and for the foreseeable future students likely will continue to select collegiate programs that hold promise of challenging employment. In 1984 a study group commissioned by the National Institute of Education (NIE), judging undergraduate professional preparation to be narrow and to overemphasize specialized or technical education, called for increasing attention to assessment of outcomes (NIE 1984). A second national report also criticized narrow specialization but held forth the possibility that a professional education could, if properly directed, be a liberal education as well (Association of American Colleges 1985). In general, these recommendations and the subsequent discussions have tended to bypass dialogue among educators in the specific professional fields. Critics have devoted little time to actually examining professional preparation yet have made assertions about the processes and outcomes of professional-type study that cry out for substantiation. This report takes a first step toward improved articulation of goals and outcomes in various fields of professional preparation by (1) identifying generic outcomes of professional preparation, (2) exploring the emphasis these outcomes receive among professional educators, (3) summarizing some problems that concern professional educators, and (4) providing some recommendations for future action and study.

Enrollments in programs that prepare students for professional occupations . . . now have surpassed enrollments in liberal studies programs. . . .

The Potential for Collaboration and Cooperation

This report was written for three audiences: (1) college and university administrators who wish to achieve better comparative understanding of professional preparation programs; (2) professional program and liberal arts faculty who desire to understand issues and trends in professional fields; and (3) researchers who may be encouraged to address a variety of important related issues, such as balancing liberal and professional study, integrating theoretical and practical education, developing more sensitive program review criteria, or fostering cooperative efforts within universities.

Previous AAHE-ERIC Higher Education Research Reports (Anderson 1974; Nyre and Reilly 1979) dealt with the topic of professional education. According to the 1974 report, "In spite of a significant literature in the various fields of professional education, the process of becoming educated in the professions has received limited attention. . . . Comparative studies, discussion of common policies and practices . . . are rare" (Anderson 1974, p. 1). Drawing from the sociological literature to define "profession," the 1974 report compared, across educational programs, processes such as student selection, curriculum, instruction, and student socialization as well as the relation of professional schools to society, institutions, and accreditors. Data presented documented the increasing numbers of workers in professional occupations and the emerging trend for baccalaureate education to be concerned with professional preparation.

The 1979 report reviewed literature defining a profession and took the pragmatic stand that professional education was "an amorphous conglomerate" not easily defined except by the existence of educational programs directed at entrance to certain occupations (Nyre and Reilly 1979). Accepting this ambiguity, the authors updated the 1974 work by reporting research on admissions, the professional school experience, curricular development, labor market prospects, continuing education, and accreditation. Finally, they provided recommendations for the future of professional education, stressing both evidence of and need for integrating the theoretical and the practical and increasing cooperation across professional education programs. These two foci were believed to be influences that would command the attention of professional schools in the eighties, replacing the emphasis on expansionism of the seventies.

As Nyre and Reilly predicted, the integration of theory and practice has become a focal point of discussion in the eighties. For example, recommendations for improved integration have been made directly in several self-study reports issued by the professional fields themselves (American Bar Association 1980; American Pharmaceutical Association 1984; Association of American Medical Colleges

1984) and more obliquely in general reports like *Integrity in the College Curriculum* (Association of American Colleges 1985). Since this literature review was begun, prominent educational statesmen have stressed the potential benefits of integration across the liberal and professional study areas as well as within professional programs (Curtis 1985; Rhodes 1985). Indeed, as such scholars point out, to advocate that the liberal and professional spheres of education should be separated may be based on a lack of realism about today's societal context.

Although conditions during the 1980s certainly have presented the challenge for cross-program cooperation among professional fields that Nyre and Reilly foresaw, discussion devoted to this issue has been less obvious. As resources have become increasingly scarce, undoubtedly some colleges and universities have examined the possibilities of interprogram cooperation as a preferred method of retrenchment and reallocation of resources. In many cases, however, decision makers have moved directly to program closure as the most feasible and expeditious solution to budgetary problems. The failure of professional program personnel to recognize possibilities for collaboration and the need of administrators to move forward rapidly to reduce budgets have foreclosed some opportunities for interprogram cooperation.

Furthermore, efforts to allocate resources have been conducted without benefit of comparative research, which could assist professional program faculty and administrators in understanding commonalities and differences in programs. Clearly, programs independently seeking to collaborate, or mandated to do so, need to strive for enhanced understanding. And review criteria used by administrators to assess program dimensions like centrality, quality of faculty and graduates, work opportunities for graduates, and cost-effectiveness depend on the decision makers' best efforts to understand the program's special goals, emphases, and curricular dilemmas.

A parallel may be drawn between potential outcomes of failure to develop communication across fields of professional study within universities and failure to develop cultural understanding of other countries with whom we must cooperate in a global society. To extend the analogy further, just as citizens misunderstand the intent of those who do not share their customs, faculty members and administrators may unwittingly apply review criteria derived from a few high-demand fields to other fields where they are less appropriate. In short, neither cross-program cooperation nor program review decisions have benefited from research-based attempts to discover the similarities and differences across various professional fields.

Both previous Higher Education Research Reports mentioned the broad range of published educational literature applying to each professional field, but they more frequently summarized material from secondary sources or comparative syntheses. Both covered a wide range of topics, treated them briefly, and provided valuable resources to the administrator or researcher seeking a broad introduction to professional education. The literature synthesis in this report was begun to develop a deeper understanding of the educational issues and challenges that face diverse professional preparation programs.

This report uses two approaches to explore the outcomes of professional preparation and the strategies used to achieve them. The primary approach is an integrative review of the literature relating to professional preparation. A secondary approach uses preliminary results of a survey of faculty in 10 of the 12 professional fields with respect to their emphases on preferred outcomes and educational activities. First, however, it is necessary to apprise the reader of what is meant by "professional preparation" and a notion of the size of this enterprise in American higher education.

What Is a Professional Preparation Field?

Progress toward better understanding and improvement of education dictates that we deal with what society views as reality rather than with scholarly abstractions. This report therefore considers programs that are at least four years in length and frequently referred to as "professional" in everyday campus parlance (to separate them from the study of nonoccupationally directed liberal arts programs).

Most students attending a college or university program in nursing, business, or engineering, to name only a few fields, see themselves as enrolled in professional preparation programs. Similarly, most faculty members teaching in fields that attempt to relate theory to practice and that have reasonably well-defined occupational entrance points for graduates see themselves as professional program faculty (although of the fields to be discussed, journalism educators are least likely to accept the idea that they teach in a "professional program"). In casual campus conversation, college and university administrators refer to programs that consume four or more years of students' time and are directed at a designated area of employment as "the professional programs or schools." And when liberal arts colleges debate the appropriateness of adding "professional programs," the studies under consideration typically are business, teacher education, social work, journalism, or computer science. Thus, although it is recognized that the term "professional" frequently evokes a legitimate definitional debate, the term is used in this report in this common sense.

Previous research reports have dealt at length with the dimensions of the debate surrounding use of the term "professional" as applied to educational programs (Anderson 1974; Nyre and Reilly 1979). Briefly, the debate stems from several sources: (1) an extensive scholarly literature that has attempted to define a profession; (2) a definition used by the U.S. Department of Education in its Higher Education General Information Survey (HEGIS) that restricts the term "first professional degree" to postbaccalaureate degrees granted in theology, law, medicine, dentistry, pharmacy, and a few other health-related fields; and (3) recruitment concerns of colleges that cause them to label their programs as professional, or to avoid the term, depending upon the image they desire to project. Authoritative sources such as the Carnegie Foundation (1977) and the NIE study group (1984) recently ignored all of these issues, the Carnegie Foundation stressing increasing enrollments in a large group of undergraduate programs they termed professional and the NIE study group criticizing as unduly narrow a seemingly extensive group of undefined undergraduate professional programs offered by colleges.

What, then, is "professional"? Having considered and rejected several synonyms, the authors concluded that "professional" is the most efficient term, encompassing as it does the understanding and curricular assessment of heavily enrolled college programs that lead to occupations in fields commonly viewed by the public as professional.

As this report emphasizes academic collegiate-level work, the authors chose to use the term "professional preparation" rather than "professional education," which may imply no skill component, or "professional training," which may imply skill development at the expense of theoretical learning (Anderson 1974). The term "professional preparation" is intended to encompass the totality of professional study—learning academic concepts, learning necessary professional skills, integrating concepts and skills, and becoming socialized into the profession.

In addition to casting a broad net at the undergraduate level, the authors used the term "entry-level" or "preservice" professional preparation to include as well traditional professional programs that historically have followed the baccalaureate degree. This decision was based on two factors, one pragmatic and one more idealistic.

Pragmatically, the distinction between undergraduate and graduate professional education has become very fuzzy, and "whenever one tries to delimit the range of graduate education, one is likely to discover that the exceptions overwhelm the rule" (Millard 1984, p. 41). Some universities, for example, offer social work, library science, and business administration as undergraduate programs; others offer these fields only at the graduate level. Despite exhortations to the contrary, the student pursuing any of these graduate-level specialties is not guaranteed to have completed a broad program of liberal study while an undergraduate. Students have long had the option of applying to law or dental school without completion of a baccalaureate degree, pharmacy education has recently been extended in length, and a national campaign is being waged to extend initial education for teacher preparation into the graduate years. At the other end of the spectrum, some universities are experimenting with shortened premedical/medical curricula that integrate and encompass liberal and professional training. Given the wide variety of patterns in American higher education, some believe it more productive to soften the outdated barriers between traditional levels than attempt to make the definitions clearer but potentially more rigid (Albrecht 1984, p. 19).

More idealistically, professional programs that traditionally have followed a period of general or liberal education can contribute vast experience that should be shared.

Some of these programs are taking renewed interest in the relation of the components of a liberal education to professional development. For example, a recent report by the Association of American Medical Colleges (AAMC) refers to the "general professional education" of physicians to encompass the entirety of collegiate-level education and includes recommendations concerning outcomes of both premedical and medical schools (AAMC 1984). The report treats many ideas that seem to be just germinating in the literature of other professional fields. Although a few traditionally graduate programs may refrain from discussing certain issues that they believe to be strictly the province of earlier educational levels, the trend seems to be in the opposite direction. Thus, a comparative study aimed primarily at cross-fertilization of ideas rightfully includes the broad range of patterns through which professional education is acquired and integrated with liberal education.

Given these broad criteria for defining a professional program, the number of professional-type programs included in any comparative study could be extensive. The focus of this report has arbitrarily been narrowed to provide a manageable project, and it includes a few programs common in the nation's larger colleges and universities. The literature search included professional preparation programs from different degree levels and from three emphases: (1) helping (dentistry, medicine, nursing, pharmacy, social work); (2) enterprising (architecture, business, engineering, law); and (3) informing (education, journalism, library science). This classification is not the only possible one that might have been chosen. Some have referred, for example, to the "service" professions and the "production" professions, based on a perceived orientation toward clients (Anderson 1974), or to the "enablers" and "exploiters," according to the degree of altruism exhibited toward clients (Reeck 1982). Other fields might have been included, too: art, chiropody, forestry, music, optometry, osteopathy, podiatry, public health, public relations, religion, research, various sciences, computer sciences, or veterinary medicine (Nyre and Reilly 1979).

Comparative study aimed primarily at cross-fertilization of ideas rightfully includes the broad range of patterns through which professional education is acquired and integrated with liberal education.

The Size of the Professional Preparation Enterprise

Table 1 provides estimates of the numbers of degrees granted annually in each of the professional preparation

TABLE 1
U.S. DEGREES GRANTED IN SELECTED PROFESSIONAL FIELDS, 1981–82[a]

	Degrees	Percent of Total	Percent Change over 1970–71	Percent Women[b]	Percent at Private Colleges[b]
Bachelor's Level Programs					
All degrees in U.S.	952,998	100	+13	50	33
Architecture[c]	9,728	1	+75	30	23
Business/management	212,474	22	+87	39	35
Communications[d]	32,428	3	+214	56	28
Education[e]	101,113	11	−43	76	23
Engineering	67,021	7	+49	11	25
Nursing[f]	32,794	3	NA	95	36
Social work[g]	14,000	1	NA	45	NA
Total	455,558	48	NA		
Master's Level Programs					
All degrees in U.S.	295,546	100	+28	51	38
Library science[h]	4,506	2	−36	82	29
Social work[g]	11,000	4	NA	38	34

First Professional Degrees[i]

	All degrees in U.S.				
	73,600	100	+94	28	59
Law[j]	35,991	49	+107	34	60
Medicine	15,814	21	+76	25	39
Dentistry	5,282	7	+40	15	40
Pharmacy[k]	1,047	1	NA	42	48

[a] Traditionally, the National Center for Education Statistics provides figures showing changes with respect to the federal census year most recently available. Thus, this table includes percent change in degrees granted since 1970–71. Because of estimates and changes in categories, some change figures have not been provided.

[b] Rounded estimates based on data available.

[c] Some institutions confer the master's degree in architecture or environmental design as a first degree at the end of five years of study. These degrees are not included.

[d] Recent transitions from journalism programs to broader degree programs called "communications" make data difficult to compare. In 1979–80, 73 percent of the degrees in communications were given in the subfield of journalism. Some institutions report both journalism and communications programs, however, where the degree given is in liberal arts.

[e] Education degrees do not include degrees given in a teaching field of arts and sciences accompanied by teacher certification. Institutional practice varies widely, but, in general, education degrees reflect primarily those in elementary education, physical education, and special education.

[f] For 1980–81.

[g] Social work degrees are not reported separately but are given in "social sciences," in "public affairs" (social and helping services), and under "clinical social work" in health professions. Estimates based on these data are provided but do not allow any guesses about the percent of degrees granted by private colleges.

[h] In 1981–82, 307 undergraduate degrees in library science also were given. Such programs, not included here, are nonaccredited and most often associated with school librarianship.

[i] Those degrees classified as "first professional" include law (51 percent), medicine (21 percent), theological professions (9 percent), dentistry (7 percent), other health fields (optometry, osteopathy, podiatry, chiropractic—total of 7 percent), veterinary medicine (3 percent), and pharmacy (1 percent).

[j] Although most law schools grant the Juris Doctor or Doctor of Jurisprudence degree, 846 law degrees were classified as bachelor's degrees in 1981–82.

[k] Bachelor's degrees are also granted in pharmacy, and the distinctions between the bachelor's and first professional degrees vary among institutions. In 1981–82, 625 bachelor of pharmacy degrees were reported separately.

Sources: National Center for Education Statistics, *Condition of Education, 1984*; National Center for Education Statistics, *Earned Degrees Conferred in 1981–82.*

programs examined in this report as well as information concerning recent enrollment trends. Estimating the number of degrees granted in each professional preparation field and the number of existing programs is no easy task. Not all professional preparation degrees, as defined here, are designated separately in HEGIS data. In addition, universities use a wide variety of degree designations to indicate similar academic work. College sourcebooks intended for prospective students also use varying terminology. Specialized accrediting agencies release no records of existing programs that have not sought accreditation. Finally, different universities offer similar programs at different levels. To illustrate, social work is offered at either the undergraduate level (B.A., B.S., B.S.W.) or graduate level (M.S.W.), depending on a college's philosophy. Similarly, while some colleges offer a degree designated as bachelor of science in journalism, others group journalism majors

TABLE 2

ESTIMATED FREQUENCY OF SELECTED PROFESSIONAL PROGRAMS IN THE MOST COMPREHENSIVE U.S. COLLEGES AND UNIVERSITIES[a]

Professional Program	Original Estimate of Number of Programs[b]	Accredited Programs Not Confirmed[c]	Confirmed Programs[d]	Estimated Number of Programs[e]
Architecture	88	18	66	84
Business	499	52	355	407
Dentistry	–	–	–	58[e]
Education[f]	463	78	358	436
Engineering	247	39	191	230
Journalism	278	12	177	189
Law	157	33	106	139[e]
Library science	79	9	48	57
Medicine	–	–	–	112[e]
Nursing	339	57	227	284
Pharmacy	73	11	44	55
Social work (undergraduate)[g]	316	14	215	229
Social work (master's)	36	11	27	38

TABLE 2 (continued)

[a]The set of 540 colleges and universities used as the population included all classified by the Carnegie Council (1976) as research universities, doctorate-granting universities, and comprehensive colleges (I). While professional-type programs occur in comprehensive colleges (II) and liberal arts colleges, they are typically small and concentrated in one or two fields, namely business and education. Including these programs would have expanded the population substantially without producing new information.

[b]Original estimates for programs occurring within the selected classifications of colleges and universities were made from various college guidebooks.

[c]Programs not confirmed directly by colleges but listed by specialized accrediting agencies as having approved programs.

[d]A confirmed program is one verified by the institution's registrar or other official whether accredited or not and irrespective of its listing in other sources.

[e]Known accredited programs plus confirmed programs. Estimates are generally low. For medicine and dentistry, the number of institutions awarding degrees is taken from *Digest of Educational Statistics, 1982* and is for 1979–80. This source reports 179 law schools granting degrees in 1979–80. This figure differs from the authors' estimate because they omitted schools not located within a college or university.

[f]Institutions offering only graduate degrees in education were excluded from the population even when those degrees provided initial entrance to teaching.

[g]When an institution offered both undergraduate and graduate programs in social work, the institution was included with undergraduate programs. Thus, master's level social work includes only those institutions offering no lower degree.

with liberal arts graduates in English, communications, or other fields.

A review of college guidebooks and a 76 percent response to an inquiry of registrars at all colleges included in three Carnegie classifications (research universities, doctorate-granting universities, comprehensive colleges and universities I) give a reasonable sense of the frequency of occurrence of most of the programs in these 540 institutions. These data are shown in table 2.

Study Methods
Identifying outcomes
Most lists of outcomes for professional preparation have been derived from an early definition of "professional" that included a knowledge base, craftsmanship, a measure of control over the educational process, a standard of ethical conduct, and the use of peers' judgment of professional competence (Flexner 1915). Building upon this definition,

various analysts have attempted to confirm the characteristics of a profession, and from this base comes the limited literature comparing professional preparation across fields of study. Because the two previous research reports (Anderson 1974; Nyre and Reilly 1979) reviewed the handful of major efforts, summaries of those works are not repeated here (see, for example, Becker and Carper 1956; Blauch 1955; Boley 1977; Gartner 1976; Haber 1974; Hughes et al. 1973; Larson 1977; McGlothlin 1960, 1964; Mayhew and Ford 1974; National Society for the Study of Education 1962; Schein and Kommers 1972; Vollmer and Mills 1966). This report instead draws upon this and other literature (for example, Bucher and Stelling 1977; Hoppmann, Liu, and Rivello 1980; Houle 1980; Sherlock and Morris 1967) to describe a set of outcomes of professional preparation that seem to be generic to all fields. The list of outcomes was derived using a "grounded theory" approach, alternating between literature reviews and discussions with professional program faculty. A detailed discussion of the derivation and the place of the outcome list in a broader conceptual framework for studying preservice professional preparation programs is found elsewhere (Stark et al. 1986).

The professional preparation outcomes that appear to be sufficiently specific to allow the examination of programmatic differences fall into two categories. One category, called "professional competence," corresponds to the common notion of the "technically competent practitioner" but has six important facets, each of which may be the target of specific educational processes. The second category, called "professional attitudes," encompasses five dimensions of professional commitment (McGlothlin 1960, 1964; Sherlock and Morris 1967). Table 3 provides a brief definition of each dimension within the two broad categories of professional competence and professional attitudes.

The literature review
Using the definitions of generic professional preparation outcomes, the authors explored the literature published in educationally focused journals of the various professional preparation fields to identify articles that defined, described, measured, or exhorted professional educators to

TABLE 3
PROFESSIONAL PREPARATION OUTCOMES

Professional Competences
- *Conceptual competence*—Understanding the theoretical foundations of the profession
- *Technical competence*—Ability to perform tasks required of the professional
- *Contextual competence*—Understanding the societal context (environment) in which the profession is practiced
- *Interpersonal communication competence*—Ability to use written and oral communication effectively
- *Integrative competence*—Ability to meld theory and technical skills in actual practice
- *Adaptive competence*—Ability to anticipate and accommodate changes (for example, technological changes) important to the profession

Professional Attitudes
- *Career marketability*—The degree to which a graduate becomes marketable as a result of acquired training
- *Professional identity*—The degree to which a graduate internalizes the norms of a profession
- *Ethical standards*—The degree to which a graduate internalizes the ethics of a profession
- *Scholarly concern for improvement*—The degree to which a graduate recognizes the need to increase knowledge in the profession through research
- *Motivation for continued learning*—The degree to which a graduate desires to continue to update knowledge and skills

consider one of the outcome categories. They also examined books dealing specifically with education in particular professional preparation fields, accreditation guidelines, and major reports published by professional associations or groups of professional schools. Although this report draws upon all of these sources, it draws most extensively from the educational journal literature of 12 fields.

Library sources like *Resources in Education* led to many journals that are primarily or partially devoted to discussions of educational practices and issues in the various professions. Based on the space they devoted to educational concerns and on discussions with colleagues in professional fields, one (in one case, two) journal from each field was selected for detailed examination. As shown in table 4, those choices were generally coincident with journals professional faculty read to become informed about issues of educational practice as reported in a later survey (see Appendix A for details).

Nearly 3,000 articles published in 14 different journals from January 1979 through December 1984 were examined, of which 660 were selected for detailed review. The details of selection are given in Appendix A.

This review confirms earlier statements (Anderson 1974; Nyre and Reilly 1979) that medical educators and teacher educators are among the most prolific writers of literature focusing on issues of professional preparation. Dental and pharmacy education are other fields where educational lit-

TABLE 4

CONGRUENCE BETWEEN JOURNALS PROFESSIONAL FACULTY READ AND JOURNALS SELECTED FOR REVIEW

Journal	Reviewed	Number of Faculty Members in Field Naming at Least One Journal	Percent- age of First Mentions[a]	Percentage of First and Second Mentions
J of Architecture Education	*	84	67.9	40.3
Architecture			4.8	11.4
ACSA Journal			10.7	10.7
No business administration journal was named by at least 10 percent of the survey respondents.				
J of Teacher Education	*	422	15.2	11.4
Phi Delta Kappan			26.1	22.1
Engineering Education	*	203	26.6	18.0
IEEE Spectrum			11.8	12.2
J of the American Society of Engineering Education			7.4	21.7
Journalism Educator	*	190	43.7	32.5
Journalism Quarterly			24.2	23.1
J of Legal Education	*	176	96.0	77.6
American Bar Association Journal			1.7	12.1

TABLE 4 (continued)

J of Education for Librarianship	*		33.1	20.9
J of Education for Library/ Information Science			32.4	20.0
Nurse Educator	*	343	9.9	11.3
J of Nursing Education	*		38.5	28.5
Nursing Research			5.5	10.3
Nursing Outlook			23.3	23.0
J of Pharmaceutical Education	*	92	83.7	58.1
American Pharmacy			1.0	13.2
J of Education for Social Work	*	204	56.9	36.8
Social Work			27.5	36.3
J of Dental Education	*	No Survey Information		
J of Medical Education	*	No Survey Information		

[a]As described in Appendix A, faculty members were asked to contribute the names of up to two journals. Because some provided only one journal name and because the journal named second by some faculty members was a first mention for others, two columns of data are provided. "Percentage of first mentions" indicates the percentage of responding faculty in the field who mentioned the journal first. "Percentage of first and second mentions" indicates the percentage of mentions the journal received from the combined set of first- and second-named journals. Only first and second mentions greater than 10 percent are included.

erature is abundant. In contrast, no single journal dealing with educational issues for business administration could be found, and, in this survey, even 10 percent of faculty in business did not name a journal. Each subspecialty of business (marketing, accounting, organizational studies, and so on) has some type of publication devoting space to educational practice, but business administration faculty named none of them consistently in a manner parallel to journals like the *Journal of Medical Education* or the *Journal of Education for Social Work*.

While it seems likely that articles published in the established education journals of each field reflect current discussions within each field of professional preparation, several factors may call such an assumption into question. Journal sponsorship varies, as do editorial and manuscript acceptance policies. In some cases, published articles may presage changing practices in the field; in other cases, they may reflect primarily past trends or merely the "publish or perish" pressure on faculty members. Because this review seeks to describe broad trends in the literature, the authors made no attempt to evaluate the articles, beyond exclusion of those that were clearly not helpful.

The literature on professional education is so extensive that delimiters are necessary in any brief report. Except where it was difficult to draw the line, this report was restricted to articles about initial professional preparation (whether at the undergraduate or graduate level) and did not review the extensive literature on continuing professional education. Articles that were reports of curricular experiments, unless they dealt with the broad outcomes in this framework rather than with specific content or teaching methods, were also excluded. In addition, labor market trends in the various professional fields have not been dealt with.

Three broad questions guided the literature review. What does the literature in education journals from the respective professional fields have to say about the generic outcomes? Is the outcome framework feasible for use in identifying special and common aspects of preparation? What practical implications for faculty, administrators, and researchers are suggested by a comparative literature review?

Faculty Views of the Emphasis on Outcomes
By the time the literature review was finished, survey responses from 2,217 faculty members in 732 professional programs representing 10 of the 12 professional fields were available (see Appendix A for information about the survey population and response). These data provided information about the emphasis faculty thought "ideally" should be given to each generic professional preparation outcome and faculty descriptions of educational activities designed to achieve the outcomes. Because the literature review, rather than the survey, was the primary source and because a detailed analysis of the survey is still underway, the authors have not made formal statistical comparisons between the emphasis in the journals and faculty perceptions gathered in the survey. Nonetheless, the traditional

literature review was supplemented with some preliminary survey results to give the reader a notion of the extent to which the discussions in the literature reflect outcomes faculty in various fields perceive as important. Thus, for each outcome are listed the fields with the most extensive and least extensive journal discussion, the fields in which faculty perceive the outcome to be of greatest and least importance, and the fields in which the highest and lowest percentage of faculty said that specific formal or informal activities intended to achieve the outcomes existed in their program. The reader is cautioned that the professional fields included in the survey were not identical to those for which literature was reviewed, the estimates of emphasis given to a topic in the journal literature are not precise, and the reasons why a topic may be widely discussed in journals but appear less important on campus (or the reverse) are still under study.

Summary
A profession "may be a fundamental social process embedded in the relationship between society and those who practice certain expert occupations" (Forsyth and Danisiewicz 1985, p. 60). The use of the term "expert" implies competent performance; thus, it is not surprising to find that a frequently expected outcome of professional education is to produce competent practitioners. This comprehensive outcome, shared by all preparation programs, probably leads to the widely accepted assertion that professional education is technical education. Yet it is far too simplistic a definition. This analysis of the literature, as well as the preliminary analysis of the authors' survey of faculty in 10 professional fields, indicates that professional preparation is a much more complex concept encompassing several components involving knowledge, skill, and attitudes.

PROFESSIONAL COMPETENCE

Developing competent professional workers is the primary objective of professional education programs. From earlier studies and discussions, six types of professional competence have been identified that appear to be sought in all or most professional programs: (1) conceptual competence, (2) technical competence, (3) contextual competence, (4) interpersonal communication competence, (5) integrative competence, and (6) adaptive competence (Stark et al. 1986). [The sense in which the term "competence" is used is the level of proficiency that professional program faculty expect a new entrant to the profession to demonstrate. While some have suggested that professional "proficiency" would be a better term (as competence implies a minimal level of performance), others suggest a performance continuum from competence to proficiency to mastery, with mastery resulting from considerable work experience (Scheffler 1965).]

Developing competent professional workers is the primary objective of professional education programs.

Certainly, the degree to which individual graduates achieve the expectations faculty hold for them vary as do the expectations in different programs. Although variations exist among fields, reactions of 2,230 professional program faculty members in 10 fields to statements describing graduates in terms of each of these competences indicate that all of these outcomes are quite important. (The 10 fields surveyed included architecture, business administration, education, engineering, journalism, law, library science, nursing, pharmacy, and social work. Medicine and dentistry were not surveyed.) Of the articles concerned with outcomes in the professional journals reviewed, about 38 percent were classified as dealing with technical competence, about 22 percent with conceptual competence. Each of the other competences accounted for less than 15 percent of the outcome-related articles. Adaptive competence was the outcome represented least frequently; less than 10 percent of the articles were classified as discussing it.

Conceptual Competence
Graduates may be considered conceptually competent if they have learned the generally accepted foundational knowledge upon which professional practice is based. (Other terms for this knowledge domain include "theoretical foundations," "professional science," and "professional knowledge base.") Partly because of a rapidly

---

TABLE 5
CONCEPTUAL COMPETENCE

Relative Proportion of Journal Articles[a]	Importance of Professional Outcome[b]		Program Has Educational Activities to Achieve Outcome[c]
High	**High**		**High**
Social work	Nursing	84%	
Law	Social work	79%	*No data*
Medicine			
Low	**Low**		**Low**
Engineering			
Pharmacy	Architecture	49%	*No data*
Library science	Business	46%	

[a]A "high" proportion of articles indicates that over the five-year period examined, the percentage of outcome articles devoted to this competence was above the third quartile of percentages of all fields examined; a "low" proportion indicates the percentage of articles in the field fell below the first quartile. Because the number of articles reviewed varied widely by field, because not all journals were included, and because the purpose of the review was integration of ideas rather than precise classification of articles, this level of precision is appropriate to convey the level of discussion.
[b]Percentage of faculty members in the survey who answered "7" on a seven-point scale when asked what emphasis would "ideally" be placed on the outcome in their professional preparation program.
[c]For most outcomes, this information includes the percentage of faculty members in the survey who reported that their program had formal or informal educational activities intended to foster the outcome. Because the authors presumed that all programs would have educational activities designed to lead to conceptual competence, faculty responding to the survey were not asked to describe such activities for this outcome.

changing technological society, faculty members in professional fields do not fully agree on the content that makes up the knowledge base. Even in the least debated fields (business and engineering), over 40 percent of faculty members believe a lack of consensus exists concerning the conceptual knowledge base (Stark, Lowther, and Hagerty 1985). Thus, as might be expected, conceptual competence receives substantial attention in the literature about professional preparation.

As indicated in table 5, relative to other fields, journals directed at educators in social work, law, and medicine published the greatest proportion of articles dealing with conceptual competence, while journals aimed at educators in engineering, pharmacy, and library science published the smallest proportion. The survey results indicate, however, that the proportion of articles published does not necessarily correspond to views of faculty in the field concerning the importance of conceptual competence. In the survey, nursing and social work faculty viewed conceptual competence as most important, while faculty in architecture and business perceived it as less important.

A pervasive, frequently contentious, problem for professional educators is the amount of conceptual content to include in the entry-level curriculum. In recent years, this problem has been exacerbated for all professional fields by at least three influential factors: (1) the rapid growth of specialized knowledge, (2) the application of new technologies to practice, and (3) the expansion of professional obligations to include new clients or recipients of service. These factors have modified the priorities of professional preparation and have provoked searching analyses of the curriculum in all fields, particularly in relation to conceptual competence. In dentistry, for example, the expansion of the service framework is reflected in assertions that dentists should be sensitive ''to the needs of all the people—the economically, physically, and emotionally disadvantaged'' (Dworkin 1981, p. 693). Similarly, in engineering, ''the computer has revolutionized engineering course content and instructional methods'' (LeBold 1980, p. 407). Such developments have profound implications for the attainment of conceptual competence and, as discussed later, of contextual and technical competences as well. Dental educators must find space in the course of study to include content from the behavioral sciences; engineering educators struggle with the social ramifications of new technologies. These same two phenomena, an ecological view of the client and an expanding technology, stimulate major curriculum debates (and sometimes changes) in most professional fields.

Consequently, the literature about conceptual competence, that is, the literature that examines the fields' theoretical foundations or fundamental knowledge base, often is characterized by uncertainty and disputation and occasionally by heroic rhetoric about mission. Questions emerge about the purpose and thrust of the profession itself, about what knowledge is fundamental to the field, about the relationship between theory and practice, and about how to meld the program into a meaningful and rational whole.

For the purposes of this discussion, different sets of literature about conceptual outcomes have been identified. One set of articles addresses the broad issue of program validity, that is, the rationale or integrity of the total preparation program. Do all the courses and experiences link together into an intellectually coherent entity? What is the appropriate overall strategy for preparing a person for entry-level practice? Is one conceptual framework "best" for professional preparation? Of course, all of these questions hark back to the essential query: What is the purpose or mission of the field? These questions, in fact, form the bulk of the literature dealing with conceptual competence, far surpassing that providing more specific discussions of conceptual competence, means for achieving student outcomes, or empirical examination of outcomes achieved.

A second set of articles addresses knowledge or theory as foundational bedrock for the attainment of all other competences. Such articles assume that practice is indeed guided by theory and must be preceded by mastery of relevant concepts. Much of this literature, devoted as it must be to the particular concepts to be taught and learned, is occupationally specific, and frequently it is difficult for nonmembers of the profession to distinguish discussions of conceptual competence from those concerning technical or skill competence. This report focuses on that literature in which several fields discuss similar problems.

A third set of articles focuses on conceptual competences that do not reside specifically in knowledge or theory but can be characterized as integral to the person: They must be present for successful attainment of other competences and for practice. They include such attributes as values, attitudes, and cognitive capabilities, which include, for example, problem-solving skills, creative capabilities, and critical thinking skills. Such internal competences are called "entry-level characteristics," which may or may not be present in the student but are conceptual fundamentals for subsequent education and practice (Bloom 1976). Thus, they are distinguished from "professional attitudes." Although professional attitudes are developed during professional study, the prerequisite student characteristics are classified as conceptual because they underlie performance in the professional preparation program and may serve as a basis for distinguishing classes of students' performance (very creative, a good problem solver, and so on).

Program validity
On the education of pharmacists, some writers have observed that "we have yet to decide which science(s) and at what depth are relevant to professional practice instruction" (Vogt, Montagne, and Smith 1981, p. 237). Similarly, in law:

> *One can say without fear of serious contradiction that legal education taken as a whole is best described as a craft that has been dead in the water since the late fifties. Changes there have been—clinical education has grown, seminars have appeared at the smallest schools, women have appeared everywhere in great numbers— but the fundamental structure of legal education remains essentially as it was at the elite schools in the immediate post-war years* (Schlegel 1984, p. 103).

These two statements from writers describing quite different preparation programs illustrate a mood of self-assessment and uncertainty that appears in all fields to some degree. Concerns, observations, and recommendations are expressed about such general preparation issues as program mission, direction, and control (Alofsin 1983; Auerbach 1984; Bakalinsky 1982; Barondess 1981; Cantor, Schroeder, and Kurth 1981; Cavers 1983; Cramton 1982; Dinerman 1982; Dostoglu 1983; Frumkin 1979; Gianniny 1982; Hacker 1982; Hartman 1980; Huling and Hall 1982; Isakson and Ellsworth 1979; Ivey 1982; Jarrett 1979; Jordon 1979; Klare 1982; Kroll and Mikellides 1981; LeBold 1980; LeBold, Lindenlaub, and Seibert 1980; Loe 1981; Meunier 1979; Pye 1982; Richardson and Hernon 1981; Rowles 1982; Roy 1979; Schlegel 1984; Smith, Johnson, and Johnson 1981; Snyder and Anderson 1980; Teigiser 1983; Terkla 1981; Vernon 1983; Vogt, Montagne, and Smith 1981; White 1982; Wodarski 1979; Zeichner 1983).

The recommendations in these overall statements range from the very broad to the very narrow and usually reflect experience-based opinion rather than conclusions drawn from systematic research. On the one hand, such broad self-critical statements of concern may represent some degree of instability and uncertainty about professional preparation. On the other hand, such expressions of self-doubt may, in fact, be healthy qualities suggesting educational maturity, confidence, and a willingness to entertain criticism and recommendations without defensive posturing.

Knowledge of theoretical foundations

As described earlier, another set of articles focused on conceptual outcomes, many of which were field-specific. Some issues, however, appear to bridge several of the professions, and this discussion is organized around three such generic themes:

1. The value and role of certain academic courses;
2. The incorporation of social science content as a conceptual foundation;
3. Changes in practitioners' roles that imply needs for new theoretical foundations.

Value and role of certain courses and content. Professional educators in several fields appear to be questioning the theoretical utility of traditional foundations courses. Most frequently targeted for criticism are courses treating historical and/or philosophical foundations of the particular profession. Architecture educators have questioned the contribution made to effective practice by the study of architectural history (Abbey and Dripps 1982; Creese 1980; Hubbard 1980); journalism educators have raised similar issues. Perhaps, however, the most searching review of required courses in history and philosophy of a field comes from teacher educators. A number of teacher educators have argued that these courses are not basic to the field as suggested by the name "foundations" (Nash and Agne 1982; Warren 1982). They assert that the current content is superficial and highly abstract and tends to induce ideological "platitudinizing."

We have argued that contemporary social and professional conditions have put the foundational disciplines in

*a precariously defensive position; in some cases, foun-
dational studies have been deleted entirely from professional programs* (Nash and Agne 1982, p. 6).

As might be expected, advocates of such courses have
responded with their own claims of intent (Green 1981;
Williams 1982).

*The foundations area, by studying the school within a
social context and by analyzing the problems from an
interdisciplinary approach, provides an excellent opportunity to promote cultural thought, the basic ingredient
of a true education* (Williams 1982, p. 34).

Interestingly, similar debates about traditional foundations study exist in many of the professional fields, illus-
trating the crowded nature of the curriculum and the dilemmas of pruning. At the same time, however, many fields
have begun to introduce social science content directly into
their professional knowledge core, while others are seeking
to expand the contextual horizons of graduates through liberal education and interdisciplinary avenues. It is possible
that the agents of change target their pleas for examination
less at the concepts to be included in the curriculum than
at the particular style and teaching format these foundational courses have gradually acquired over the years.
Another feasible explanation is that the threat of college
and university retrenchment encourages faculty to maintain foundational courses in separate professional study
areas although they could be taught in a more interdisciplinary format.

Incorporation of social science content. In examining potential physicians, the National Board of Medical Examiners
now includes questions drawn from the behavioral sciences
in an attempt to demonstrate "the interaction of biological,
psychological, and social factors in the onset and treatment
of illness" (Begun and Ricker 1980, p. 181). As a consequence, "medical educators agree that the behavioral sciences are important in medical education, but translating
this affirmation into an effective curriculum has proven to
be a complex task" (Carr 1981, p. 667). The inclusion of
behavioral science as contributing to conceptual compe-

tence in medicine is a phenomenon shared by a number of other professional preparation programs (AAMC 1984; Bailey 1979; Brusich 1980; Dolinsky 1979; Dworkin 1981; Gianniny 1982; Johnson and Wertheimer 1979; Jordon 1979; Jvhasz 1981; Leighninger and Leighninger 1980; Mohan 1980; Priest 1983; Seidel 1981; Shreve et al. 1980; Shuck 1983; Svarstad 1979; Sze, Keller, and Keller 1979).

The expansion of the conceptual base to include more social science or behavioral theory responds to an expanded vision of clients' needs and an attempt to provide a basis for clients' interaction that will maximize the delivery of quality service. Its inclusion, however, creates both issues of curricular volume and instructional dilemmas. Who, for example, should provide the instruction? The professional program faculty? Faculty drawn from other units? Does social science content actually advance professional practice? Can nonprofessional faculty members modify content to make it relevant to the particular needs of the professional school?

Changing roles of practitioners. A number of articles propose emphasis on new roles for practitioners to serve new clients—for example, human service workers in education, health educators in nursing (Graham and Gleir 1980) and in pharmacy (Fedder and Beardsley 1979), public health pharmacists (Bush and Johnson 1979), public agency workers and child welfare workers in social work (Gibelman 1983; Stein 1982). But the introduction of new specialty areas within established preparation programs tends to exacerbate the problem of appropriate conceptual content.

Students' attitudinal and cognitive attributes
One area of the literature treats attributes of students, such as values, attitudes, and cognitive capabilities as prerequisite to effective practice and, indeed, to successful professional preparation. The preparation program may attempt to foster the development of such attributes, if the student does not possess them. For example, in engineering, suggestions are made regarding ways to advance students on the Perry scheme of intellectual development (Culver and Hackos 1982), to teach holistic ways of thinking and the use of higher levels of intellect (Williamson and Hudspeth 1982), and to structure students' learning goals to meet the

goals of engineering education (Smith, Johnson, and Johnson 1981). Journalists propose the need to focus on problem solving (Bennett 1984), while in library science, a suggestion is made to enhance students' awareness of their own learning processes as a prerequisite for improving the ability to learn relatively independently at high levels (Ford 1984). Medicine addresses issues of problem solving: "Reasoning from the premise that highly developed problem-solving skills are requisite to effective clinical practice, many medical schools have incorporated some form of problem-based instruction or assessment into their curricula" (McGaghie 1980, p. 912). Furthermore, medical educators have developed a taxonomy to evaluate the overall cognitive performance of medical students (Buckwalter et al. 1981). In part, the increased concern about such attributes represents awareness among professional faculty of the advancing research about metacognition and styles of learning. Emphasis on development of these attributes seems intended to accomplish two purposes: improving students' conceptual capabilities and providing a vehicle for socializing the student into the modes of thought associated with the profession. For example, "with respect to law school, deliberate, technical socialization is generally agreed to be the acquisition of information, concepts, and intellectual skills—often summed up as learning 'to think like a lawyer' " (Schwartz 1980, p. 440).

Values, attitudes, and cognitive capabilities [are] prerequisite to effective practice and, indeed, to successful professional preparation.

Technical Competence

Technical competence refers to a graduate's ability to perform fundamental skills required of the professional. In the various professions, technical competence is closely related to conceptual competence; thus, the "craft" aspect of professional preparation is clearly unique to each field. Because skills needed by an architect are distinguishable from those needed by a nurse or a lawyer, for example, less opportunity seems available to find commonalities across professional preparation programs with respect to technical competence than in most other aspects of competence. Further, it is more difficult for individuals who are not trained in the professions to understand the literature written about technical competence, contributing to the view that professional education is narrow. Historians of the professions point out, however, that preparation for

TABLE 6
TECHNICAL COMPETENCE

Relative Proportion of Journal Articles	Importance of Professional Outcome		Program Has Educational Activities to Achieve Outcome[a]
High	**High**		**High**
Journalism	Social work	79%	*No data*
Social work	Journalism	71%	
Library science	Education	63%	
Low	**Low**		**Low**
Nursing	Library science	35%	*No data*
Pharmacy	Architecture	32%	
Engineering	Law	25%	

[a]The authors, presuming that all fields would have activities to develop technical competence, did not ask faculty to describe such activities.

most professional fields migrated from apprenticeship status to university status when the conceptual base of an occupation had expanded so that on-the-job training in skills no longer sufficed to produce a competent professional (Bullough 1970). Today, most fields that more heavily emphasize technical competence compared to conceptual competence would not be judged "professional."

As shown in table 6, three fields, library science, journalism, and social work, devoted a considerably higher proportion of journal articles to technical competence than did other fields. Nursing, engineering, and pharmacy, which the casual observer might judge to be more concerned with the development of skills, devoted a low proportion of journal articles to this outcome. A similar pattern emerged in the survey of professional field faculty. Faculty members in architecture and law were the least likely to believe technical competence should be emphasized. In fact, faculty in some fields, such as law, felt that the development of skills currently receives more emphasis than it should. Perhaps recent criticisms have caused professional educators to be reluctant to discuss skill development so as not to appear excessively vocational. Alternatively, one can speculate that basic skills needed by new professionals are fairly well established in many fields and firmly entrenched in licensing and certification examinations where they exist, and that continued discussion is little needed.

This discussion focuses on identifying a few categories of technical skills that seem common to several fields. Three such generic types of technical skills are addressed in the professional journals: (1) psychomotor skills, (2) interpersonal skills, and (3) special cognitive skills.

Psychomotor skills

The journal literature does not heavily emphasize psychomotor and technological skill outcomes, although some fields describe entire new curricula for required skills (Heymann and Roberson 1984). Others describe specific skills required of their graduates. For example, one library science article discusses training in on-line cataloging (Downing 1981), while dental educators describe specific techniques required of students, such as endodontic skills (Goerig 1980). Other articles discuss methodologies for evaluating technical outcomes defined as competencies. In the area of measuring competency, one article in social work lists 87 specific competencies to be evaluated. Educators in pharmacy describe domain-referenced tests and practice rating scales (Grussing, Cyrs, and Silzer 1979; Holloway 1979); authors in dentistry discuss the need for feedback from students and competency requirements for state board examinations (Terkla 1981). Nursing education literature describes employers' competency ratings of new graduates (Bolin and Hogle 1984).

Interpersonal skills

For most purposes, interpersonal skills are viewed in this monograph as a separate category called "interpersonal communication competence." Differences are apparent, however, between interpersonal skills as techniques specific to particular fields and a more general competence that allows one to be adept in interpersonal communication. Particularly in the helping professions, specific training is required for interaction with clients like the elderly, the handicapped, and minorities (Corcoran 1981; Salley 1980; Toseland and Spielberg 1982; Wright 1981). Similarly, in fields like journalism and law, communication skills might be viewed as technical competence that extends beyond a general level.

Special cognitive skills

Special cognitive skills include behaviors specific to a field (design skills in architecture, for example) (Meunier 1979) and more general skills used by several fields (statistics and literature reading, for example) (Riegelman, Povar, and Ott 1983). These types of special skills allow the new professional to perform certain tasks or procedures that enhance professional practice. Such a classification also includes "creative" skills, which may be nurtured in fields such as architecture, journalism, and some aspects of engineering (Merrill 1980; Meunier 1979).

Society sanctions professional practice based on technical competence, that is, those skills necessary to ensure the provision of safe, quality service to clients. Yet the literature contains negligible discussion of technical competence as a component for defining a professional field. Indeed, professions appear to use their skills and technical base of practice to expand their boundaries and to define more inclusively their arena of practice. As economic constraints increase, clients and employers of professionals appraise the cost effectiveness of professional practice, based in part, on its technical components. Thus, in spite of the apparent reluctance of professional educators to focus on technical competence, this outcome may be influenced by pressing issues with respect to the nature, effectiveness, and efficiency of professional practice in all fields.

Contextual Competence

"Contextual competence" signifies an understanding of the broad social, economic, and cultural setting in which the profession is practiced (McGlothlin 1964). It refers not only to the professional's specific work setting, but also to the larger environments, both social and natural, within which the work is embedded. The acquisition of this competence implies that the student can examine the environmental context from a variety of vantage points: historical, social, economic, psychological, political, and philosophical. The capability to adopt multiple perspectives allows the student to comprehend the complex interdependencies between the profession and society, thus fostering both increased professional social awareness and more effective citizenship (Smith, Johnson, and Johnson 1981). The achievement of contextual competence allows the student to transcend egocentric or parochial levels of thought in interpreting contemporary life. In this fashion, the needs of society and of the professions are met in a complementary way. By fostering breadth of vision and understanding through multiple perspectives, contextual competence serves to counter the accusation that professional education is excessively narrow and intellectually confining (Torgersen 1979).

Typically, the task of implementing contextual competence has resided with liberal arts and, particularly, with educators in the humanities. Yet this obligation has long been surrounded by debate within professional fields about the appropriate amount and nature of nonprofessional or contextual course work required (Raths 1980) and whether liberal arts courses are the appropriate curricular vehicle to achieve the objective (Hodges and Lichter 1980). Recently, this debate has been accompanied by a growing awareness that society's moods and needs generate powerful forces for most professions that may disrupt established professional life (AAMC 1984; Porter 1979). For example, some professions are subject to widespread discontent about what is seen as self-serving behavior (Larson 1977; Schon 1983), and the point is vividly made: "The blunt, inexcusable fact is that this nation, which prides itself on efficiency and justice, has developed a legal system that is the most expensive in the world, yet cannot manage to protect the rights of most of its citizens" (Bok 1983, p. 574).

For the teaching profession, numerous public agencies are attempting to remedy what they perceive as contextual deficiencies in teacher training through legislation, testing, and revision of licensing standards. Such considerations imply that increased emphasis on contextual competence may positively influence societal/professional relationships, thus serving the needs of both constituents. Consequently, the literature suggests that professional educators are reassessing their commitment to contextual competence as well as the ways in which that competence may be achieved.

As shown in table 7, relatively high proportions of journal articles concerning contextual competence are found in architecture and law, relatively low proportions in library science, nursing, business, and pharmacy. Faculty in social work, journalism, and nursing believe contextual competence should be emphasized to a substantial degree, while faculty in business, pharmacy, law, and engineering rank it

TABLE 7
CONTEXTUAL COMPETENCE

Relative Proportion of Journal Articles	Importance of Professional Outcome		Program Has Educational Activities to Achieve Outcome	
High	**High**		**High**	
Architecture	Social work	70%	Social work	93%
Law	Journalism	59%	Nursing	91%
	Nursing	55%	Architecture	85%
Low	**Low**		**Low**	
Library science	Business	36%	Business	66%
Pharmacy	Pharmacy	34%	Law	61%
Nursing	Law	28%	Engineering	60%
Business	Engineering	19%		

quite low among the competences a graduate should possess. According to this survey, those fields in which contextual competence is least emphasized also cite fewer activities to achieve it.

The literature about contextual competence was grouped according to three themes: (1) the liberal arts connection, (2) the social and environmental content within the professional curriculum, and (3) the recognition of social diversity.

The liberal arts connection
The literature describing the role of liberal arts or the humanities in professional preparation programs ranges from a conception (in journalism and law) of the professional program as a liberal arts discipline and as a professional study (DeMott 1984; Lindley 1984; Stone 1984; White 1982) to concern (in engineering, for example) about whether the tight professional curriculum can accommodate even a small number of liberal courses within four years (VanderMeer and Lyons 1980). Further, graduate professional programs like medicine see their role as the "shaping" of the baccalaureate program to include social sciences, natural sciences, and humanities through modification of perceived and required admissions criteria (AAMC 1984). Underlying all these discussions is a convic-

tion that professional education can benefit from the liberal arts tradition (Dovey 1981; Neidle 1980; Reid 1979; Smith 1979; Torgersen 1979). What may be at issue is the best form of implementation. Questions are raised frequently about the appropriate contextual content, the contributions of various liberal arts disciplines, and the proper ratio between such courses and professional studies. One national sample of the attitudes of engineering faculty toward liberal arts in the engineering curriculum found that most faculty favor no growth or a reduction in liberal arts courses. Further, they are not inclined to be prescriptive about what disciplines ought to be represented (Vander-Meer and Lyons 1980). Such attitudes, the authors concluded, are fostered partly by rapid advances in engineering knowledge and by the constraints of a four-year program. This issue seems most acute in those professional programs where entry-level professional preparation frequently is provided in a four-year period culminating in a bachelor's degree—that is, education, nursing, engineering, journalism, and social work. In part, of course, such attitudes may also reflect distrust among faculty in professional fields about the way in which liberal arts are taught:

> *Devotees of the humanities and social sciences generally have failed to develop an understanding of their own subject matter as essentially action guiding. The liberal studies appear to have been singularly unsuccessful in either enriching or illuminating the lives of the large mass of citizenry in democratic societies, much less the activities of highly trained technical professionals* (Hodges and Lichter 1980, p. 817).

Despite such accusations and the fact that liberal arts courses account for only about 20 percent of the engineering student's total coursework, the liberal component in engineering education has a long history and contemporary vitality (Torgersen 1979).

Some professional teacher education programs, having emerged from the liberal arts tradition, continue to rely very heavily on that coursework for as much as two-thirds of the total curriculum. Currently, however, this traditional relationship is being penetrated with seams of doubt. Several factors may help to account for this reexamination of the liberal arts relationship: the growing vocationalism of students in education, the dramatic increases in knowledge about teaching (Tymitz-Wolf 1984), and questions about the outcomes of general education (Raths 1980). As might be expected, strong liberal arts advocates deplore the perceived drift away from the liberal arts tradition to vocationalism (Carbone 1980; Webb and Sherman 1983), and recently national reports and government officials have begun to as well. Although the general education component of teacher training seems well established, what some professional teacher educators are proposing is that the field be more prescriptive about appropriate courses and more specific about intended student outcomes (Carbone 1980; Raths 1980). Like engineers, teacher educators have proposed expanding the program to five years, but the proposal has not been widely adopted (Kluender 1984).

Journalism faces special dilemmas as a consequence of its professional accrediting agency's rule that only 25 percent of total coursework may be professional in nature (Stone 1984; Zagano 1983). Furthermore, journalism educators are challenged by assertions from some magazine and newspaper editors that professional or technical coursework is unnecessary and that the best preparation for practice is a liberal arts degree. Thus, a core issue for journalism educators is how to resolve the tension between expansion of technical knowledge and the perceived legitimacy of professional preparation courses (Haroldsen and Harvey 1979; Mehra 1984; Mills, Harvey, and Warnick 1980).

Professional preparation in social work can be acquired through either a four-year curriculum leading to a bachelor of social work degree or by pursuing a master of social work degree. Supporters of the M.S.W. curriculum argue that the B.S.W. too heavily erodes necessary groundwork in liberal arts. Advocates of the B.S.W. claim that undergraduate social work education, with its strong emphasis on societal problems, can serve as a vehicle for resolving a fragmented liberal education (Reid 1979).

Social/environmental content within the professional curriculum

The second major category of literature about contextual competence focuses on how it can be fostered within the professional curriculum rather than relying solely on liberal arts courses. As suggested earlier, professional educators are concerned that the liberal arts lack focus on the occupational world of the professional; that is, current liberal arts content is too abstract and too removed from reality. As a consequence, many professional educators have attempted to introduce contextual issues into their own curricula (Abramson 1979; Allen and Burwell 1980; Berman 1981; Ellis 1981; Findley 1979; Gessner, Katz, and Schimpfhauser 1981; Gitterman and Germain 1981; Grantham and Block 1983; Harris and Rosenthal 1981; Lewis 1979; Martinez-Brawley 1983; Porter 1979; Smith 1979; Vonalt et al. 1980; Von Blum 1979), and in some fields, such as medicine, faculty development programs are proposed to raise consciousness and competence concerning the professional context (AAMC 1984).

Professional educators are concerned that the liberal arts . . . content is too abstract and too removed from reality.

Much of the literature describing integration within the professional courses focuses upon how specific content was introduced in a particular course setting. For example, an interdisciplinary approach was taken in one course to foster a historical perspective (Von Blum 1979); in another setting, attempts were made to fuse social content into an entire curriculum (Gessner, Katz, and Schimpfhauser 1981). Professional educators face dilemmas as they attempt to introduce social content. On the one hand, much of the desired content is interdisciplinary, which may preclude its incorporation into existing disciplinary courses. On the other hand, general survey courses do not provide adequate depth or are unrelated to professional concerns. Last, introducing new electives may force students to choose between them and attractive skill courses. As yet, the arguments are not bolstered by much evidence that if broad issues are introduced directly into a professional program, the attitudes of faculty and students will change in the desired directions.

Social diversity
The final category of literature about contextual competence suggests a growing awareness of the wide diversity of populations served by the professions. In part, this recognition may emerge from the economic need to expand the client base (Brendtro 1980; Carlson and Lockwood 1980); more probably it represents implementation of humanitarian concern to provide service to all who require

it and to recognize clients' differing needs. Most of the professions recognize the need to introduce social realities and the necessity and moral obligation to provide service to women (Kravetz 1982; Rathbone-McCuan 1984), to the handicapped and other special populations (Cassileth and Egan 1979; Humphreys 1983; Jennings and Smith 1979; Lange and Fender 1980; Salley 1980), to the aged (Allen and Burwell 1980; Buschman, Burns, and Jones 1981; Denise and Nauratil 1984; Gessner, Katz, and Schimpfhauser 1981; Shepherd and Erwin 1983; Thomas and Ship 1981), to minority and ethnic groups (Baker and Mayer 1982; Balgopal, Munson, and Vassil 1979; Proctor and Davis 1983; Pugach and Raths 1982; Sims 1981; Steiner and Devore 1983), and to entire communities (AAMC 1984). Just as the people-oriented professions express sensitivity to diversity, architecture and engineering have introduced content about the natural and social environments and the need to integrate treatments (Comerio 1981; Dovey 1981; Ellis 1981; Gaines 1980; Hull 1979; Lewis 1979; Littman, Mayo, and Burgess 1981; Thorpe 1979; Treib 1982).

Interpersonal Communication Competence
Interpersonal communication implies the ability to communicate effectively with others through a variety of symbolic means. As a cornerstone objective of liberal study, students' achievement of these skills is not the sole responsibility of the professional faculty. Professional fields can be differentiated, however, in the extent to which they accept these goals as legitimate and ensure these applications by students in different professional settings.

In the journal literature, the greatest proportional attention to interpersonal communication competence occurs in engineering, pharmacy, and business, the smallest proportion in social work, library science, and journalism. As shown in table 8, the attention to interpersonal communication in the journal literature is not congruent with faculty members' desired emphasis. It is possible that the most extensive discussions are found in fields where these skills traditionally have been neglected. Journalism educators, for example, discuss communication competence in all articles but in a different sense from the other fields.

Despite considerable general concern about the writing skills of today's college students, faculty in several profes-

TABLE 8

INTERPERSONAL COMMUNICATION COMPETENCE

Relative Proportion of Journal Articles	Importance of Professional Outcome		Program Has Educational Activities to Achieve Outcome	
High	**High**		**High**	
Engineering	Journalism	92%	Law	95%
Pharmacy	Education	77%	Nursing	95%
Business	Law	76%	Journalism	92%
Low	**Low**		**Low**	
Social work			Pharmacy	79%
Library science	Engineering	47%	Architecture	77%
Journalism	Architecture	37%	Library science	76%

sional fields are specifically concerned about other aspects of communication. The health professions (medicine, nursing, pharmacy, and dentistry) seem particularly concerned with those interpersonal communication skills that help health professionals become empathetic and responsive to the needs and feelings of their patients. Medical care may be becoming more efficient, but it is not yet sufficiently patient-centered (AAMC 1984; Comstock et al. 1982). Because the interaction between physician and patient provides information for making clinical decisions as well as establishing a physician-patient relationship, it is viewed as critical for treatment and compliance (Stillman et al. 1983). For the medical or nursing student, the ability to obtain a complete and accurate medical history is essential to a clinical diagnosis. Additionally, however, genuineness and nonpossessive warmth, in addition to empathy, are especially important when dealing with patients (Streit-Forest 1982). If longer-term studies confirm this relationship, the development of a capacity for empathy and other personality traits among medical students may be more actively attempted.

Techniques currently used to develop the interpersonal communication skills of medical students include role playing, simulations of interviewing techniques, and videotaping actual cases of patient-staff interactions (Dickinson,

Huels, and Murphy 1983). Developing interpersonal communication skills among nursing students may include a program to promote positive attitudes among the caregivers of the elderly. Techniques in such a program include game playing, trigger films, guided fantasies, and the use of analogy, with the intent to recognize self-feelings, become aware of misconceptions, and develop positive attitudes toward working with the elderly—and ultimately to improve patient care.

In a field quite different from medicine, educators in library science have special approaches to teach students to deal with disabled persons. The critical factor is educating librarians to promote positive attitudes so that disabled persons come alive as individuals of ability (Lucas 1983). Several courses stress library services to people who are blind and physically handicapped, mentally retarded, learning disabled, or emotionally disabled. Learning approaches include simulations of disabilities, volunteer projects with disabled or institutionalized people, and site visits to libraries in institutions.

Pharmacy also pays considerable attention to interpersonal skills, possibly because pharmacists increasingly are involved in patient and physician contact. The 1975 report of the Millis Commission, in its sweeping analysis of the state of pharmacy and pharmacy education, cites the need for pharmacists to become health educators (Lezberg and Fedo 1980). The pharmacist's role is expanding, moving toward a more service-oriented, clinical role; dispensing drugs must incorporate communicating information about the drugs to patients. Patients often do not comply with instructions, and pharmacists therefore need to become more assertive and better able to communicate the importance of their message. A systematic program of classroom instruction to reduce apprehension about communication in pharmacy students is one example of an attempt to improve interpersonal relations (Berger and McCroskey 1982). Role playing and assertiveness training have been successfully implemented as techniques to improve the communication skills of pharmacy students (Kimberlin 1982).

Studies of dental students reveal their need for instruction in diverse interpersonal areas, including communication with staff, coping with patients' fears, humane collection procedures, and reconciling patients' needs (Godwin et al. 1981). Various techniques have been successful, including one-to-one feedback with dental students and their patients and videotaped simulations of interactions between dentists and patients. Analysis of actual situations can provide students with insight into both the patient and the provider that appears unattainable by other techniques.

Educators and social workers are concerned with changing and expanding roles in society. Teaching interpersonal skills to undergraduates in social work can be viewed as one effort within a larger thrust to identify and teach technical skills (Toseland and Spielberg 1982). Without specific training in these helping skills, students remain at low levels of helpfulness.

Architecture, business, and engineering frequently translate interpersonal communication into the ability to work with a team, but these professions are also concerned with writing skills. Engineers are said to spend almost one-third of their time in some kind of writing, and the ability to write effective letters, reports, memoranda, and proposals is very important. Keeping journals is one way of incorporating writing in an engineering course (Selfe and Arbabi 1983); such journals give engineering students an opportunity to practice the communication skills that the field demands.

In accounting, faculty are concerned that students know how to conduct one-to-one sessions, how to make presentations to large and small groups, how to prepare presentations for conferences, and how to write memos and summaries for executives. Benefits of this type of training include the recognition of interpersonal interactions that occur in group activities (Coe 1983). Because the inability to communicate is often cited as the greatest deficiency in junior staff accountants, assertiveness training for accountants is a technique that can improve interpersonal skills. Programs have been developed that integrate the teaching of effective writing skills with regular accounting courses (May and Arevalo 1983). Assignments resemble on-the-job technical writing tasks a professional accountant might encounter. In addition, role playing and internships with accounting firms offer students experience in interpersonal communications. The Federation of Schools of Accountancy's first lyceum focused on the development of interpersonal skills in a simulated professional setting. The program was designed to help bridge the transition from the classroom to the practice of accounting (Williams 1983).

The characteristic that is believed to make law a profession, rather than a science or a technique, is its dealing with people's problems rather than objects or objective phenomena (Hunsaker 1980). Thus, law school curricula involve communication skills as well as cognitive skills and other types of competence. Interpersonal communication skills offered in some law curricula include interviewing, counseling, negotiation, mediation, legal decision making, and group processes.

Integrative Competence

Integrative competence is the ability to meld conceptual, contextual, technical, and interpersonal competence so as to make informed judgments about appropriate professional strategies to be employed in practice. Integrative competence has also been defined as "professional judgment" (Anderson 1974), but among professional educators, the use of the word "integration" relates more closely to the process by which this competence is acquired. Exhibiting integrative competence implies that a cognitive process has occurred, employing capabilities such as reasoning, decision making, and problem solving acquired through prior knowledge and experience. Such a process involves not only decisions about which strategy should be employed but also decisions concerning issues of magnitude like "how much" and "in what sequence." Although little is known about this process when specifically focused on problems of professional practice, it may be assumed similar to other applications of problem solving. In general, educators and psychologists are concerned with developing a better understanding of such cognitive processes and how they can be developed.

A hallmark of university-level professional preparation programs, one that distinguishes them from occupational programs in general, is the conscious attempt to integrate theory and practice. This challenge also differentiates college or university professional study from the basic disciplines concerned primarily with theoretical knowledge. Although the distinction may grow fuzzy at advanced levels in some fields (chemistry, for example), the professional fields are clearly unique among departments in a university in their responsibility to provide real or simulated opportunities for integration to undergraduate or beginning professional students. Despite extensive experience in arranging such opportunities, in the judgment of some, "those looking to professional education as a model for integrating careerism and vocational training with the more traditional modes of undergraduate and graduate education will also find it wanting" (Nyre and Reilly 1979, p. 38).

One problem is that work experience is an important element in the perfection of integrative competence. Although their mastery may remain incomplete, students can be directly taught the necessary conceptual knowledge and technical skills through standard academic procedures. But factors such as judgment and problem-solving skill are more difficult to nurture within the time constraints of entry-level professional preparation programs. Professional educators expect new graduates to have begun to develop integrative competence, but they typically would not judge them to have fully achieved this expertise, which may continue to develop with professional maturity to the point of mastery (Jarvis 1983).

After a career has begun, however, integrative competence may be a crucial factor in distinguishing the merely competent professional from the acknowledged expert. A recent study of practitioners in the fields of engineering, architecture, management, psychotherapy, and town planning, for example, found that a kind of "reflection-in-action" characterized outstanding professional practice (Schon 1983). Others who have examined physicians' behavior in medical problem solving report that considerable variability exists in the range of clinical reasoning and inquiry, qualities that are associated with integrative competence (Elstein, Shulman, and Sprafka 1978).

Given the importance of integrative competence, its acquisition by students should be a significant and carefully defined outcome of professional preparation programs. Yet, viewed as a competence, it presents dilemmas for program developers. More typically, integration is seen as a "process" rather than an outcome, fostered by providing students with opportunities for application in a clinical or field setting intended to represent the real world of practice. Such opportunities provide a connection between the world of professional preparation and the world of the professional practitioner that changes the student in usually undocumented ways.

As field or clinical experiences provide opportunities for integrative competence to develop, they also serve the function of socialization by providing mediated entry into the world of work (Lortie 1975). During such experiences, students may recognize dichotomies that had not previously come to their attention. To illustrate, students may notice that faculty sometimes do not integrate their own roles but separate their interests along dimensions of theory or practice. As integrative competence is fostered under the guidance of clinical faculty, students confront issues of the relevance and utility of conceptual knowledge as well as uncertainties faced by practitioners. Introducing such experiences into the curriculum means that students must be provided with appropriate supervision to help them deal with these new and often perplexing observations. Unquestionably, unusual academic burdens are sometimes placed upon clinical or field experiences and on students' abilities to cope.

In terms of the percentage of journal articles devoted to integrative competence, education and engineering publish such articles relatively more frequently than other disciplines, while architecture and social work are relatively less likely to publish articles on this outcome (see table 9). In this survey, faculty members in nursing and social work believe integrative competence should be very highly emphasized. Faculty in journalism, business, and law are least likely to sponsor integrative activities, but even so over 80 percent of the faculty in these fields report some formal or informal educational activities.

Most of the literature about integrative competence focuses on matters related to mediated work entry. With the exception of law and journalism, the professional preparation programs provide clinical and field experiences within the curriculum. In fields that provide clinical work, such matters as the extent of clinical experiences, the management of activities, the appropriateness of practice settings, the roles of clinical faculty, the evaluation of students' performance, and the usefulness of real world simulation frequently are addressed. This discussion is organized around two sets of fields: professional studies

TABLE 9
INTEGRATIVE COMPETENCE

Relative Proportion of Journal Articles	Importance of Professional Outcome		Program Has Educational Activities to Achieve Outcome	
High	**High**		**High**	
Education	Nursing	76%	Architecture	98%
Engineering	Social work	74%	Social work	97%
			Nursing	97%
Low	**Low**		**Low**	
Architecture	Business	51%	Law	88%
Social work	Architecture	51%	Journalism	86%
	Law	50%	Business	82%
	Engineering	44%		

without institutionalized field experiences and those with such experiences.

Professional studies without institutionalized field experiences
The literature in law and journalism reveals continuing debate about whether field or clinical education should be formally incorporated into the curriculum (Condlin 1983; Garrison 1983). In law, such discussions about the need for clinical education reveal the theory/practice dichotomy in the purpose of legal education (Hegland 1982). Some legal educators believe that the training of practitioners is a secondary function of law schools. Law faculty, they assert, should engage in legal scholarship rather than in teaching skills (Hegland 1982; Summers 1984), and clinical instructors contribute little to legal scholarship (Leleiko 1979). Advocates of clinical legal education claim, however, that education based on traditional legal scholarship is sterile and far removed from the world of work, examining theoretical issues rather than preparing students to be effective practitioners (Condlin 1983; Leleiko 1979; Snyman 1979; Summers 1984).

Traditionally, law students were expected to find a summer clerkship for their clinical experience. Within the last 10 years, however, many law schools have incorporated clinical experiences into their curricula to the point where they are well entrenched and no longer marginal (Condlin 1983). Advocates argue that clinical experiences expose faculty and students to the daily operation of law, thus enhancing the objectives of both legal scholarship and preparation. Yet one analyst claims that clinical law builds too narrowly on teaching "how to" skills at the expense of underlying theoretical foundations of lawyering (Vernon 1983), contending that clinical legal education should be the forum where the "how" and the "why" become integrated. The debate about the contribution of clinical legal education reflects ambiguity about educational purpose. The issue is sometimes couched in terms of whether law school should be a "liberal and liberating study" or a professional, technical endeavor (Stevens 1983).

Like law, journalism faces issues arising from the theory/practice dichotomy, with some editors claiming that preparation programs are too theoretically based and lack sufficient exposure to the news environment (Fosdick 1979; Harvey 1982; Roosenraad and Wares 1983). Professional journalism educators, supported by the Accrediting Council on Education in Journalism and Mass Communication (which states that internships for credit may not account for more than 10 percent of the total hours in the major field), advance opinions that internships should be extracurricular to the substantive program (Garrison 1983). In effect, traditional journalism educators seem to rely on the development of integrative competence following employment, even though little attention is paid to such an outcome during the preparation program (Garrison 1983). A few programs require a credit-based internship for graduation where the grade may or may not be counted in computing the grade point average, and many provide noncredit experience in publishing student newspapers. The majority, however, offer or encourage internships as a student's summer or extracurricular responsibility. As in law, advocates of a required credit-based internship suggest that the experience will introduce a healthy reality into preparation programs and that students and professional educators will benefit (Fosdick 1979; Garrison 1983).

In recognition of wide debate concerning internships, the Accrediting Council on Education in Journalism and Mass Communication established an interim committee to produce guidelines and recommendations, yet the debate continues. At the heart of the matter may be the fundamental issue of the professional credibility of journalism education. Some educators, as well as some practitioners, do not view journalism as a professional study, claiming that its skills are best acquired through on-the-job training following a liberal education. Such attitudes may foster reluctance on the part of professional journalism educators to recognize the possible value of field experience in the student's overall academic program. Perhaps this debate illustrates the problems of lifting crafts from apprenticeship status and embedding them in the college or university setting. The issue becomes that of professional identity: What are journalists? What are lawyers? What is their role in society? What education allows them to best fill the role? Should the nature of education be determined by practitioners?

Should the nature of education be determined by practitioners?

Professional studies with institutionalized field experience
Although law and journalism debate the role of clinical and field experiences in the professional program, professional educators in other areas seem to have resolved that issue and have incorporated such activities into the curriculum. In architecture, dentistry, education, engineering, library science, medicine, nursing, pharmacy, and social work, some kind of mediated work entry forms an important element of professional preparation.

In addition to the dimensions of time and experience that must be considered in program development and implementation is the factor that responsibility for instruction sometimes is shifted from the professional faculty to practitioners who act as clinical or field instructors. Confounding relationships between the two groups are perceived discrepancies in authority, remuneration, status, and attitudes toward preparation and practice. The literature about practice settings and integrative competence addresses a number of these factors in all of the fields.

In some health-related professions, such as dentistry, medicine, and nursing, internships and clinical experiences have a long tradition and are widely accepted as a vital curricular element (Keen and Dear 1983; Schofield 1984). The literature in these areas is characterized by concern about the evaluation of clinical performance competencies

(Anderson and Botticelli 1981; AAMC 1984; Davidge, Davis, and Hall 1980; Lee 1979; Wigton 1980), the impact of the experience on personal and professional attitudes (Burgess 1980; Cassidy, Swee, and Stuart 1983; Cotanch 1981; Dear and Keen 1982; Herman, Veloski, and Hojat 1983; Kahn et al. 1981; Olson, Gresley, and Heater 1984; Suess, Schweitzer, and Williams 1982), and how clinical experiences can foster clinical judgment (Bucher and Stelling 1977; del Bueno 1983; Elstein, Shulman, and Sprafka 1978; McKenzie 1980; Mazzuca, Cohen, and Clark 1981; Suess, Schweitzer, and Williams 1982).

Although pharmacy is considered part of the health care service continuum, pharmacy educators are discussing a somewhat different set of issues about integrative competence. In part, this difference seems to grow out of uncertainty about the role of the pharmacist. As late as the 1960s, pharmacists were prepared as technologists with a focus upon preparing and dispensing drugs. This role, however, served a less important purpose as drug manufacturers began to prepare materials in various dosage forms (Vogt, Montagne, and Smith 1981). Consequently, pharmacy educators introduced the concept of clinical pharmacy education, which placed less emphasis on quantitative and physical skills and more emphasis on the medical aspects of pharmacy.

Current programs are designed to permit pharmacists to make clinical judgments about patients' treatment; thus, students take clerkships in surgery and other medical specialties. These courses, supporting a medical orientation, were incorporated into the curriculum at the expense of earlier foundations courses. Consequently, the current scene reflects attempts to resolve the theory/practice dichotomy, with many suggestions about how to achieve rapport between basic and clinical faculty (Russo et al. 1983; Smith and Swintosky 1983).

A common characteristic of the education of teachers and social workers is a strong component of field experience. In many teacher education programs, at least half of the professional coursework may occur in classroom observation or in practice teaching. Similarly, master of social work programs strongly emphasize practicums as important educational vehicles designed to provide mediated entry into the work world. Recognizing their importance, the literature in education and social work suggests that guidelines for students' expected performance need to be more clearly specified and integrative field experiences more effectively linked to other aspects of the preparation program (Alvermann 1981; Dwyer and Urbanowski 1981; Hodges 1982; Judah 1979; Kettner 1979; Larsen and Hepworth 1982; Simpher, deVoss, and Nott 1980).

In both education and social work, relationships among university or college faculty, professional practitioners, and clinical faculty represent areas of concern and uncertain expectancies (Applegate and Lasley 1982; Conte and Levy 1980; Frumkin 1980; Goodman 1983; Kilgore 1979; Kolevzon and Biggerstaff 1983). As in other professional preparation programs involving real-world experiences, for example, the attitudes of the clinical or field faculty about education and technique may differ widely from those held by the professional faculty. Views are diverse about whether such discrepancies weaken or strengthen the program (Alvermann 1981; Applegate and Lasley 1982; Conte and Levy 1980; Judah 1979; Kilgore 1979; Shur 1979; Zeichner and Tabachnick 1981).

Many teacher educators (and practitioners) argue that the amount of time given to practice teaching is far too short in relation to expectancies associated with the experience and suggest increased amounts, including full-year internships (Kunkel and Dearmin 1981). The timing of such activities is also at issue, with suggestions that field contacts made early in the program are likely to enhance the value of the conceptual coursework (Denton 1982).

Engineering and architecture are both applied fields with a focus on creation and problem solving in the natural environment. Although some engineering skills can be applied in class settings using a variety of simulation devices (Nadler and Seireg 1982), many engineering educators advocate the use of cooperative internships with employers as a means of enhancing students' professional development (Houze and Simon 1981; Pierce and Birmingham 1981).

In a number of fields, modern technology may help to bridge the gap between theory and practice in a way that presents a compromise for proponents and adversaries of field experiences. Educators have proposed the use of games to simulate reality for students of architecture (Bender 1979; Bonta 1979; Sanoff 1979) and the use of videotapes as a resource to supplement and extend clinical experiences (del Bueno 1983; Liu et al. 1980; Schoonover et al. 1983). Perhaps outcomes of integrative activities can be more easily defined and ensured by working within particular domains where students can find opportunities to gradually understand practice settings. For example, one could imagine progressive experience in three domains: laboratory or class versions of the real world, simulations of the real world through technology, and practice in real-world settings. The 1970s saw universities accede to students' demands for more integrative experiences to increase relevance and a real-world sense of becoming a professional (Nyre and Reilly 1979). Perhaps the 1990s will combine advances in technology with new understandings from cognitive psychology to produce new ways to structure such activities and to ensure the development of professional problem-solving skills.

Adaptive Competence

Adaptive competence is the graduate's ability to adjust to new conditions inherent in a rapidly changing technological society. Because professional practice is dynamic rather than static, adaptive competence implies a futuristic problem-solving orientation so that graduates can anticipate and prepare for changes that might affect their work. More specifically, adaptive competence is the propensity to modify, alter, or change elements of professional practice or professional community; it is a capacity advocated as a mechanism to ensure relevant and controlled professional change (Hughes et al. 1973). It may be viewed as an extension of integrative competence.

Adaptive competence is a three-part process: (1) sensing and detecting changing conditions in the internal or external environment that affect practice; (2) acknowledging the need to alter or adapt some mode of functioning; and (3) taking steps to initiate or accommodate the changes required, such as learning new skills (technical), embracing new knowledge (conceptual), or, perhaps, refocusing practice to meet new market demands (contextual). Thus, adaptive competence allows one to initiate or implement changes either as an individual practitioner or in the professional community (Colson 1980).

Discussion of adaptive competence in professional preparation incorporates two major themes: (1) those changes affecting society that are likely to change the qualities and skills needed in the profession; and (2) new modes of teaching that use technology and thus are transmitted to students as new professionals.

Societal changes affecting professional practice
Technological advance clearly has exerted intensive pressure on professional preparation. The strong influence of technology on professional preparation, either directly in the classroom or indirectly through such ramifications as increased costs, is evident in the literature of each professional program. As changes occur in the workplace, educational curricula and faculty attempt to keep pace with the advances; in fact, journalism students must be prepared for new technology even before its development (Adler and VandenBergh 1984). Many authors lament the slow progression and adoption of technological innovation in the preparation programs (C. Anderson 1983; Roepke 1982; Romney 1983; Ronald 1979; Schroeder, Cantor, and Kurth 1981; Speedie 1980; Wallert 1982), and the Association of American Medical Colleges has recommended that its members establish an organizational unit with specific concern for expanding technology (AAMC 1984).

In the area of societal and professional changes, one focus is on use of technology for the practice of the future (Loe 1981), another on new specialty areas and new systems for delivering services. Medicine is concerned with the need for improved information management that assists physicians in scientific analysis of clinical issues (Barondess 1981). Library science educators question who their service recipients are and should be and how technology will define this issue (Association of American Library Schools 1981). Pharmacists embrace changes in technology and service delivery to expand their practice into such areas as pharmacy psychology, behavioral pharmacy, and public health pharmacy (Bush and Johnson 1979; Dolinsky 1979; Johnson and Wertheimer 1979). Social work educators discuss the preparation program with respect to the changing nature of public agency practice (Gibelman 1983).

Indeed, adaptive competence requires that educators in the professions consider the ways in which students are taught to cope with sweeping technological and societal changes and the resulting complexity. Many authors believe it can be accomplished by facilitating more versatile skills of scientific inquiry.

New modes of teaching

Some professional educators stress the importance of teaching real-world "solution finding"—how to ask the right questions, gather the pertinent information, and promulgate life-long learning (Nadler and Seireg 1982). Others believe that liberal education is required to produce a versatile graduate able to deal with diversity and change (Hodges and Lichter 1980). Indeed, one can speculate that an emphasis on adaptive competence might be a key to bridging the traditional gap between liberal studies and specialized professional education. In architecture, for example, the teaching of history can help students better understand their professional heritage and envision potential future scenarios (Creese 1980; Hubbard 1980). Dental students can be taught criteria for examining the reliability of information and developing a healthy skepticism for dogma and unfounded fad (Loe 1981). In education, writers espouse the need for "generative teachers who can take any environment under any circumstances, with any budget, and work with any child," using internalized theories, a philosophical basis, innovation, and self-assessment (Jordan 1979, p. 14). Nursing educators, for example, fault professional education that consists of a body of content evoking responses to a narrow range of clinical cues (Cantor, Schroeder, and Kurth 1981). In essence, students and graduates must be able to think about familiar problems in unfamiliar ways (Rango 1981).

Adaptive competence is also manifested in narratives in nursing, pharmacy, architecture, dentistry, and social work that describe and advocate improved communication and collaboration among professional fields (Collier 1981; Curiel et al. 1979; Goyan 1981; Scott et al. 1983; Turnbull 1982). Contrary to previous competitive modes, professionals appear to be exploring interdisciplinary collaboration as a means to address multifaceted, complex problems. In one team model, for example, multiple disciplines work together in educational and practice settings to solve particular dilemmas (May 1979). And, in an increasingly small world, preparation for international involvement is assuming new importance in the curriculum as students in various fields study languages, international relations, and government (Knepler 1982; Wakeland 1982).

The professions appear to be confronting substantial social changes and to be tugged by multiple forces, including changing knowledge and values, external demands of society, and more aware, educated consumers (Bennett 1984; Gessner, Katz, and Schimpfhauser 1981; Loe 1981; Meskin 1980; Porter 1979). In dealing with the complexities and dilemmas of practice, educators increasingly recognize the need to help graduates develop more flexibility and problem-solving capabilities. Thus, a frequently raised issue is how professional preparation programs will provide the education required for complex, multidimensional tasks (Goodman 1981).

Although a large amount of literature on change processes appears relevant to the practicing professional, fewer articles in the educational journals directly discuss how to incorporate a sense of the need for future change as part of students' professional preparation. Nursing, library science, engineering, and business address this issue most frequently, law, dentistry, and journalism least frequently (see table 10). Interestingly, engineering and business faculty see this competence as relatively unimportant for new professionals and cite few educational activities directed at its attainment.

The area of adaptive competence appears to be a fruitful one for future consideration and study in professional education. Although a substantial need is apparent to develop this competency, few authors have addressed its multiple components or the educational practices designed to facilitate its development for students. Much of the literature that represents adaptive competence focuses on specific elements such as the use of computers or interdisciplinary collaboration. While descriptions of particular teaching methods and some visionary rhetoric are evident, empirical studies examining any outcome akin to adaptive competence are lacking.

Summary
Although authors devote most attention to competences that are field-specific, such as conceptual knowledge and

TABLE 10
ADAPTIVE COMPETENCE

Relative Proportion of Journal Articles	Importance of Professional Outcome		Program Has Educational Activities to Achieve Outcome	
High	**High**		**High**	
Nursing	Library science	57%	Nursing	72%
Library science	Nursing	52%	Architecture	60%
Engineering			Social work	58%
Business			Library science	58%
Low	**Low**		**Low**	
Dentistry	Engineering	37%	Business	34%
Law	Business	37%	Pharmacy	30%
Journalism	Architecture	33%	Engineering	29%
	Law	27%		

technical skills, all professional fields are concerned with educating students about the context within which their profession is practiced and with the development of various interpersonal communication skills. All fields examined in this survey are actively debating the nature and function of experiences that assist students to integrate theory, practice, context, and interpersonal communication skills. Much less discussion focuses on the necessity to adapt professional practice as society changes.

PROFESSIONAL ATTITUDES

The six facets of professional competence described in the previous section are based on reasonably distinct spheres of behavior and knowledge that influence professional practice. Although some overlap occurs among professional competences, the notions professional educators have about them are reasonably clear. Explicit curricular experiences are designed to teach most of the professional competences, and in some areas procedures exist to test whether graduates have achieved them.

The professional outcomes discussed in this section are more elusive dimensions that are often considered to be part of "becoming professional." Academic programs may or may not consciously articulate these attitudinal objectives, and, frequently, no specific curricular experiences are designed to achieve them. Rather, the development of professional attitudes is part of a relatively informal socialization process that may begin when the student decides to pursue preprofessional or professional education and continues through at least an early stage of his or her career.

On the average, professional attitudes are less frequently discussed in professional journal literature than are professional competences. Overall, slightly more than 10 percent of the articles reviewed for this monograph were devoted to professional attitudes. Although professional educators in the socially oriented and helping fields view these attitudes as quite important for graduates to possess, they are rated as much less important by the enterprising fields, such as engineering, business, architecture, and law. In general, these attitudes—career marketability, professional identity, professional ethics, scholarly concern for improvement of the profession, and motivation for continued learning—receive less emphasis in all professional preparation fields than the more widely recognized and more readily measurable professional competences.

The development of professional attitudes is part of a relatively informal socialization process. . . .

Career Marketability

Career marketability is defined here as a broad attitudinal outcome, to distinguish it from job market forces that influence professional preparation. The concept suggests that graduates not only can meet professional entry standards but also are competitive candidates for professional practice and have an education that makes them reflective about the future course of their own careers. This outcome is, of course, related to job market factors, but it implies additionally a graduate's ability to realistically assess the market, consciously develop knowledge and skills that are most essential to a professional future, present his or her credentials effectively, and plan ahead so that, as the market changes, opportunities will be enhanced rather than restricted. Because this responsibility is placed upon students rather than left to the winds of economic and social change, career marketability is classified as an attitude to be nurtured rather than as a competence. For the professional preparation program, nurturing such an attitudinal outcome requires conscious assessment of and responsiveness to the dynamics of the professional job market as well as substantial program guidance for students. In rapidly changing professional fields, the concept of career marketability may overlap with that of adaptive competence.

Faculty were queried regarding the emphasis that should be placed on achieving qualifications that exceed basic entry-level requirements to make graduates competitive applicants for positions. Faculty in most professional preparation programs think of career outcomes in fairly concrete terms—for example, how many graduates pass the bar examination, how many obtain positions with prestigious firms or agencies. Similarly, few articles in the literature could be classified as discussions of "career marketability" as defined here rather than as articles focused on job supply and demand or obtaining an initial position. Perhaps the concept of marketability must be rephrased to encompass more clearly its dimensions for guidance.

One might expect the greatest concern with career guidance to be found in professional fields where the level of supply and demand is becoming problematic. A search of the literature does not confirm this expectation, however. The highest proportion of journal articles regarding career marketability are in library science, medicine, and business. In this survey, nursing, social work, and journalism reported the highest ideal emphasis on this outcome, while faculty in education, nursing, and architecture most frequently reported particular educational activities designed to assist students in "being marketable" (see table 11).

Some professional fields devote attention in journals to the long-term career implications of changing qualifications needed by their graduates. Professional educators in

TABLE 11
CAREER MARKETABILITY

Relative Proportion of Journal Articles	Importance of Professional Outcome		Program Has Educational Activities to Achieve Outcome	
High	**High**		**High**	
Library science	Nursing	59%	Education	89%
Medicine	Social work	58%	Nursing	85%
Business	Journalism	56%	Architecture	82%
Low	**Low**		**Low**	
Too few articles	Engineering	31%	Law	53%
to distinguish	Architecture	26%	Business	44%
	Law	25%	Journalism	41%

library science, for example, appear to be acutely aware of the importance of socialization in producing librarians who are better equipped to face their constantly evolving work environment. Electronic technology is seen as the single most important influence on the library science curriculum as library education makes the transition to library and information science education. Thus, library science educators are concerned that librarians of the 1980s are skilled in computer use as well as in cataloging and classification (Downing 1981). Because many library science graduates are not working in libraries but in business and industry (Gleaves 1982), library educators are discussing whether joint or separate graduate programs provide better career potential for graduates (Marchant and Wilson 1983).

The need for graduates of teacher education programs to be able to function in an expanding array of settings is particularly obvious. The literature reflects the recent period (1979 to 1984) when as many as one-third to one-half of new education graduates accepted positions (sometimes education-related) outside traditional school settings. Under such circumstances, a change of emphasis in teacher education programs can provide graduates with more choice upon graduation as well as open up new fields of inquiry (Brandt and Covert 1980).

New fields of emphasis also appear to be important in accounting education—but for different reasons. New rules and regulations in accounting are so numerous that accounting educators can barely keep pace (W. Anderson 1983). Teaching techniques stemming from such changes include preparing students directly for professional examinations, using more fully professors' prior professional experiences, teaching communication skills, incorporating computers in the classroom, and considering the problem of job supply and demand. New curricula focus on the student's career requirements, forcing faculty to examine the probable careers students will pursue and to design courses in the skills needed for those careers (Wilson 1982). For example, programs in personal financial planning are being implemented because job possibilities have increased dramatically in that field (Higgins 1983). Accounting educators are initiating job counseling for students, requiring that professors understand how to assess the market. Based on experiences of graduates and surveys of prominent employers, students are assisted in improving their presentation of themselves in seeking a job.

Based on belief that survival depends on the kinds of skills graduates have acquired, articles in engineering journals focus on the career survival of students after employment. Engineering is concerned with the need for the United States to have competent engineers to compete internationally. To help maintain and enhance the competitiveness of U.S. industries, engineering educators believe they need to continue to examine and evaluate the trade-offs and compromises in the curriculum between the new technology (software engineering, for example) and the traditional skills on which industrial competitiveness still strongly depends (manufacturing processes and design, for example) (Alic, Caldwell, and Miller 1982). Engineers need more research skills and training in the real world before entering the job market (Alic, Caldwell, and Miller 1982), and preparing engineering students for consulting is becoming more common so that graduates can take advantage of opportunities in this growing field, particularly in environmental systems and engineering technology (Manzo 1979).

Several professional fields are considering career guidance earlier in a student's educational program. For example, pharmacy educators recommend early identification of interests so that students are exposed to relevant research and graduate opportunities (Brink 1982). Although dental educators do not devote, proportionately, a great deal of attention to career marketability in journal articles, several authors express concern about dentistry's image in the marketplace, particularly with respect to the quality of student applicants for admission (Smith 1981), and some recommend career counseling for dental students. Most dental students are so busy meeting the demands of schooling that they have little time to explore the diverse opportunities in the field or to plan their future. Dental schools have placed minimal attention on acquainting students with the large number and variety of activities that could enrich their professional lives and allow a much needed change of pace from the daily routine of private practice. Career counseling as part of the curriculum could help alleviate this problem (Zucker, Selby, and Garbee 1980).

Social work educators seem to be developing strong student advising systems, including realistic appraisals of the job market and techniques that students can use to assist in continued career development once they are practitioners (Faver, Fox, and Shannon 1983). Social work educators are particularly concerned with sex equity in their field and emphasize new research and field placement opportunities to help broaden available career options for women.

Professional Identity
Professional identity involves the degree to which graduates integrate the profession's norms, competences, and values into a conception of role. The socialization process by which professionals come to acquire a sense of professional identity is well documented in the sociological literature. The emerging professional begins to test and accept the traditions and obligations that bind the professional community (Bucher and Stelling 1977). Eventually, a sense of professional self emerges that other members of the profession share. The process is socialization and the outcome is professional identity.

Professional identity may not be independent of other outcomes but may in fact be positively correlated with a sense of mastery of knowledge and skills in the profession (Green 1981). After a seven-year longitudinal study of dental students from predental courses through the first year of practice, researchers concluded that the outcomes of professional socialization consist of knowledge, theories and principles, technique (skills), ethics, professional culture, and career plans (Sherlock and Morris 1967). A study of residents in psychiatry and internal medicine and students in biochemistry also described the outcomes of professional identity, professional commitment, and career plans as including attitude, knowledge, and skills (Bucher and Stelling 1977). In such a view, professional identity includes all aspects of what is more broadly defined as professional competence.

Although theorists have described the abstract outcomes of professional socialization, the professional literature does not clearly describe the specific outcome expectations for students. Rhetorical articles debate the need for a better developed sense of self and values through more humanistic education (Hunsaker 1980; Weinstein 1982) versus the need for "social-technical competence" to accompany interpersonal competence (Rodenberger 1981). Rather than addressing specific outcomes for professional identity, much of the literature focuses on the process of socialization.

The term "professional identity" is also used two ways in the literature. It may refer not only to the professional identity of individual graduates but also to the identity of the profession itself. This dual use occurs particularly in professional fields where practitioners strive to achieve status, recognition, or improved compensation. Although the two affect each other, an individual practitioner need not be an active crusader for professional status to have internalized professional identity as defined here.

As shown in table 12, the highest relative proportion of articles focusing on professional identity occurs in law, nursing, and pharmacy, the lowest proportions in library science, dentistry, and journalism. In this survey, the contrast among professional fields is quite sharp. The helping and informing professions, particularly nursing, social work, and pharmacy, place strong emphasis on professional identity as an outcome of professional preparation, while the enterprising professions generally consider it of much less importance. Nonetheless, even in business, which rated the importance of professional identity quite low, 65 percent of the faculty sampled cite some type of educational activity intended to address this competence.

TABLE 12
PROFESSIONAL IDENTITY

Relative Proportion of Journal Articles	Importance of Professional Outcome		Program Has Educational Activities to Achieve Outcome	
High	**High**		**High**	
Law	Nursing	65%	Journalism	91%
Nursing	Social work	64%	Social work	91%
Pharmacy	Pharmacy	56%	Nursing	89%
Low	**Low**		**Low**	
Library science	Business	16%	Pharmacy	71%
Dentistry	Engineering	14%	Law	71%
Journalism	Architecture	10%	Business	65%

The reason why some fields so strongly espouse the importance of developing professional identity and others consider it so much less important merits investigation. One theoretically attractive explanation is that strong professional emphasis should accompany consensus on professional knowledge and skills. The fields generally considered to have least consensus, however, are precisely the ones that appear to see professional identity as a very important attitude to be nurtured among graduates. As has been discussed with regard to conceptual competence, many professional fields with a shorter history, such as education, dentistry, journalism, nursing, and social work, appear to lack structured paradigms and consensus as to the appropriate knowledge and skills required for practice (Frumkin 1979; Guidry 1979; Kilgore 1980; Lindley 1984; Matejski 1979; Mulvihill 1980; Roy 1979). A more reasonable explanation seems to be that professional identity is closely related to the type of client provided service.

In addition, expanding specializations within professional preparation programs seem to weaken professional socialization processes. Specialty group development implies socialization into smaller subgroups within the general profession and may oppose the maintenance of a holistic and internally consistent view of professional norms and practice. As mentioned earlier, many of the professions are discussing the need for expanded practice roles to cope with increased social complexities. Pharmacy, for example, is examining future practice in public health (Bush and Johnson 1979), behavior pharmacy (Johnson and Wertheimer 1979), and patient education (Fedder and Beardsley 1979). Other professions, such as dentistry and social work, are addressing whether graduates should be prepared as generalists, able to provide an array of services, or as specialists, able to provide in-depth services in a specific area of the field (Meskin 1980; Mulvihill 1980; Teigiser 1983).

The interaction of a profession and society also influences professional identity. Architecture, for example, is attempting to imbed itself in the social and political experiences of the times (Littman, Mayo, and Burgess 1981). The question of the client base to be served influences the expected outcomes of the development of professional identity. Writers question library science's image in the community and wonder how its services should be directed and used (Benavides, Lynch, and Velasquez 1980; Association of American Library Schools 1981). Social workers ponder the nature of their client base and question how to integrate social work with clients' needs (Benavides, Lynch, and Velasquez 1980). As society changes, professional identity is affected as professionals confront the need to provide their services where the need exists.

Professional educators are interested in whether the personalities of entrants are congruent with the "ideal professional personality" (Cain et al. 1983). Consequently, some empirical studies have examined changes in students' attitudes and values throughout the course of study. One investigator found that few changes occurred in dental students' personality traits and values throughout the educational process (Cain et al. 1983), but studies of attitude changes among medical students suggest that they become more conservative and less concerned with patients' needs, reflecting a greater realism about their ability to help others (Leserman 1980). A comparison of physicians' attitudes toward the practice of pharmacy found physicians to be more understanding and supportive of pharmacists than pharmacy students anticipated (Voris, Anderson, and Kimberlin 1982).

Different processes are used in assisting students to acquire a sense of professional identity. Most professions emphasize the use of the practice setting as a mechanism for developing identity. In medicine, the residency is viewed as the time when professional identification is consolidated (Brent 1981). The practicum plays a parallel role in nursing (Dear and Keen 1982; Olson, Gresley, and Heater 1984). Educators in medicine, education, and nursing address the anticipatory socialization of students, that is, their ability to think about the role, imagine themselves in it, and explore their beliefs and attitudes related to it (Cotanch 1981; Harvill 1981; Lasley 1980; Pataniczek and Isaacson 1981).

Although the practice setting appears to be the major mechanism for instilling professional identity, how it occurs or what exactly is supposed to occur remains unclear. Pharmacy students have more confidence and feel better prepared as professionals following an internship than before (Nuessle and Levine 1982). Despite such findings, some advocate that the process could be improved by the better integration of attitudinal objectives with knowledge and skill objectives (Kahn et al. 1981).

In contrast with architecture, law, engineering, and business, the helping professions (nursing, social work, medicine, pharmacy) attach far more importance to professional identity (see table 12) and more frequently seem to be struggling for the better integration of attitudes and values into their practice world. Even so, the specific outcomes related to professional identity are seldom identified in the literature. Rather, it is assumed that professional identity will be developed through practice.

Closely related to the issue of professional identity is the appropriate model for preparation in the various fields. The self-examinations underway in nearly all professional fields question what models (including structure, curriculum volume, and time frame) facilitate professional competence (Anderson, Kimberlin, and Hodsall 1979; Boatsman 1983; Kunkel and Dearmin 1981; Leighninger and Leighninger 1980; Merrill 1980; Rodenberger 1981). As these broader issues are resolved, the concepts of professional identity may be clarified.

Professional Ethics

Nearly every writer on professionalism discusses the need for practitioners to internalize the code of ethics agreed

The self-examinations underway in nearly all professional fields question what models facilitate professional competence.

upon by the profession. Existence of such a code, sponsoring and supporting professional norms, is considered one of the hallmarks of professionalism. The code of ethics is believed to be isomorphic with a sense of social responsibility that enables the professional to apply moral judgments to professional behaviors and decision making (Anderson 1974).

While advances in knowledge and technology have extended or improved the quality of life for many, these same issues have raised complicated ethical questions to which professionals and clients must respond. In addition to individualized choices the professional must make in practice, the ethics of power exercised by professionals acting as social collectives is an issue (Larson 1977). Some authors suggest that, in contrast to the spirit of altruism or service commonly attributed to professional status, professionals are becoming exploiters rather than enablers in society as they expend more effort in seeking rewards rather than in expending services (Reeck 1982). As a consequence of these trends and complexities, interest in ethical and moral issues has been revived in professional fields. Concurrently, the teaching of ethics and values in professional study programs is assumed to deserve a central place in curricular discussions in all fields (Callahan 1977).

In spite of the discussions about the need for such content (Engelhardt and Callahan 1980) and the apparent high value placed on professional ethics by educators in several fields (see table 13), some studies suggest that most professional schools offer little systematic coursework or content in ethics. In this survey of professional educators, a very high percentage of faculty in certain fields report activities to teach professional ethics, while other fields report few activities. Other data from the survey provide some clues. When asked to judge for their own field the truth of the statement, "The professional field has reached consensus on standards of ethical conduct," 48 percent of professional educators believe (to varying degrees) that consensus exists, 42 percent that it does not. Belief that consensus exists is strongest among professional faculty in social work (74 percent) and nursing (67 percent) but weakest in business administration (27 percent), law (31 percent), and journalism (33 percent). These results are congruent with

TABLE 13
PROFESSIONAL ETHICS

Relative Proportion of Journal Articles	Importance of Professional Outcome		Program Has Educational Activities to Achieve Outcome	
High	**High**		**High**	
No data	Social work	77%	Law	91%
	Nursing	77%	Nursing	89%
	Journalism	67%	Social work	85%
Low	**Low**		**Low**	
No data	Business	44%	Engineering	49%
	Architecture	40%	Pharmacy	48%
	Engineering	38%	Business	43%

faculty views of how much attention preparation programs pay to ethics as an outcome. In business, engineering, and pharmacy, over 50 percent of faculty say their programs have no activity designed to teach professional ethics.

The limited literature in professional education journals addresses the issue of ethics from two perspectives: (1) outcomes—the need for professional practitioners to confront and act on major ethical dilemmas in their work; and (2) processes—the teaching of ethics, including moral development, methods, and content.

Ethics as an outcome
Ethical behavior as a specifically defined outcome for the professionally prepared graduate is discussed only minimally, and descriptions of ethical outcomes for graduates of professional preparation programs are often ambiguous and abstract (Howe and Jones 1984; Martin 1981). Writers in social work and law note the need for students to assume an ethical perspective in contemporary practice (Brooks 1981; Joseph and Conrad 1983). In medicine, recent recommendations focus on "ethical sensitivity" (AAMC 1984). Authors in engineering, business, and law urge moral reasoning in problem solving (Fielder 1979; Willging and Dunn 1981; Wyer 1984), and nursing, law, and engineering educators describe achievement of moral

autonomy (Martin 1981; Munhall 1982; Richards 1981). Additional discussions involve familiarizing students with legal as well as ethical issues in practice and differentiating between them (Hamner, Scoggin, and White 1981; Jankovic and Green 1981) and guidelines concerning the use of human subjects in professional research (Jenny 1980). Although one general expectation is that graduates will adhere to their professional codes of ethics, fewer than 10 percent of graduates from professional programs have any working knowledge of their professional codes (Reeck 1982).

Ethics as a process

A few authors in the various professional fields emphasize the teaching of ethics and debate the specifics of content and methodology (Andrews and Hutchinson 1981; Brooks 1981; Hunt 1982; Odom 1982; Sallady 1981). On the other hand, a number of authors question whether or not the teaching of ethics actually results in any changes in students' behavior or perceptions, asserting that the social environment and the nature of practice may have more important effects on the development of values than the professional curriculum (Loupe, Meskin, and Mast 1979) and that little connection may exist between the nature of the relationship between ethics courses and actual responsible behaviors (Martin 1981). Some educators believe that students already know the basic difference between right and wrong and that programs should therefore teach technical ethics or the critical evaluation of societal implications and consequences (Brown 1983). Serious doubt apparently exists concerning whether hypothetical dilemmas and texts really can help students deal later with real-life ethics and values (Sallady 1981).

Some professional educators report attempts to test the outcomes of particular educational programs. For example, studies in medicine and social work demonstrate that students taking discrete ethics courses show increased reflectiveness about moral and ethical issues, compared with students who have ethical content integrated in various courses (Joseph and Conrad 1983; Siegler, Rezler, and Connell 1982). Others advocate the use of values exploration (Cassidy, Swee, and Stuart 1983; Pignaturo and McShane 1979), case studies (Mitchell 1981), and discussion of the need for independent decision making (Dirsmith

1983). Although the interest and discussion of the need to instill ethical competence in the professions are apparent, little is being explicitly described, implemented, or empirically investigated in professional studies.

Scholarly Concern for Improvement
Graduates of professional programs who exhibit scholarly concern for improvement support the research necessary to improve the profession's knowledge base and can adapt practice to those new findings. Graduates who have adopted this attitude are dynamic rather than static professionals, are aware that professional practice is constantly changing, and feel a sense of obligation to facilitate that change. Such an attitude implies the ability to use basic research skills and interpret the results and implications of research for professional practice.

Among the professional educators surveyed (which did not include medical and dental educators), this attitude is given the lowest emphasis of all the competences and attitudes among all preservice professional preparation programs. Faculty members in nursing, social work, and library science see this attitude as deserving higher emphasis than do faculty members in law, business, and engineering. The highest proportion of articles dealing with scholarly concern for improvement is found in education, engineering, and dentistry (see table 14).

Although it may be considered less important than other attitudes, most professions acknowledge in some way the importance of transmitting scholarly concern to students at all levels of professional study. The literature indicates some attempt to do so through preparation for basic research. Understanding the scientific method for the purposes of critical inquiry, data collection, data analysis, and interpretation; development of inferences; and evaluation of practice issues are viewed as necessary parts of the educational process (AAMC 1984; Downs and Robertson 1983; Fleming 1980; Loe 1981; Zahorik 1984). For the most part, students are not expected to be experts in the design and implementation of rigorous research studies. Instead, it is anticipated that they will use scientific method in daily practice and demonstrate skills in critically reading research studies.

TABLE 14
SCHOLARLY CONCERN FOR IMPROVING THE PROFESSION

Relative Proportion of Journal Articles	Importance of Professional Outcome		Program Has Educational Activities to Achieve Outcome	
High	**High**		**High**	
Dentistry	Nursing	45%	Nursing	92%
Education	Social work	36%	Social work	78%
Engineering	Library science	34%	Library science	72%
Low	**Low**		**Low**	
Too few	Law	12%	Education	33%
articles	Business	12%	Business	31%
to distinguish	Engineering	12%	Journalism	29%

Educators in many professional fields are concerned that, although this professional attitude and its concomitant base of skills are necessary and vital to professionalism, its development is often little emphasized or encouraged. Climates within the professional preparation programs tend to support teaching content and practice skills rather than the integration of scholarly concern for improvement among individual students (Cramton 1982; Downs and Robertson 1983; Fisher 1981). In some respects, this finding is surprising in view of the history of professionalism that has thrust certain fields of study into the college and university setting where inquiry is highly valued.

This paradox is partially explained by the segmented approach to research and scholarly development apparent in the professional education literature. On the one hand, some educators in nursing, law, medicine, education, and social work insist that research and scholarly awareness are integral parts of professional practice and basic preparation (Corrigan 1981; Cramton 1982; Lawson and Berleman 1982; Riegelman, Povar, and Ott 1983; Rinke 1979). On the other hand, other discussion in dentistry, law, and medicine focuses on research and scholarly concern as a separate specialization and career track, even at the level of basic preparation (Bickel and Morgan 1980; Leleiko

1979; Santangelo 1981). While research study is sometimes relegated to graduate-level programs, professionals in many fields practice without pursuing additional formal study. The apparent polarity between generating and using research continues to broaden the gap between research and practice. A key issue in all the fields is how research could be integrated into courses focusing on content and technical skills. Some professional educators believe that such integration should be part of every course (Castles 1984), while others view research as the separate domain of the faculty and of little concern to preservice students (Allen 1983). Graduate professional programs believe that the foundation of scholarly concern is built in an appropriately intellectual liberal education preceding professional preparation (AAMC 1984).

Motivation for Continued Learning
Motivation for continued learning is characterized by new graduates' interest in their own professional development and commitment to enhancing and updating their knowledge and skills. Such enhancement may take place through a variety of mechanisms—attending conferences, acquiring advanced degrees, and reading professional literature, for example. Inherent in an awareness that such learning activities will be necessary as well as in a positive attitude toward them is the recognition that the profession is dynamic rather than static and that the delivery of services changes as new knowledge, skills, and technologies become available.

Professionals' commitment to their own development and to maintaining currency in practice has long been viewed as an integral component of professionalism (Houle 1980). Not only do the professions expect members to keep abreast of new developments that improve the quality of services provided; clients expect professionals to monitor and adopt new practices that promote their investment in service. Indeed, the strongest motivation for continued learning seems to be professionals' need to update practice, while motivators like approval by peers, mandated attendance, and social interaction are secondary (Houle 1980).

In spite of the extensive literature that addresses motivation for continued learning for practitioners and graduates, the inculcation of this attitude at the basic professional

TABLE 15
MOTIVATION FOR CONTINUED LEARNING

Relative Proportion of Journal Articles	Importance of Professional Outcome		Program Has Educational Activities to Achieve Outcome	
High	**High**		**High**	
Pharmacy	Nursing	67%	Nursing	68%
Law	Pharmacy	59%	Library science	64%
Medicine	Social work	56%	Pharmacy	63%
Low	**Low**		**Low**	
Too few	Architecture	37%		
articles	Law	35%	Architecture	43%
to distinguish	Business	35%	Engineering	41%
	Engineering	31%	Business	38%

preparation level is documented or discussed very little. Occasionally, the need for incorporating the idea of continued learning in the curriculum, for integrating it into a senior capstone-type course (American Dental Association 1980; C. Anderson 1983), or for singling out for special assistance those students who appear to lack inherent motivation (AAMC 1984) is referred to in general terms. Studying the emphasis on continued learning in pharmacy programs, Walker and Lowenthal (1981) discovered that, although students agree it is important, only a very small percentage have participated in any outside learning activity.

In the journal literature, pharmacy, law, and medicine show the highest proportion of articles related to motivation for continued learning (see table 15). In this survey of faculty, nursing, pharmacy, and social work educators rate the importance of this outcome most highly, while faculty in architecture, law, business, and engineering rate it lowest. Nursing, library science, and pharmacy educators most often note the existence of educational activities designed to achieve this outcome, whereas faculty in architecture, engineering, and business report fewer such activities. The contrast between these two groups in the extent of activities reported, however, is much less sharp than for some of the other attitudinal outcomes.

The apparent lack of emphasis on promoting continued professional learning at the preservice level may be partially explained by the fact that continuing education is viewed as a practitioner's issue. Formalized continued learning is mandated for some professional fields, and professional norms make it the sina qua non in other fields. In some professions (business, for example), employers are likely to bear the significant costs of continued learning of professionals, while in others (education, for example), individual practitioners meet such costs wholly or partially. Participation in informal modes of continuing education may be deemphasized because it competes or conflicts with professional school program offerings that provide crucial program income. In fact, colleges and universities place much more emphasis on obtaining advanced degrees than on pursuing other types of continued learning (Walker and Lowenthal 1981).

Herein lies the complexity of the issue of continued learning. Rather than focusing on continued learning as a professional attitude to be cultivated, continued learning has come to be defined as a mechanism for quality control. Debate about mandatory versus voluntary learning has become dominant despite research demonstrating that professionals' inner standards of achievement are more important than mandated continuing education in enhancing knowledge and skills (Crabtree and Geiger 1983; Houle 1980; Richards and Cohen 1980; Walker and Lowenthal 1981). Clearly, important differences exist between those fields that have externally imposed requirements for continued learning (education for continuing certification, medicine for a certain number of continued education hours) and those fields with no such requirements. Perhaps, too, some fields where preparation is already at the post-baccalaureate level (law and dentistry) may feel that they have more time within the initial preparation program to prepare proficient, rather than merely competent, graduates. In medicine, specific recommendations have been made to reduce the scheduled time for students and require more independent learning that may foster the habit of independent inquiry and professional development (AAMC 1984). Certainly, the process by which motivation for continued learning is transmitted to students within the professions is an area ripe for further discussion and research.

Summary

The journal literature devotes considerably less attention to the attitudinal dimensions of education than to other professional competences. Outcomes of professional socialization are believed most important in the helping and informing professions and least important in the enterprising fields, such as business, architecture, law, and engineering. As might be expected in preservice professional preparation programs, educators seem more immediately concerned with developing professional identity than with stimulating among students longer-range attitudes, such as concern for continued individual and collective professional improvement.

SUMMARY AND IMPLICATIONS

Common Themes in Professional Preparation

In all fields of professional preparation, educators are re-examining the way they prepare graduates for entry into professional practice. In several fields (architecture, journalism, law, pharmacy, dentistry, medicine, and social work), one or two primary professional journals devoted to educational issues provide a rich array of articles dealing with the outcomes expected of professionals. Such journals appear to provide a forum for faculty discussion about issues of professional education. In other fields (education, library science, nursing, and engineering), a number of journals, often based upon specialties within the general field, deal with different aspects of education. It appears that no more than 25 percent of the faculty in each field would find a common forum for discussion of educational concerns. One field, business administration, appears to have no published forum to address concerns of professional education, although faculty keep up with societal influences and technical aspects of their field by reading sources like *Business Week* and *The Wall Street Journal.*

In discussing outcomes of professional preparation, educators devote the bulk of their time to discussing the conceptual knowledge base that students should learn, the technical aspects of skill development, and the means of integrating concepts and skills through field experiences. In those fields of professional study commonly offered in a four-year undergraduate program, considerable concern is apparent about the problem of fitting all of the essential or desirable experiences into four years. Such concerns are exacerbated by the responsiveness of the professional preparation programs to a changing society. Nearly all of the fields, but especially those providing health or information services, show increased sensitivity to dealing with clients' diverse needs and to accompanying demands for skills in interpersonal communication. Communication skills needed by new professionals clearly are judged to extend well beyond basic skills of reading and writing to include skills in group relations, a capacity for teamwork, empathy, and listening skills. Professional educators are sensitive as well to the extensive changes that technology is bringing in professional practice. These three major issues—the diversification of clients, a growing conceptual knowledge base, and the impact of technology—have

Nearly all of the fields . . . show increased sensitivity to dealing with clients' diverse needs and to . . . skills in interpersonal communication.

caused each field to engage in continual self-examination of the role and nature of professional preparation. Professional preparation is struggling to keep abreast of changes that already have significantly affected the competence that graduates must exhibit. Thus, educators seem to be devoting comparatively little attention or specific activities to "adaptive competence," that is, to explicitly calling students' attention to the need to think in advance about rapid future societal changes.

This review of educational literature in the professions found little evidence to support accusations that professional educators are unconcerned about the supporting role that liberal education plays in the preparation of professionals. In fact, while struggling with the problem of how much material can fit into the curriculum to meet the current demands of society and of employers for adequately prepared beginning professional workers, professional educators are acutely conscious and concerned that students understand the context in which professional practice occurs. Such issues seem likely to receive more, rather than less, discussion in professional settings where diverse clients and technology exert heavy impacts. Concern exists as well about how the necessary contextual competence should be achieved. Except in those fields like law, where students are already assumed to have completed a liberal arts education, professional educators show widespread discontent about current methods of providing contextual learning for students. This discontent is focused both on the seeming detachment of liberal arts courses from the real-world issues that professional graduates will face and on the contextual foundations courses offered within the professional study programs themselves. The challenge appears to be integration of liberal and professional study in such a way that the student is assisted in making meaningful or relevant translations of contextual courses with potential to undergird decisions in the practice setting.

As the student attempts to integrate conceptual knowledge, technical skills, and an awareness of the societal context in which professional practice occurs, professional educators focus on field experiences as a source of both strength and weakness in their programs. In two fields, law and journalism, active debate concerns more systematic provision of integrative field experiences. In engineering and architecture (and probably in business, although the lack of journal literature causes one to speculate), possibilities for simulated practice experiences (including laboratory or studio work on practical problems) and cooperative work programs currently appear to satisfy the need for field experience. In fields like education, nursing, social work, medicine, and dentistry, where field or clinical experiences are an established part of the educational program, attention focuses more closely on the design of that experience, the assessment of its actual outcomes, and improving links between field settings and supervisors. The balance of theory and practice seems to be less an issue than how to integrate the two.

A review of the literature in professional journals gives one the sense that socialization of students is somewhat less important than teaching them conceptual or technical skills. For most professional programs, especially those in the helping and informing fields, much of the socialization process is assumed to take place during field experience. Yet discussions focusing on the various attitudinal competences that can be viewed as products of the socialization experience lack clarity. Several structures of the educational setting influence socialization: (1) the selection of students, (2) the isolation of students from outside influences, (3) the consistency of institutional or program goals, (4) the explicitness of values and role models, (5) the provisions of opportunities for practicing responses, and (6) the provision of both positive and negative sanctions as feedback to students (Bragg 1976, p. 14). Of these elements, the greatest attention seems to focus on provision of opportunities for practice. Problem areas connected with placing the major burden of professional attitude development on field experience include lack of consistency in program goals and lack of consistency in the feedback provided to students. Relationships with supervising practitioners appear to need strengthening to model appropriate behaviors for students. In this sense, debates about whether professional ethics can be taught in the classroom pale in relation to the seeming lack of consensus in some fields between and among educators and practitioners about what ethical standards should be.

Usefulness of the Professional Preparation Outcome Framework

Drawing on previous work concerned with professions and professional preparation, this work began with a framework that envisioned the outcomes of professional preparation as being comprised of six aspects of competence and five aspects of attitude. This framework served as a guide for the examination of the professional education literature. Simultaneously, the authors were interested in determining the usefulness of the framework to facilitate discussions of instructional collaboration and assumed that such collaboration might be enhanced by examining dimensions of professional preparation in more detail than the simple dichotomy of "theory and practice," which tends to ignore the integrative and socialization aspects of professional study.

By pilot testing a survey instrument, the authors found that faculty could distinguish the 11 professional preparation outcomes when expressed in the form of competence statements for graduates. This ability to see the outcome dimensions as distinct was sustained in a survey across 10 professional fields, the details of which are forthcoming. In reviewing literature, the authors were able to categorize reliably most articles as dealing primarily with one or two of the outcomes. While the outcomes may be separable for some purposes, however, the literature review clearly shows that the outcomes are integrally linked in the thinking of professional education faculty. Furthermore, most professional fields have not articulated a relationship between specific outcomes and specific educational activities. For example, one type of educational activity—the field experience, clinical experience, or internship—carries more than the burden of assisting the student to combine conceptual knowledge and technical skills. It also is assumed that during this experience the student will draw on contextual background, visualize the possible adaptations the profession may need to make to future societal changes, and develop attitudes like a professional identity, professional ethics, and motivation to continue personal and professional development. Even so, those fields without systematic provisions for internships (law and journalism, for example) express concern that inappropriate use of these activities will weaken the preparation program and steer it in the direction of trade education.

Based on a literature review alone, the framework would need to be reconstructed to recognize more fully the overlaps and links among the various outcomes of professional preparation. One could speculate, for example, that for some professional fields the attitudes called "professional identity," "professional ethics," and "motivation for continued learning" cannot exist separately from "integrative competence" because it is the integrative field experience that primarily nurtures such attitudes. Yet some educators in fields of professional study that do not incorporate a field experience as a regular part of the program would insist that their students nonetheless develop the socialized attitudes to professional practice considered appropriate. In retrospect, the attitudinal outcome termed "career marketability" may be better seen as a process, namely career guidance. Such a process is receiving increasing attention in some professional fields.

While common themes and trends have been uncovered across the professional study fields on which collaboration conceivably can be built, one can envision that overlaps of the different outcomes of professional preparation may be distinctive for different fields. It is clear that the various relationships among outcomes for different fields may depend highly upon other aspects of the environment in which professional preparation exists. Such factors as societal influences, university support and interrelationships, and internal differences in programs appear related to the amount of discussion about outcomes and the direction that discussion may take at various times. Such issues are worthy of further exploration.

Implications for Faculty, Administrators, and Researchers
The uniqueness of the conceptual knowledge base and the even greater specificity of the technical skills taught in the various professional areas make these competence areas appear to be unfertile ground for beginning most discussions of collaboration across fields. Faculty members across professional programs may not be aware, however, that changing trends in society (to which they are responding in conceptual, technical, and communication courses in their programs) reflect new educational foci also relevant to their colleagues in quite different professional fields. Some opportunities for interdisciplinary teamwork among

professional fields and with liberal arts faculty in contextual areas are readily identified. To some extent, the concept of teamwork within the health professions has encompassed such interdisciplinary efforts, but the collaborative net could be stretched much more widely. An infinite number of such opportunities exist, but this discussion is limited to three such possibilities, in addition to the obvious potential for collaboration in the area of developing technology.

The issue of paying more specific attention to diverse clients pervades all fields. To take one example only, all professional study fields—from social work to architecture and business—recognize the aging of the American population. Courses are being introduced separately into each professional study program to review the basic problems that face the elderly before dealing with specific professional problems. It is not difficult to imagine the challenge and curricular coherence of an interdisciplinary course, perhaps called "Professional Challenges of an Aging Population," with a general core of concepts drawn from the medical, behavioral, and social sciences. Such a general core could be supplemented by discussion groups to focus issues for students in various professional programs. Undoubtedly, such courses are already in developmental stages, representing an alternative to liberal arts courses considered too abstract by professional faculty.

While developing competence in interpersonal communication, one can envision a similar interdisciplinary venture among virtually all professional fields and faculty members in English or communications, where interviewing clients becomes an important professional skill. The issue of what one conveys to the client by various verbal and nonverbal gestures and by listening behaviors involves the enterprising professions that wish to retain the confidence of fee-paying clients as well as the helping and informing professions, where establishing empathy or rapport is essential to serving or treating clients.

Finally, and at a slightly different level, benefits would accrue from discussion across professional preparation fields and with social and behavioral faculty from the arts and sciences about all aspects of student socialization. Despite the differences in settings, what can be learned about the development of simulated and real practice settings, the role modeling of desirable behavior, the provision of feedback to students, and the establishment of appropriate relationships with field supervisors? Such concerns about field experiences and their role in inculcating attitudes considered desirable to advancement of the professional fields are pervasive, even in those fields where integration of theory and practice is left to students' initiative.

Administrators, of course, must develop some sense of the common threads to cultivate among professional faculty a sense of freedom to experiment with collaboration that may be educationally effective as well as cost effective. Additionally, however, for the purposes of program review and consolidation, administrators need to be aware and sympathetic to the particular struggles to improve their programs that professional faculty experience. One frequently hears speculative accusations directed at various professional educators regarding the expansion of curricular content. Engineering faculty, for example, sometimes are accused of seeking to deflect their students from contextual courses in favor of technical preparation; concerns of education faculty for a five-year program have been attributed to a quest for more credit hours (and ultimately maintenance of faculty positions) in a time of declining enrollments. Such broad-scale accusations reflect a lack of understanding of the struggles of faculty in professional preparation with the problem of curricular volume, their desire to build a sense of commitment to the professional field, and, most important, their concern for the complete and liberal education of professionals. For administrators and the public to view these struggles as a sign of weakness or self-serving behavior is erroneous. As "a profession is a sociocultural construct whose contours are constantly shifting . . ." (Geison 1983, p. 8), turbulence in professional education is in fact a sign of strength.

Administrators have a responsibility as well to listen carefully to professional educators when developing program review criteria so that they can select appropriate measures of quality. Examples of possible errors that could result from lack of discussion are particularly obvious in the area of job placement statistics. As presently conceived, journalism educators are least likely of all the professional fields to consider their programs as prepara-

Administrators . . . must develop some sense of the common threads to cultivate among professional faculty a sense of freedom to experiment with collaboration.

tion for a specific vocation. Given the emphasis of their accrediting agency on restricting rather than expanding professional courses and the fact that many employers select individuals without specific training for journalism positions, it might be quite inappropriate to judge a journalism program by its record of placing graduates in traditional communication posts. Similarly, nursing attempts, more than most other fields, to give undergraduate students a strong sense of what research can do to improve the profession, provides many opportunities for specific continuing education, and has few programs for doctoral-level degrees. It would be patently unfair to judge a nursing program on the basis of how many students immediately enter graduate school. Adjusting program review criteria to reflect the varying needs and orientation of professional fields is a time-consuming task requiring a sincere effort by administrators and faculty review committees to understand a professional field different from their own. Given its potential for relieving some current university tensions, however, it is a worthwhile effort.

As mentioned earlier, most of the articles concerning the outcomes of professional preparation are exhortative rather than empirically based, which is surprising, because professional preparation is typically in a better position to demonstrate that students achieve concrete outcomes than are general or liberal education programs. A substantial number of followup studies of graduates, exploring nearly every dimension of competence and attitudes, have been conducted in the health professions, particularly medicine and dentistry. One may assume that such active research programs are the result of federal support of evaluative activities within the context of various grants for medical education.

The evaluation studies in the health professions, which would merit treatment in a separate research report, provide a model that other professional fields have not followed. In most other fields, the studies were parochial and idiosyncratic and typically the effort of one or two interested faculty members or a doctoral student.

The literature contains little evidence that professional preparation has accepted the challenge of defining student outcomes and designing research to verify their achievement. Nor, would it seem, have college and university administrators been likely to fund research and development that would enable use of a common outcome and data collection framework across professional fields—with appropriate modifications for the special aspects of that field. Despite the fact that over 50 percent of college students generally are pursuing professional programs, most discussions of outcomes, even in large universities, seem to focus on the outcomes of the first year or two of liberal or general education presumed to be common to all students. In professional preparation, few studies encompass broad enough samples of students, graduates, or programs to begin to build models.

Professional schools may be assumed to pay more attention to outcomes because of accreditation and licensing or certification procedures. A review of the accreditation guidelines for the professional fields indicates that the outcomes discussed here are made explicit only in the field of architecture (Hagerty and Stark 1986). This finding causes one to question the common assumption that accreditors are rapidly introducing specifications or measures for outcomes.

Articulation of the desired outcomes is a necessary precursor to measurement. The framework used here for categorizing educational outcomes has helped to clarify that many assumptions about the extent to which graduates possess "desirable" outcomes are untested. The issue of whether educational processes assumed to foster the outcomes actually do so is even more ambiguous. Research is needed to assess the major work being conducted in colleges and universities, namely, the education of graduates prepared for occupations commonly thought of as professional. Several steps are necessary: (1) specification of the competences and attitudes to be developed among professional graduates, generally and specifically, for each professional field; (2) assessment of the extent to which graduates achieve the outcomes; (3) identification of links among specific educational processes and specific outcomes; and (4) better understanding of the extent to which the outcome is actually useful and important in professional practice.

APPENDIX A

METHODOLOGY FOR THE STUDY

Review of Journal Articles

Professional preparation fields to examine were chosen largely on pragmatic grounds: The objective was to view 12 fields commonly referred to as "professional programs" offered at both public and private collegiate institutions, for which relevant educational journals could be located at the researchers' university library. This pragmatic criterion eliminated such fields as theology (seldom offered at public universities) as well as agriculture and veterinary medicine (because library resources were not available). Fields such as art and music were not included because, although careers in the arts certainly may be viewed as professional, these programs are seldom referred to on campuses as being among the professional programs.

An initial list of 30 journals potentially containing articles pertinent to educational issues in the 12 fields was constructed by examining the frequency of indexing in the ERIC data base and by consulting with professional colleagues and librarians. Members of the research team examined all of the potential journals for a particular field. Next, they defended to the team the rationale for including one or two journals devoted to the educational issues included in the broader theoretical framework guiding the research (see Stark et al. 1986). Twelve journals representing 11 fields were selected for further study. For the field of business administration, the team located no currently published journal that devotes substantial space to educational issues but did review occasional articles in the *Journal of Accounting* dealing with issues broader than specific classroom procedures.

Using a decision tree coding scheme, four members of the research team coded all articles published during 1979 in the selected journals to represent their primary and secondary thrusts: professional preparation outcomes; external, internal, or "within university" influences; or specific curricular recommendations and studies. Within each of these general categories, they also coded articles for designated subcategories. Thus, for articles dealing with outcomes, the coder selected one or more of 10 professional outcomes discussed in this report. (At that time, the theoretical framework grouped professional ethics and professional identity as one category.) Based on recoding a random selection of 30 articles by other members of the team, intercoder reliability was found to be over 90 percent. The need for revision and clarification of some categories was noted and implemented.

Using the revised coding scheme, all articles in the same journals published from January 1980 through December 1984 were then coded. Because highly reliable coding was not essential to the purpose of identifying issues and trends in professional preparation, individual members of the team exclusively read and classified two or more related fields of professional preparation as closely allied as possible to their own academic backgrounds (information-providing professions, helping professions, and enterprising professions). This procedure undoubtedly sacrificed objectivity but allowed team members to become familiar with terminology unique to the particular professions, to identify trends and issues in potentially similar professional fields, and to concentrate reading from other related sources in a few fields. The number of articles coded is shown in table A-1.

A computer sorting program was used to calculate frequencies of articles' occurrence by professional field as well as the selection of subsets of coded articles. The percent of articles dealing with professional preparation outcomes and, more specifically, with professional competences and professional attitudes was calculated for each field. Despite early evidence of intercoder reliability, these percentages are not reported, lest they imply greater precision in classifying the articles than is warranted. Rather, the interquartile deviation (semi-interquartile range) of the percentages of articles focusing on each professional preparation outcome was calculated (the deviation around the median percentage). The tables in this report show those professional fields where the percent of articles devoted to an outcome was "high" (above the third quartile of percentages) or "low" (below the first quartile of percentages).

Some outcomes of professional preparation (for example, technical competence) showed substantial differences in the percentage of journal articles devoted to the discussion in different professional fields. Other cases showed little diversity, typically because discussion of the outcome was not common in the journals of any field. The interquartile deviations and percentage ranges for each outcome of professional preparation are given in table A-2.

Following discussion of the coding results, team members returned to articles they had coded to annotate each article and classify it as A (very important), B (important), C (some possible value), or W (worthless), according to how directly it addressed one of the categories and subcategories in the theoretical framework of professional preparation. Articles classified as worthless were generally detailed, methodological, or technical articles (for example, "how to prepare slides for a laboratory experiment," "how to evaluate student journals fairly"), articles that dealt with outcomes of graduate, postservice, or continuing education (excluded from the study by prior agreement), or articles reporting on professional preparation in countries other than the United States.

The principal investigator then reviewed the entire file of 2,933

TABLE A-1
ARTICLES REVIEWED BY FIELD[a]

Field	Year of Publication						Total
	1979	1980	1981	1982	1983	1984	
Architecture	18	30	24	23	9	–	104
Business administration[b]							26
Dentistry	87	85	83	54	33	24	366
Education	54	56	57	47	48	20	282
Engineering	50	47	31	36	23	6	193
Journalism	19	35	31	29	33	15	162
Law	17	15	30	27	24	9	122
Library science	27	13	14	16	16	4	90
Medicine	76	158	142	155	142	46	719
Nursing	81	91	83	76	86	46	463
Pharmacy	43	50	59	44	55	–	241
Social work	38	38	16	31	26	16	165
Total							2,933

[a]It was possible for an article to be classified as dealing with both outcomes and some other topic, for example, influences of external forces on the professional preparation field.
[b]A few pertinent articles from the *Journal of Accounting Education* were reviewed.

INTERQUARTILE DEVIATIONS AND PERCENT OF JOURNAL ARTICLES ACROSS ELEVEN FIELDS FOR EACH PROFESSIONAL PREPARATION OUTCOME

	Quartile Deviation	Range of Percent of Articles	Median Percent of Articles
Professional Competences	8.5	10–62	26
Conceptual competence	4.5	8–38	22
Technical competence	14.0	8–68	38
Contextual competence	6.5	1–50	17
Interpersonal communication competence	4.5	1–35	14
Integrative competence	8.5	1–33	17
Adaptive competence	2.0	1–20	6
Professional Attitudes	**2.0**	**0–25**	**9**
Career marketability	2.0	0–15	2
Professional identity[a]	4.0	5–35	12
Scholarly concern for improvement	2.0	0–12	5
Motivation for continued learning	3.0	0–12	4

[a]Includes professional ethics.

bibliographic entries, including annotations and codewords, and, to be inclusive rather than exclusive, restored to the outcome file those articles that might merit reexamination. In particular, restored articles focused on curricular studies and recommendations that appeared to have potential to illuminate articles dealing more explicitly with outcomes. The classification of articles at this point is given in table A-3.

Subsequently, it became clear that the space limitations of this review would not allow even cursory treatment of all 986 potentially useful, outcome-related articles. The purposes of this review seemed best served by reviewing in detail only those articles classified as A or B in terms of relevance to issues and trends. Although the review is based on those 660 articles, not all of them are cited in the discussion.

Survey Data

Data are reported representing faculty views of the ideal emphasis on various professional outcomes and the extent to which

TABLE A-3
ARTICLE CLASSIFICATION

Category	1979	1980	*Year of Publication* 1981	1982	1983	1984	Total
Outcome Related							
A	20	43	48	38	47	15	211
B	84	105	91	66	71	32	449
C	57	54	70	65	53	27	326
W	93	118	93	86	57	23	470
Nonoutcome Related	242	285	251	279	320	100	1,477
Total	496	605	553	534	548	197	2,933

their programs sponsor educational activities to achieve the outcomes. These data come from a 1985 survey of a national population of faculty in the 540 most comprehensive colleges and universities that offer programs of professional study (Carnegie classifications "research universities," "doctoral universities," and "comprehensive colleges and universities I"). Ten fields were included in the study: architecture, business administration, education, engineering, journalism, law, graduate library science, nursing, pharmacy, and social work (bachelor's and master's programs surveyed separately). Upon finishing this review, analysis of the full survey was not complete.

The sampling unit was the program, and the population included 1,814 programs whose existence was confirmed by college registrars after a mail inquiry and one followup. Although no precise data base identifies all accredited and nonaccredited programs in each field, it is estimated that this survey population included approximately 76 percent of all existing programs in the 10 fields (see table 3 in the text).

The survey sample was selected from separate sampling frames for each field with programs stratified by Carnegie classification, type of control (public or independent), and expected enrollment decline in the state where the institution is located. For fields with fewer than 125 programs in the confirmed national population, all confirmed programs were surveyed; for the more commonly offered programs, a 50 percent random sample was drawn from each stratification cell. Surveys were distributed through program administrators (deans or department chairs), who were asked to respond to the survey and to request responses from faculty who, in their judgment, were most closely involved in and knowledgeable about the preservice professional preparation program. The number of full-time faculty responses requested was proportional to the annual number of program graduates supplied by the college registrar. As student/faculty ratios varied dramatically within fields, different ratios were used for different fields to result in approximately 4.65 responses for the program of mean size in each study field.

A total of 2,230 timely faculty responses from 732 programs in 346 different colleges were obtained after two followups, representing an overall response rate of 69.8 percent of the programs from which response was requested and of 46 percent of the desired faculty sample. The program response rate varied from 56 percent for architecture to over 95 percent for library science and social work. Faculty response rates varied from 31 percent for architecture to 62 percent in nursing and library science. The respondent sample was unbiased with respect to the characteristics of the population surveyed and the stratification parameters (see table A-4).

TABLE A-4
SUMMARY OF SURVEY RESPONSES

Professional Field	Programs Responding		Faculty Responding		Mean Institutional Enrollment	Mean Number of Graduates
	N	%	N	%		
Architecture	36	56.3	90	30.8	18,490	89
Business administration	102	57.6	268	34.6	12,368	376
Education	144	81.8	441	53.9	13,019	233
Engineering	60	61.9	222	46.6	20,365	436
Journalism	66	70.2	207	48.5	20,904	123
Law	59	56.7	185	36.3	18,706	225
Library science	43	95.6	145	62.2	23,069	61
Nursing	96	85.0	356	62.5	14,857	98
Pharmacy	31	73.8	96	50.8	21,491	94
Social work–B.S.W.	69	63.9	145	38.9	15,564	38
Social work–M.S.W.	26	99.9	62	49.2	22,838	116
Total	732	69.8	2,217	46.1		

Within the more extensive survey, faculty respondents were asked to provide, on a seven-point Likert-type scale, their view of the emphasis each of the professional outcomes ideally should receive in their field. The fields with highest and lowest percentages of faculty selecting a rating of "7" on the scale are reported in tables 5 through 15 in the text. In a separate question, faculty were asked to describe briefly specific formal or informal learning experiences directed at various outcomes their program sponsored. The fields in which the highest and lowest percentages of faculty reported such experiences are reported in tables 7 through 15 in the text.

In the survey, faculty also were asked to name one or two journals a faculty member in that profession would be likely to read to be informed about the field's *educational* practice issues (teaching methods, curricular emphasis, competencies expected of new professionals, and so on). Although a tally of this question was available only after the literature review was completed, the data in table 4 show that for most fields the authors had correctly identified the most widely read journals.

A more complete report of the survey results is available from the authors.

REFERENCES

The ERIC Clearinghouse on Higher Education abstracts and indexes the current literature on higher education for the Office of Educational Research and Improvement's monthly bibliographic journal, *Resources in Education*. Most of these publications are available through the ERIC Document Reproduction Service (EDRS). For publications cited in this bibliography that are available from EDRS, ordering number and price are included. Readers who wish to order a publication should write to the ERIC Document Reproduction Service, 3900 Wheeler Avenue, Alexandria, Virginia 22304. When ordering, please specify the document number. Documents are available as noted in microfiche (MF) and paper copy (PC). Because prices are subject to change, it is advisable to check the latest issue of *Resources in Education* for current cost based on the number of pages in the publication.

Abbey, Bruce, and Dripps, Robert. 1982. "Analyzing Organizational Schemes." *Journal of Architectural Education* 35 (2): 14–16.

Abramson, Elliot M. 1979. "Law, Humanities, and the Hinterlands." *Journal of Legal Education* 30 (1–2): 27–42.

Adler, Keith, and VandenBergh, Bruce. 1984. "Advertising Graduates Need to Prepare for New Technologies." *Journalism Educator* 39 (1): 27–29.

Albrecht, Paul A. 1984. "Opportunity and Impediment in Graduate Program Innovation." In *Keeping Graduate Programs Responsive to National Needs*, edited by M. J. Pelczar and L. C. Solmon. New Directions for Higher Education No. 46. San Francisco: Jossey-Bass.

Alic, John A.; Caldwell, Martha; and Miller, R. R. 1982. "The Role of Engineering Education in Industrial Competitiveness." *Engineering Education* 72 (4): 269–73.

Allen, Francis A. 1983. "Legal Scholarship: Present Status and Future Prospects." *Journal of Legal Education* 33 (3): 403–5.

Allen, Josephine A., and Burwell, N. Yolanda. 1980. "Ageism and Racism: Two Issues in Social Work Education and Practice." *Journal of Education for Social Work* 16 (2): 71–77.

Alofsin, Anthony. Fall 1983. "Toward a History of Teaching Architectural History: An Introduction to Herbert Langford Warren." *Journal of Architectural Education* 36: 2–7.

Alvermann, Donna E. 1981. "The Possible Values of Dissonance in Student Teaching Experience." *Journal of Teacher Education* 32 (3): 24–25.

American Association for Higher Education. 1982–83. "Liberal Learning and Career Preparation." Current Issues in Higher Education No. 2. Washington, D.C.: AAHE. ED 240 948. 54 pp. MF–$0.97; PC–$7.14.

American Bar Association. 1980. *Law Schools and Professional Education: Report and Recommendations of the Special Committee for a Study of Legal Education*. Chicago: ABA. ED 200 077. 127 pp. MF–$0.97; PC–$12.96.

American Dental Association. 1980. *Report of the Special Higher Education Committee to Critique the 1976 Dental Curricular Study*. Chicago: ADA.

American Pharmaceutical Association and the National Professional Society of Pharmacists. 1984. *The Final Report of the Task Force on Pharmacy Education*. Washington, D.C.: American Pharmaceutical Association.

Anderson, Alexander S., and Botticelli, Max G. 1981. "Evaluating M.D. Level Competence in Internal Medicine." *Journal of Medical Education* 56 (7): 587–92.

Anderson, Cheryl A. 1983. "Computer Literacy: Changes for Teacher Education." *Journal of Teacher Education* 34 (5): 6–9.

Anderson, G. Lester. 1974. *Trends in Education for the Professions*. AAHE-ERIC Research Report No. 7. Washington, D.C.: American Association for Higher Education. ED 096 889. 58 pp. MF–$0.97; PC–$7.14.

Anderson, Robert J.; Kimberlin, Carole; and Hodsall, Ronald. 1979. "Perceptions of Pharmacy Practice—B.S. vs. PharmD Students." *American Journal of Pharmaceutical Education* 43 (3): 209–11.

Anderson, Wilton T. 1983. "Suggested Changes in Accounting Education to Meet the Demand of the Professor." *Journal of Accounting Education* 1 (2): 5–10.

Andrews, Sam, and Hutchinson, Sally A. 1981. "Teaching Nursing Ethics: A Practical Approach." *Journal of Nursing Education* 20 (1): 6–11.

Applegate, Jane H., and Lasley, Thomas J. 1982. "Cooperating Teachers' Problems with Preservice Field Experience Students." *Journal of Teacher Education* 33 (2): 15–18.

Association of American Colleges. 1985. *Report of the Project on Redefining the Meaning and Purpose of Baccalaureate Degrees: Integrity in the College Curriculum*. Washington, D.C.: AAC.

Association of American Library Schools. 1981. "Task Force on the Implications of the White House Conference on Library and Information Science." *Journal of Education for Librarianship* 21 (3): 246–62.

Association of American Medical Colleges. 1984. *Physicians for the Twenty-first Century*. Washington, D.C.: AAMC.

Auerbach, Carl A. 1984. "Legal Education and Some of Its Discontents." *Journal of Legal Education* 34 (1): 43–72.

Bailey, Roger. 1979. "A New School." *Journal of Architectural Education* 33 (2): 42–46.

Bakalinsky, Rosalie. 1982. "Generic Practice in Graduate Social Work Curricula: A Study of Educators' Experiences and Attitudes." *Journal of Education for Social Work* 18 (3): 46–54.

Baker, C. M., and Mayer, G. G. 1982. "One Approach to Teaching Cultural Similarities and Differences." *Journal of Nursing Education* 21 (4): 17–22.

Balgopal, Pallassana R.; Munson, Carlton E.; and Vassil, V. Thomas. 1979. "Developmental Theory: A Yardstick for Ethnic Minority Content." *Journal of Education for Social Work* 15 (3): 28–35.

Barondess, Jeremiah A. 1981. "The Future Physician: Realistic Expectations and Curricular Needs." *Journal of Medical Education* 56 (5): 381–89.

Becker, H. S., and Carper, J. W. 1956. "The Development of Identification with an Occupation." *American Journal of Sociology* 61 (4): 289–98.

Becker, Howard S.; Geer, Blanche; Hughes, Everett C.; and Strauss, Anselm L. 1961. *Boys in White: Student Culture in Medical School.* Chicago: University of Chicago Press.

Begun, J. W., and Ricker, P. P. 1980. "Social Science in Medicine." *Journal of Medical Education* 55 (3): 181–85.

Benavides, Eustolio, III; Lynch M. M.; and Velasquez, J. S. 1980. "Toward a Culturally Relevant Fieldwork Model: The Community Learning Center Project." *Journal of Education for Social Work* 16 (2): 55–62.

Bender, Richard. 1979. "Operational Games in Architecture and Design." *Journal of Architectural Education* 33 (1): 2–6.

Bennett, John. 1984. "Diverse Sequence of Course Focuses on Problem Solving." *Journalism Educator* 39 (1): 23–26.

Berger, B. A., and McCroskey, J. C. 1982. "Reducing Communication Apprehension in Pharmacy Students." *American Journal of Pharmaceutical Education* 46 (2): 132–36.

Berman, Louise. 1981. "Teacher Education and the Expanding Role of the Schools." *Journal of Teacher Education* 32 (4): 7–9.

Bickel, James, and Morgan, Thomas E. 1980. "Research Opportunities for Medical Students: An Approach to the Physician-Investigator Shortage." *Journal of Medical Education* 55 (7): 567–73.

Blauch, Lloyd, ed. 1955. *Education for the Professions.* Washington, D.C.: U.S. Government Printing Office.

Bledstein, B. J. 1976. *The Culture of Professionalism: The Middle Class and the Development of Higher Education in America.* New York: Norton.

Bloom, B. S. 1976. *Human Characteristics and School Learning.* New York: McGraw-Hill.

Boatsman, James R. 1983. "American Law Schools: Implications for Accounting Education." *Journal of Accounting Education* 1 (1): 93–117.

Boaz, Martha. 1981. *Issues in Higher Education and the Professions in the 1980s.* Littleton, Colo.: Libraries Unlimited.

Bok, Derek C. 1983. "A Flawed System of Law Practice and Training." *Journal of Legal Education* 33 (4): 570–85.

Boley, Bruno A. 1977. *Crossfire in Professional Education: Students, the Professions, and Society.* Elmsford, N.Y.: Pergamon Press.

Bolin, S. E., and Hogle, E. L. 1984. "Relationship between College Success and Employer Competency Ratings for Graduates of a Baccalaureate Nursing Program (Research)." *Journal of Nursing Education* 23 (1): 15–20.

Bonta, Juan Pablo. 1979. "Simulation Games in Architectural Education." *Journal of Architectural Education* 33 (1): 12–13.

Bragg, Ann K. 1976. *The Socialization Process into Higher Education.* AAHE-ERIC Research Report No. 7. Washington, D.C.: American Association for Higher Education. ED 132 909. 54 pp. MF–$0.97; PC–$7.14.

Brandt, Richard M., and Covert, Robert C. 1980. "Emerging Markets for Educators." *Journal of Teacher Education* 31 (5): 15–18.

Brendtro, Larry K. 1980. "Bridging Teaching and Treatment: The American Educator." *Journal of Teacher Education* 31 (5): 23–24.

Brent, David A. 1981. "The Residency as a Developmental Process." *Journal of Medical Education* 56: (5): 417–22.

Brink, C. J. 1982. "Postgraduate Educational Plans of Wisconsin Pharmacy Students and Recent Graduates: A Social Psychological Approach." *American Journal of Pharmaceutical Education* 46 (2): 126–32.

Brooks, Richard. 1981. "The Future of Ethical Humanism: The Reintroduction of Ethics into the Legal World: Alan Gewirth's Reason and Morality." *Journal of Legal Education* 31 (3–5): 287–305.

Brown, Franklyn K. 1983. "Technical Ethics." *Engineering Education* 73 (4): 298–300.

Brusich, Judy. 1980. "Social Learning Theory as a Basis for Teaching Decisions." *Journal of Nursing Education* 19 (5): 27–31.

Bucher, R., and Stelling, J. G. 1977. *Becoming Professional.* Beverly Hills, Cal.: Sage Publications.

Buckwalter, Joseph A.; Schumacher, Rex; Albright, John P.; and Cooper, Reginald. 1981. "Use of an Educational Taxonomy for Evaluation of Cognitive Performance." *Journal of Medical Education* 56 (2): 111–15.

Bullough, V. L. 1970. "Education and Professionalization: An Historical Example." *History of Education Quarterly* 10 (2): 160–69.

Burgess, G. 1980. "The Self-Concept of Undergraduate Nursing Students in Relation to Clinical Performance and Selected Bio-graphical Variables." *Journal of Nursing Education* 19 (3): 37–44.

Buschman, M. B.; Burns, E. M.; and Jones, F. M. 1981. "Student Nurses' Attitudes toward the Elderly." *Journal of Nursing Education* 20 (5): 7–10.

Bush, Patricia J., and Johnson, Keith W. 1979. "Where Is the Public Health Pharmacist?" *American Journal of Pharmaceutical Education* 43 (3): 249–52.

Cain, M. J.; Silberman, S. L.; Mahan, J. M.; and Meydreeh, E. F. 1983. "Changes in Dental Students' Personal Needs and Values." *Journal of Dental Education* 47 (9): 604–8.

Callahan, Daniel. 1977. *The Teaching of Ethics: A Preliminary Inquiry*. Special Supplement: Hastings Center Report. Hastings-on-Hudson, N.Y.: The Hastings Center.

Campbell, Dale F., and Korim, Andrew S. 1979. *Occupational Programs in Four-Year Colleges: Trends and Issues*. AAHE-ERIC Research Report No. 5. Washington, D.C.: American Association for Higher Education. ED 176 645. 44 pp. MF–$0.97; PC–$5.34.

Cantor, Marjorie M.; Schroeder, Deborah M.; and Kurth, Susan W. 1981. "The Experienced Nurse and the New Graduate: Do Their Learning Needs Differ?" *Nurse Educator* 6 (7): 17–22.

Carbone, Peter F., Jr. 1980. "Liberal Education and Teacher Preparation." *Journal of Teacher Education* 31 (3): 13–17.

Carlson, Jean B., and Lockwood, James R. 1980. "Human Service Educators in the Business World." *Journal of Teacher Education* 31 (5): 27–30.

Carnegie Council on Policy Studies in Higher Education. 1976. *A Classification of Institutions of Higher Education*. Berkeley, Cal.: Author.

Carnegie Foundation for the Advancement of Teaching. 1977. *Missions of the College Curriculum*. San Francisco: Jossey-Bass.

Carr, John F. 1981. "Teaching Behavioral Sciences in Medical Education: A Ten-Year Progress Report." *Journal of Medical Education* 56 (2): 667–69.

Carr-Saunders, A. M., and Wilson, P. A. 1933. *The Professions.* Oxford: Clarendon Press.

Cassidy, Robert C.; Swee, David E.; and Stuart, Marian R. 1983. "Teaching Biopsycho-Ethical Medicine in a Family Practice Clerkship." *Journal of Medical Education* 58 (10): 778–95.

Cassileth, Barrie R., and Egan, Thomas A. 1979. "Modification of Medical Student Perceptions of the Cancer Experience." *Journal of Medical Education* 54 (10): 797–802.

Castles, Mary Reardon. 1984. "Teaching Research Methods in Schools of Nursing." *Journal of Nursing Education* 23 (3): 120.

Cavers, David F. 1983. "Signs of Progress: Legal Education, 1982." *Journal of Legal Education* 33 (1): 33–47.

Clark, Charles A., and Vanek, Eugenia P. 1984. "Meeting the Health Care Needs of People with Limited Access to Care." *Journal of Dental Education* 48 (4): 213–16.

Coe, Teddy L. 1983. "Student Management Consulting Projects in the Accounting Curriculum." *Journal of Accounting Education* 1 (2): 97–105.

Collier, Idolia M. 1981. "Educational Cooperation among Nursing, Medicine, and Pharmacy: A Success Story." *Journal of Nursing Education* 20 (7): 23–26.

Colson, John Calvin. 1980. "Professional Ideals and Social Realities: Some Questions about the Education of Librarians." *Journal of Education for Librarianship* 21 (2): 91–108.

Comerio, Mary C. 1981. "Pruitt Igoe and Other Stories." *Journal of Architectural Education* 34 (4): 26–31.

Comstock, Loretto M.; Hooper, Elizabeth M.; Goodwin, Sean M.; and Goodwin, James S. 1982. "Physician Behaviors that Correlate with Patient Satisfaction." *Journal of Medical Education* 57 (2): 105–12.

Condlin, Robert J. 1983. "Clinical Education in the Seventies: An Appraisal of the Decade." *Journal of Legal Education* 33 (4): 604–12.

Conte, Jon R., and Levy, Rona L. 1980. "Problems and Issues in Implementing the Clinical-Research Model of Practice in Educational and Clinical Settings." *Journal of Education for Social Work* 16 (3): 60–66.

Corcoran, Ellen. 1981. "Transition Shock: The Beginning Teacher's Paradox." *Journal of Teacher Education* 32 (3): 19.

Corrigan, Dean C. 1981. "Creating the Conditions for Professional Practice: Education's Unfinished Agenda." *Journal of Teacher Education* 32 (2): 26–32.

Cotanch, H. 1981. "Self-Actualization and Professional Socialization of Nursing Students in the Clinical Laboratory Experience." *Journal of Nursing Education* 20 (8): 4–14.

Crabtree, Vaun, and Geiger, John O. 1983. "Who Cares about What: 13 Organizations Look at Teacher Education." *Journal of Teacher Education* 34 (5): 30–33.

Cramton, Roger C. 1982. "The Current State of the Law Curriculum." *Journal of Legal Education* 32 (3): 321–35.

Creese, Walter. 1980. "Reflections on How to/How Not to Teach History." *Journal of Architectural Education* 34 (1): 11–14.

Culver, Richard S., and Hackos, JoAnn R. 1982. "Perry's Model of Intellectual Development." *Engineering Education* 7 (3): 221–26.

Curiel, Hermon; Brockstein, Joan R.; Cheney, Clark C.; and Adams, George L. 1979. "Interdisciplinary Team Teaching in a Barrio Primary Care Mental Health Setting." *Journal of Education for Social Work* 15 (3): 44–50.

Curtis, Mark H. 1985. "Confronting an Ancient Dichotomy: A Proposal for Integrating Liberal and Professional Education." *Phi Kappa Phi Journal* 65 (3): 10–12.

Davidge, A. M.; Davis, W. K.; and Hall, A. L. 1980. "A System for the Evaluation of Medical Students' Clinical Competence." *Journal of Medical Education* 55 (1): 65–67.

Davis, Howard. 1983. "Individual House and in Groups: The Pattern Language in a Teaching Studio." *Journal of Architectural Education* 36 (3): 14–19.

Dear, Margaret R., and Keen, Mary Frances. 1982. "Role Transition: A Practicum for Baccalaureate Nursing Students." *Journal of Nursing Education* 21 (2): 32–37.

del Bueno, Dorothy J. 1983. "Doing the Right Thing: Nurses' Ability to Make Clinical Decisions." *Nurse Educator* 8 (3): 7–11.

DeMott, John. 1984. "Journalism Courses Are an Essential Part of Liberal Education." *Journalism Educator* 39 (3): 31–33.

Denise, Laurent G., and Nauratil, Marcia J. Winter 1984. "Library Science Students' Commitment to Library Service for Older Adults." *Journal of Education for Librarianship* 24: 183–88.

Denton, Jon J. 1982. "Early Field Experience Influence on Performance in Subsequent Coursework." *Journal of Teacher Education* 33 (2): 19–23.

Dickinson, M. Lee; Huels, Michelle; and Murphy, M. Dianne. 1983. "Pediatric House Staff Communication Skills: Assessment and Intervention." *Journal of Medical Education* 58 (8): 659–61.

Dinerman, Miriam. 1982. "A Study of Baccalaureate and Master's Curricula in Social Work." *Journal of Education for Social Work* 18 (2): 84–92.

Dirsmith, Mark W. Fall 1983. "Obedience in the Classroom." *Journal of Accounting Education* 1 (2): 41–50.

Dolinsky, Donna. 1979. "Pharmaceutical Psychology." *American Journal of Pharmaceutical Education* 43 (3): 261–66.

Dostoglu, Sibel. 1983. "Lincoln Cathedral versus the Bicycle Shed." *Journal of Architectural Education* 36 (4): 10–15.

Dovey, Kim. 1981. "Public Service Architecture: An Interview with Sandy Hilshen." *Journal of Architectural Education* 35 (1): 28–31.

Downing, Mildred H. 1981. "Training in On-Line Cataloging in an Academic Setting." *Journal of Education for Librarianship* 21 (4): 327–36.

Downs, William R., and Robertson, Joan E. 1983. "Preserving the Social Work Perspective in the Research Sequence: State of the Art and Program Models for the 1980s." *Journal of Education for Social Work* 19 (1): 15–22.

Dworkin, Samuel F. 1981. "Behavioral Sciences in Dental Education: Past, Present, and Future." *Journal of Dental Education* 45 (10): 692–93.

Dwyer, Margaret, and Urbanowski, Martha. 1981. "Field Practice Criteria: A Valuable Teaching/Learning Tool in Undergraduate Social Work Education." *Journal of Education for Social Work* 17 (1): 5–11.

Ellis, William Russell. 1981. "The Social in the Studio." *Journal of Architectural Education* 34 (3): 29–31.

Elstein, Arthur S.; Shulman, Lee S.; and Sprafka, Sarah A. 1978. *Medical Problem Solving: An Analysis of Clinical Reasoning.* Cambridge, Mass.: Harvard University Press.

Engelhardt, H. Tristram, and Callahan, Daniel. 1980. *Knowing and Valuing: The Search for Common Roots.* Hastings-on-Hudson, N.Y.: Hastings Center Institute.

Faver, Catherine A.; Fox, Mary Frank; and Shannon, Coleen. 1983. "The Educational Process and Job Equity for the Sexes in Social Work." *Journal of Education for Social Work* 19 (3): 78–87.

Fedder, Donald O., and Beardsley, Robert S. May 1979. "Preparing Pharmacist Health Educators." *American Journal of Pharmaceutical Education* 43 (2): 127–29.

Fielder, J. H. 1979. "Philosophy and Engineering." *Engineering Education* 69 (7): 705–8.

Findley, Roger W. 1979. "Environmental and Planning Studies at the University of Illinois." *Journal of Legal Education* 30 (1–2): 213–18.

Fink, Arthur E.; Pfouts, Jane H.; and Dobelstein, Andrew W. 1985. *The Field of Social Work.* 8th ed. Beverly Hills, Cal.: Sage Publications.

Fisher, Waldo R. 1981. "Medical Student Research: A Program of Self-Education." *Journal of Medical Education* 56 (11): 904–8.

Fleming, J. 1980. "Teaching Nursing Research: Content." *Nurse Educator* 5 (1): 124–27.

Flexner, A. S. 1910. *Medical Education in the United States and Canada*. Boston: Updyke, Merrymount Press.

——— .1915. "Is Social Work a Profession?" In *Proceedings of the National Conference of Charities and Corrections*. Forty-second Annual Session, May 12–19, Baltimore, Maryland. Chicago: Hildmann Printing Co.

Ford, Nigel. Winter 1984. "Intellectual Development and the Organization of Knowledge." *Journal of Education for Librarianship* 24 (3): 157–73.

Forsyth, P. B., and Danisiewicz, T. J. 1985. "Toward a Theory of Professionalization." *Work and Occupations: An International Sociological Journal* 12 (1): 59–76.

Fosdick, James A. 1979. "Post-interns Change Views of the Media, J-education." *Journalism Educator* 34 (2): 22–25.

Fowler, Gilbert L., Jr. 1983. "Community Journalism Program Responds to Needs." *Journalism Educator* 38 (4): 39–41.

Frumkin, Michael L. 1979. "The Human Service Delivery System Curriculum: A Conceptual Framework." *Journal of Education for Social Work* 15 (1): 20–28.

——— .1980. "Social Work Education and the Professional Commitment Fallacy: A Practical Guide to Field-School Relations." *Journal of Education for Social Work* 16 (2): 91–99.

Gaines, Merrill C. 1980. "Teaching a Contextual Architecture." *Journal of Architectural Education* 33 (3): 212–16.

Garrison, Bruce. 1983. "Internships Vary Widely in Structure and Academic Status." *Journalism Educator* 38 (1): 3–7.

Gartner, Alan. 1976. *The Preparation of Human Service Professionals*. New York: Human Sciences Press.

Geison, Gerald L., ed. 1983. *Professions and Professional Ideologies in America*. Chapel Hill: University of North Carolina Press.

Gessner, Peter K.; Katz, Leonard A.; and Schimpfhauser, Frank T. 1981. "Sociomedical Issues in the Curriculum: A Model for Institutional Change." *Journal of Medical Education* 56 (12): 987–93.

Gianniny, O. Allan, Jr. November 1982. "Engineering: A Liberating Education for a High-Technology World." *Engineering Education* 73: 159–65.

Gibelman, Margaret. 1983. "Social Work Education and the Changing Nature of Public Agency Practice." *Journal of Education for Social Work* 19 (3): 21–28.

Gitterman, Alex, and Germain, Carol B. 1981. "Education for Practice: Teaching about the Environment." *Journal of Education for Social Work* 17 (3): 44–51.

Gleaves, Edwin S. 1982. "Library Education: Issues for the Eighties." *Journal of Education for Librarianship* 22 (4): 260–74.

Godwin, William C.; Starks, David D.; Greer, Thomas G.; and Koran, Andrew, III. 1981. "Identification of Sources of Stress in Practice by Recent Dental Graduates." *Journal of Dental Education* 45 (4): 220–21.

Goerig, Albert C. 1980. "Technique Models: An Endodontic Teaching Aid." *Journal of Dental Education* 44 (6): 334–35.

Goodman, Leonard. 1983. "An Analysis of the Effectiveness of Public Accounting Internship Programs at Major New York City CPA Firms." *Journal of Accounting Education* 1 (2): 159–62.

Goodman, Percival. 1981. "Architecture Responsive to Human Needs and the Ecological Imperative." *Journal of Architectural Education* 35 (1): 46–50.

Gouldner, A. 1979. *The Future of Intellectuals and the Rise of the New Class.* New York: Seabury Press.

Goyan, Jere E. 1981. "The Relationship of Basic Science Departments in Medical Schools for Other Professional Schools." *Journal of Dental Education* 45 (12): 786–89.

Graham, B., and Gleir, C. 1980. "Health Education: Are Nurses Really Prepared?" *Journal of Nursing Education* 19 (8): 4–6.

Grantham, Emily V., and Block, Marvin J. 1983. "Effect of Extramural Experiences on Dental Students' Attitudes." *Journal of Dental Education* 47 (10): 681–84.

Green, Thomas G. 1981. "Dental Student Response to Moral Dilemmas." *Journal of Dental Education* 45 (3): 137–40.

Grussing, Paul G.; Cyrs, Thomas E., Jr.; and Silzer, Robert F. 1979. "Development of Behaviorally Anchored Rating Scales for Pharmacy Practice." *American Journal of Pharmaceutical Education* 43 (2): 115–20.

Guidry, Rosalind. 1979. "A Design for Teaching Human Behavior in Generalist Undergraduate Programs." *Journal of Education for Social Work* 15 (2): 45–50.

Haber, Samuel. 1974. "The Professions and Higher Education: A Historical Overview." In *Higher Education and the Labor Market,* edited by Margaret S. Gordon. New York: McGraw-Hill.

Hacker, Andrew. 1982. "The Shame of the Professional Schools." *Journal of Legal Education* 32 (2): 278–81.

Hagerty, Bonnie M. K., and Stark, Joan S. 1986. "A Comparison of Accreditation Standards in Selected Professional Fields." Mimeographed. Ann Arbor: University of Michigan.

Hall, R. H. 1969. *Occupations and the Social Structure*. Englewood Cliffs, N.J.: Prentice-Hall.

Hamner, Martin E.; Scoggin, J. Allen; and White, Bruce David. 1981. "The Basis for Ethico-Legal Instruction in the Pharmacy Curriculum." *American Journal of Pharmaceutical Education* 45 (1): 25–28.

Haroldsen, Edwin O., and Harvey, Kenneth E. 1979. "Frowns Greet New J-Grads in Magazine Job Market." *Journalism Educator* 34 (2): 3–8.

Harris, Cyril M., and Rosenthal, Albert J. 1981. "The Interdisciplinary Course in the Legal Aspects of Noise Pollution at Columbia University." *Journal of Legal Education* 31 (1–2): 128–33.

Hart, F. L., and Turkstra, C. J. 1979. "Senior Projects Supervised by Consulting Engineers." *Engineering Education* 69 (7): 747–48.

Hartman, Ann. 1980. "But All Knowledge Is One: A Systems Approach to the Dilemmas in Curriculum Building." *Journal of Education for Social Work* 16 (2): 100–107.

Harvey, Kenneth E. 1982. "News Executives Reaffirm: They're Ready to Help." *Journalism Educator* 37 (3): 51–52.

Harvill, L. M. 1981. "Anticipatory Socialization of Medical Students." *Journal of Medical Education* 56 (5): 431–33.

Hastings Center. 1980. *The Teaching of Ethics in Higher Education*. Hastings-on-Hudson, N.Y.: Author.

Hegland, Kenney J. 1982. "Moral Dilemmas in Teaching Trial Advocacy." *Journal of Legal Education* 32 (1): 69–86.

Herman, Mary W.; Veloski, Jon J.; and Hojat, Mohammadreza. 1983. "Validity and Importance of Low Ratings Given Medical Graduates in Noncognitive Areas." *Journal of Medical Education* 58 (11): 837–43.

Heymann, Harold O., and Roberson, Theodore M. 1984. "Using Survey Information for Curriculum Review." *Journal of Dental Education* 48 (3): 166–68.

Higgins, David D. Fall 1983. "Integrating a Personal Financial Planning Major into Existing Curricula." *Journal of Financial Education* 12: 31–36.

Hodges, Carol. 1982. "Implementing Methods: If You Can't Blame the Cooperating Teacher, Who Can You Blame?" *Journal of Teacher Education* 33 (6): 25–29.

Hodges, M., and Lichter, B. 1980. "The Union of Theory and Practice." *Engineering Education* 70 (8): 816–21.

Holloway, Richard L. 1979. "The Development of a Domain-Referenced Test of Pharmacy Competence." *American Journal of Pharmaceutical Education* 43 (2): 112–14.

Hoppmann, W. H., II; Liu, James; and Rivello, J. Roberta. 1980. "Models of Professions: Law, Medicine, and Engineering." *Mechanical Engineering* 102 (5): 44–49.

Houle, Cyril. 1980. *Continuing Learning in the Professions*. San Francisco: Jossey-Bass.

Houze, R. Neal, and Simon, Rebecca J. 1981. "Cooperative Education: Three on a Tightrope." *Engineering Education* 71 (4): 283–87.

Howe, Kenneth R., and Jones, Martha S. 1984. "Techniques for Evaluating Student Performance in a Preclinical Medical Ethics Course." *Journal of Medical Education* 59 (4): 350–52.

Hubbard, William Q. 1980. "History Synchrony." *Journal of Architectural Education* 34 (1): 22.

Hughes, Everett C.; Thorne, Barrie; DeBaggis, Agostino; Gurin, Arnold; and Williams, David. 1973. *Education for the Professions of Medicine, Law, Theology, and Social Welfare*. New York: McGraw-Hill.

Huling, Leslie, and Hall, Gene E. 1982. "Factors to Be Considered in the Preparation of Secondary School Teachers." *Journal of Teacher Education* 33 (1): 7–12.

Hull, D. M. 1979. "Technical Education to Meet New Demands in Energy." *Engineering Education* 69 (7): 798–802.

Humphreys, Griffith E. 1983. "Inclusion of Content on Homosexuality in the Social Work Curriculum." *Journal of Education for Social Work* 19 (1): 55–60.

Hunsaker, David M. 1980. "Law, Humanism, and Communication: Suggestions for Limited Curricular Reform." *Journal of Legal Education* 30 (4): 417–36.

Hunt, Todd. 1982. "Raising the Issue of Ethics through the Use of Scenarios." *Journalism Educator* 37 (1): 55–58.

Isakson, Richard L., and Ellsworth, Randy. 1979. "Educational Psychology: What Do Teachers Value in Its Content?" *Journal of Teacher Education* 30 (4): 26–28.

Ivey, Elizabeth S. 1982. "Engineering at Smith College." *Engineering Education* 7 (3): 235–37.

Jankovic, Joanne, and Green, Ronald K. Spring 1981. "Teaching Legal Principles to Social Workers." *Journal of Education for Social Work* 17 (3): 28–35.

Jarrett, James L. 1979. "Teacher Education as a Liberal Art." *Journal of Teacher Education* 30 (6): 25–28.

Jarvis, Peter. 1983. *Professional Education*. London: Croom Helm.

Jennings, Glen H., and Smith, Mary K. 1979. "The Pharmacist and Human Sexuality." *American Journal of Pharmaceutical Education* 43 (1): 44–45.

Jenny, Joanna. 1980. "Ethical and Legal Considerations in Dental Caries Research Using Human Subjects: Conference Summary." *Journal of Dental Education* 44 (6): 338–40.

Johnson, C. Anderson, and Wertheimer, Albert. 1979. "Behavioral Pharmacy." *American Journal of Pharmaceutical Education* 43 (3): 257–61.

Johnson, Davis G. 1983. *Physicians in the Making: Personal, Academic, and Socioeconomic Characteristics of Medical Students from 1950 to 2000.* San Francisco: Jossey-Bass.

Jordan, Daniel C. 1979. "Rx for Piaget's Complaint: Science of Education." *Journal of Teacher Education* 30 (5): 11–14.

Joseph, M. Vincentia, and Conrad, Ann P. 1983. "Teaching Social Work Ethics for Contemporary Practice: An Effectiveness Evaluation." *Journal of Education for Social Work* 19 (3): 59–68.

Judah, Eleanor Hannon. 1979. "Values: The Uncertain Component in Social Work." *Journal of Education for Social Work* 15 (2): 79–86.

Jvhasz, Joseph. 1981. "The Place of the Social Sciences in Architectural Education." *Journal of Architectural Education* 34 (3): 2–7.

Kahn, Elsbeth; Lass, Sandra L.; Hartley, Russell; and Kornreich, Helen K. 1981. "Affective Learning in Medical Education." *Journal of Medical Education* 56 (8): 646–52.

Keen, Mary Frances, and Dear, Margaret R. 1983. "Mastery of Role Transition: Clinical Teaching Strategies." *Journal of Nursing Education* 70 (2): 210–12.

Kettner, Peter M. 1979. "A Conceptual Framework for Developing Learning Modules for Field Education." *Journal of Education for Social Work* 15 (1): 51–58.

Kilgore, Alvah M. 1979. "Pilot Project Shows Definite Link between Pre-Inservice Education." *Journal of Teacher Education* 30 (4): 10–12.

——— .March/April 1980. "PBTE: A Follow-up Study." *Journal of Teacher Education* 31: 55–60.

Kimberlin, C. L. 1982. "Assertiveness Training for Pharmacy Students." *American Journal of Pharmaceutical Education* 45 (2): 137–41.

Klare, Karl E. 1982. "The Law School Curriculum in the 1980s: What's Left?" *Journal of Legal Education* 32 (3): 336–43.

Kluender, Mary M. 1984. "Teacher Education Programs in the 1980s: Some Selected Characteristics." *Journal of Teacher Education* 35 (4): 33–35.

Knepler, Henry. 1982. "Technology Is Not Enough." *Engineering Education* 72 (4): 274–76.

Kolevzon, Michael S., and Biggerstaff, Marilyn A. 1983. "Functional Differentiation of Job Demands: Dilemmas Confronting the Continuum in Social Work Education." *Journal of Education for Social Work* 19 (2): 26–34.

Kravetz, Diane. 1982. "An Overview of Content on Women for the Social Curriculum." *Journal of Education for Social Work* 18 (2): 42–49.

Kroll, Lucien, and Mikellides, Byron. 1981. "Can Architecture Be Taught?" *Journal of Architectural Education* 35 (1): 36–39.

Kunkel, Richard C., and Dearmin, Evelyn Titus. 1981. "The Political and Ideological Development of a Fifth-Year Statewide Internship." *Journal of Teacher Education* 32 (1): 19–23.

Lange, Robert R., and Fender, Marilyn J. 1980. "Adult Handicapped as Resource Persons in Secondary Education Preservice Programs." *Journal of Teacher Education* 31 (2): 49–54.

Larsen, Ann, and Hepworth, Dean H. 1982. "Enhancing the Effectiveness of Practicum Instruction: An Empirical Study." *Journal of Education for Social Work* 18 (2): 50–58.

Larson, Margali Sarfatti. 1977. *The Rise of Professionalism: A Sociological Analysis.* Berkeley: University of California Press.

Lasley, Thomas J. 1980. "Preservice Teacher Beliefs about Teaching." *Journal of Teacher Education* 331 (4): 38–41.

Lawson, Thomas R., and Berleman, William C. 1982. "Research in the Undergraduate Curriculum: A Survey." *Journal of Education for Social Work* 18 (1): 86–93.

LeBold, W. K. 1980. "Research in Engineering Education: An Overview." *Engineering Education* 70 (5): 406–9.

LeBold, W. K.; Lindenlaub, J.; and Seibert, W. 1980. "Faculty and Student Views of Institutional Development and Educational Goals." *Engineering Education* 71 (3): 223–29.

Lee, Lettie A. 1979. "An Investigation of the Effects of Clinical Experience on Cognitive Gains." *Journal of Medical Education* 18 (7): 27–37.

Leighninger, Robert D., Jr., and Leighninger, Leslie. 1980. "Hail and Farewell: Undergraduate Social Work and the Social Sciences, 1974–1979." *Journal of Education for Social Work* 16 (3): 110–18.

Leleiko, Steven H. 1979. "Clinical Education, Empirical Study, and Legal Scholarship." *Journal of Legal Education* 30 (1–2): 149–65.

Leserman, J. 1980. "Changes in the Professional Orientation of Medical Students: A Follow-up Study." *Journal of Medical Education* 55 (5): 415–22.

Lewis, David. 1979. "Listening and Hearing." *Journal of Architectural Education* 33 (1): 27–30.

Lezberg, Amy K., and Fedo, David A. 1980. "Communication Skills and Pharmacy Education: A Case Study." *American Journal of Pharmaceutical Education* 44 (3): 257–59.

Lindley, William R. 1984. "Journalism Needs More Emphasis on Humanities Study." *Journalism Educator* 39 (1): 39–40.

Littman, Elliott; Mayo, James; and Burgess, Peter. 1981. "Political Knowledge and the Architectural Studio." *Journal of Architectural Education* 34 (3): 24–28.

Liu, Philip; Miller, E.; Herr, G.; Hardy, C.; Sivarajan, M.; and Willenkin, R. 1980. "Videotape Reliability: A Method of Evaluation of a Clinical Performance Examination." *Journal of Medical Education* 55 (8): 713–15.

Loe, Harold. 1981. "The Impact of Research and Technological Advances on Dental Education." *Journal of Dental Education* 45 (10): 670–75.

Lortie, Daniel C. 1975. *Schoolteacher: A Sociological Study.* Chicago: University of Chicago Press.

Loupe, Michael J.; Meskin, Lawrence H.; and Mast, Terrill A. 1979. "Changes in the Values of Students and Dentists over a Ten-year Period." *Journal of Dental Education* 43 (3): 170–75.

Lucas, Linda. 1983. "Education for Work with Disabled and Institutionalized Persons." *Journal of Education for Librarianship* 23 (3): 207–23.

Lynton, Ernest A. 1984. *The Missing Connection between Business and the Universities.* New York: MacMillan.

McGaghie, William C. 1980. "Medical Problem Solving: A Reanalysis." *Journal of Medical Education* 55 (11): 912–21.

McGlothlin, W. J. 1960. *Patterns of Professional Education.* New York: G. P. Putnam & Sons.

——— .1964. *The Professional Schools.* New York: Center for Applied Research in Education.

McGuire, C. H.; Foley, R. P.; Gorr, A.; Richards, R. W.; and associates. 1983. *Handbook of Health Professions.* San Francisco: Jossey-Bass.

McKenzie, Richard S. 1980. "Curriculum Considerations for Correlating Basic and Clinical Sciences." *Journal of Dental Education* 44 (5): 248–56.

Manzo, J. P. 1979. "Mechanical/Electrical Building Systems: A Neglected Specialty." *Engineering Education* 69 (4): 325–30.

Marchant, Maurice P., and Wilson, Carolyn F. 1983. "Joint Graduate Programs for Librarians." *Journal of Education for Librarianship* 24 (1): 30–37.

Martin, Mike W. 1981. "Why Should Engineering Ethics Be Taught?" *Engineering Education* 71 (4): 275–78.

Martinez-Brawley, Emilia E. 1983. "Interdisciplinary Aspects of the Baccalaureate Curriculum in Rural Social Work." *Journal of Education for Social Work* 19 (3): 29–36.

Matejski, Myrtle P. 1979. "A Framework for Nursing: A Concept for Practice." *Journal of Nursing Education* 18 (5): 49–58.

May, Gordon S., and Arevalo, Claire. 1983. "Integrating Effective Writing Skills in the Accounting Curriculum." *Journal of Accounting Education* 1 (1): 119–26.

May, Hayden B. 1979. "The Potentiality of Gaming: Simulation in Architecture." *Journal of Architectural Education* 33 (1): 7–11.

Mayhew, L. B., and Ford, P. J. 1974. *Reform in Graduate and Professional Education.* San Francisco: Jossey-Bass.

Mazzuca, S. A.; Cohen, S. J.; and Clark, C. M., Jr. 1981. "Evaluating Clinical Knowledge across Years of Medical Training." *Journal of Medical Education* 56 (2): 83–90.

Mehra, Achal. 1984. "Liberal Arts Help Develop Critical Judgment." *Journalism Educator* 39 (3): 33–36.

Merrill, John C. 1980. "Upside Down: Another Look at a Revolutionary Journalism Education Program First Proposed in 1975." *Journalism Educator* 35 (2): 20–22.

Meskin, Lawrence H. 1980. "Societal and Professional Forces Affecting Graduate Dental Education." *Journal of Dental Education* 44 (12): 714–24.

Meunier, John. 1979. "The Cranbrook TS: Old Albion Strikes Again." *Journal of Architectural Education* 32 (3): 12–13.

Millard, Richard. 1984. "Assessing the Quality of Innovative Graduate Programs." In *Keeping Graduate Programs Responsive to National Needs,* edited by M. J. Pelczar and L. C. Solmon. New Directions for Higher Education No. 46. San Francisco: Jossey-Bass.

Mills, Gordon; Harvey, Kenneth; and Warnick, Leland B. 1980. "Newspaper Editors Point to Journalism Grad Deficiencies." *Journalism Educator* 35 (2): 12–19.

Mitchell, J. J. 1981. "The Use of Case Studies in Bioethics Courses." *Journal of Nursing Education* 20 (9): 31–36.

Mohan, Brij. 1980. "Human Behavior, Social Environment, Social Reconstruction, and Social Policy: A System of Linkages, Goals, and Priorities." *Journal of Education for Social Work* 16 (2): 26–32.

Mulvihill, James E. 1980. "The Scope, Goals, and Objectives of Graduate Dental Education—II." *Journal of Dental Education* 44 (11): 650–73.

Munhall, Patricia L. 1982. "Moral Development: A Prerequisite." *Journal of Nursing Education* 2 (6): 11–15.

Nadler, Gerald, and Seireg, Ali. 1982. "Professional Engineering Education in the Classroom." *Engineering Education* 72 (8): 781–84.

Nash, Robert T., and Agne, Russell M. 1982. "Beyond Marginality: New Role for Foundations of Education." *Journal of Teacher Education* 33 (3): 2–7.

National Commission on Nursing. 1983. *Summary Report and Recommendations*. Chicago: American Hospital Association.

National Institute of Education, Study Group for the Conditions of Excellence in American Higher Education. 1984. *Involvement in Learning: Realizing the Potential of American Higher Education*. Washington, D.C.: U. S. Government Printing Office. ED 246 833. 127 pp. MF–$0.97; PC–$10.80.

National Society for the Study of Education. 1962. *Education for the Professions: The Sixty-first Yearbook, Part II*. Chicago: University of Chicago Press.

Neidle, Enid. 1980. "Dentistry–Ethics–The Humanities: A Three-Unit Bridge." *Journal of Dental Education* 44 (12): 693–96.

Nuessle, N. O., and Levine, D. V. 1982. "Development and Utility in Externship of a Questionnaire on Attitude toward Professional Roles of the Pharmacist." *American Journal of Pharmaceutical Education* 46 (1): 60–67.

Nyre, G. F., and Reilly, K. C. 1979. *Professional Education in the Eighties: Challenges and Responses*. AAHE-ERIC Higher Education Research Report No. 8. Washington, D. C.: American Association for Higher Education. ED 179 187. 60 pp. MF–$0.97; PC–$7.14.

Odom, John G. 1982. "Formal Ethics Instruction in Dental Education." *Journal of Dental Education* 46 (9): 553–56.

Olson, Roberta K.; Gresley, Ruth Seris; and Heater, Barbara Stewart. 1984. "The Effects of an Undergraduate Clinical Internship on the Self-Concept and Professional Role Mastery of Baccalaureate Nursing Students." *Journal of Nursing Education* 23 (3): 105–8.

Pataniczek, Dennis, and Isaacson, Nancy Sigler. 1981. "The Relationship of Socialization and the Concerns of Beginning Secondary Teachers." *Journal of Teacher Education* 32 (3): 14–18.

Pierce, Joseph H., and Birmingham, Roy J. 1981. "The Cooperative Internship Program: Giving Students the Best of Both Worlds." *Engineering Education* 71 (4): 288–93.

Pignaturo, Louis J., and McShane, W. R. 1979. "Interdisciplinary Research: Transcending Departmental Conflicts." *Engineering Education* 69 (4): 349–51.

Porter, William. 1979. "Architectural Education in the University Context: Dilemmas and Directions." *Journal of Architectural Education* 32 (3): 3–7.

Priest, George L. 1983. "Social Science Theory and Legal Education: The Law School as University." *Journal of Legal Education* 33 (3): 437–41.

Proctor, Enola K., and Davis, Larry E. 1983. "Minority Content in Social Work Education: A Question of Objectives." *Journal of Education for Social Work* 19 (2): 85–93.

Pugach, Marleen C., and Raths, James D. 1982. "Teacher Education in Multicultural Settings." *Journal of Teacher Education* 33 (6): 13–21.

Pye, A. Kenneth. 1982. "Legal Education Past and Future: A Summer Carol." *Journal of Legal Education* 32 (3): 367–82.

Rango, Nicholas. 1981. "Health and Society: Education in a Liberal Arts College—A Curriculum Strategy." *Journal of Medical Education* 56 (12): 994–1003.

Rathbone-McCuan, Eloise. 1984. "Older Women, Mental Health, and Social Work Education." *Journal of Education for Social Work* 20 (1): 33–41.

Raths, James. 1980. "Suggested Standards for General Education." *Journal of Teacher Education* 31 (3): 19–22.

Reeck, Darrell. 1982. *Ethics for the Professions*. Minneapolis: Augsburg Publishing House.

Reid, Susan. 1979. "Undergraduate Social Work Education and the Liberal Tradition." *Journal of Education for Social Work* 15 (2): 38–44.

Rhodes, Frank. 22 May 1985. "Reforming Higher Education Will Take More Than Just Tinkering with the Curriculum. *Chronicle of Higher Education:* 80.

Richards, David A. J. 1981. "Moral Theory, the Developmental Psychology of Ethical Autonomy and Professionalism." *Journal of Legal Education* 31 (3): 359–74.

Richards, R. K., and Cohen, R. M. 1980. "Why Physicians Attend Traditional CME Programs." *Journal of Medical Education* 55 (6): 479–85.

Richardson, John, Jr., and Hernon, Peter. 1981. "Theory vs. Practice: Student Preferences." *Journal of Education for Librarianship* 21 (4): 287–300.

Riegelman, Richard K.; Povar, Gail J.; and Ott, John E. 1983. "Medical Students' Skills, Attitudes, and Behavior Needed for Literature Reading." *Journal of Medical Education* 58 (5): 411–17.

Rinke, Lynn T. 1979. "Involving Undergraduates in Nursing Research." *Journal of Nursing Education* 18 (6): 59–64.

Rodenberger, Charles A. 1981. "The School of Professional Engineering: An Administrative Model." *Engineering Education* 71 (7): 671–76.

Roepke, William J., ed. Autumn 1982. "New Journalism Writing Approaches Needed, Educators Are Told." *Journalism Educator* 37: 42–44 +.

Romney, Marshall. 1983. "The Use of Microcomputers in Accounting Education." *Journal of Accounting Education* 1 (2): 11–19.

Ronald, Judith Schneider. 1979. "Computers and Undergraduate Nursing Education: A Report on an Experimental Introductory Course." *Journal of Nursing Education* 18 (9): 4–9.

Roosenraad, Jon, and Wares, Donna. 1983. "Academics vs. Experience." *Journalism Educator* 38 (2): 17–18.

Rosen, B., and Caplan, A. L. 1980. *Ethics in the Undergraduate Curriculum*. Hastings-on-Hudson, N. Y.: The Hastings Center.

Rowles, James P. 1982. "Toward Balancing the Goals of Legal Education." *Journal of Legal Education* 31 (3–5): 375–98.

Roy, Sister Callista. 1979. "Relating Nursing Theory to Education: A New Era." *Nurse Educator* 4 (2): 16–29.

Russo, Mary E.; Closson, Richard G.; McKenney, James M.; Spino, Michael; Steward, Ronald B.; Thiessen, Jake K.; and Walker, Elaine S. 1983. "Collaborative Teaching and Research between Basic and Clinical Sciences: Exploration of the Barriers to Collaboration and Suggested Approaches to Achieve Collaboration." *American Journal of Pharmaceutical Education* 47 (1): 58–61.

Sallady, S. A. 1981. "Teaching Ethics in the Psychiatry Clerkship." *Journal of Medical Education* 56 (3): 204–6.

Salley, John J. 1980. "Providing Dental Care to the Handicapped." *Journal of Dental Education* 44 (3): 136–40.

Sanoff, Henry. 1979. "Collaborative Design Process." *Journal of Architectural Education* 33 (1): 18–22.

Santangelo, Mario V. 1981. "The Dental Accrediting Process." *Journal of Dental Education* 45 (8): 513–21.

Scheffler, Israel. 1965. *Conditions of Knowledge*. New York: Scott Foresman & Co.

Schein, E. H., and Kommers, D. W. 1972. *Professional Education: Some New Directions*. New York: McGraw-Hill.

Schlegel, John Henry. March 1984. "Searching for Archimedes: Legal Education, Legal Scholarship, and Liberal Ideology." *Journal of Legal Education* 34: 103–10.

Schofield, J. R. 1984. *New and Expanded Medical Schools: Midcentury to the 1980s*. San Francisco: Jossey-Bass.

Schon, Donald. 1983. *The Reflective Practitioner: How Professionals Think in Action*. New York: Basic Books.

Schoonover, Stephen C.; Bassuk, E. L.; Smith, R.; and Gaskill, D. 1983. "The Use of Videotape Programs to Teach Interpersonal Skills." *Journal of Medical Education* 58 (10): 804–10.

Schroeder, Deborah M.; Cantor, Marjorie M.; and Kurth, Susan W. 1981. "Learning Needs of the New Graduate Entering Hospital Nursing." *Nurse Educator* 6 (6): 10–17.

Schwartz, Audrey J. 1980. "Law, Lawyers, and Law School: Perspectives from the First-year Class." *Journal of Legal Education* 30 (4–5): 437–69.

Scott, David M.; Montagne, Michael; Hakanson, Nina; and Schwanke, Robert W. 1983. "The Development and Evaluation of an Interdisciplinary Health Training Program: A Pharmacy Perspective." *American Journal of Pharmaceutical Education* 47 (1): 42–48.

Scott, Donald M. 1983. "The Profession That Vanished: Public Lecturing in Mid-nineteenth Century America." In *Professions and Professional Ideologies in America,* edited by Gerald L. Geison. Chapel Hill: University of North Carolina Press.

Seidel, Andrew. 1981. "Teaching Environment and Behavior: Have We Reached the Design Studios?" *Journal of Architectural Education* 34 (3): 8–13.

Selfe, Cynthia, and Arbabi, Freydoon. 1983. "Writing to Learn: Engineering Student Journals." *Engineering Education* 74 (2): 86–98.

Shepherd, Marvin D., and Erwin, Gary. 1983. "An Examination of Students' Attitudes toward the Elderly." *American Journal of Pharmaceutical Education* 47 (1): 35–38.

Sherlock, B. J., and Morris, R. T. 1967. "The Evolution of the Professional: A Paradigm." *Sociological Inquiry* 37 (1): 27–46.

Shreve, William B.; Mohammed, Hambi; Mealiea, Wallace L.; and Clark, William B. 1980. "Integration of the Basic, Behavioral, and Biomaterials Sciences with the Clinical Curriculum." *Journal of Dental Education* 44 (2): 76–79.

Shuck, Peter H. 1983. "Organization Theory and the Teaching of Administrative Law." *Journal of Legal Education* 33 (1): 13–32.

Shur, Edith. 1979. "The Use of the Coworker Approach as a Teaching Model in Graduate Student Field Education." *Journal of Education for Social Work* 15 (1): 72–79.

Siegler, Mark; Rezler, Agnes G.; and Connell, Karen J. 1982. "Using Simulated Case Studies to Evaluate a Clinical Ethics Course for Junior Students." *Journal of Medical Education* 57 (5): 380–85.

Simpher, Nancy L.; deVoss, Gary G.; and Nott, Deborah L. 1980. "A Closer Look at University Student Teacher Supervision." *Journal of Teacher Education* 32 (4): 11–15.

Sims, Norman H. 1981. "Reporting Cultures: Penetrates Realm of Feelings, Drives." *Journalism Educator* 36 (1): 6–7 +.

Smith, Harry A., and Swintosky, Joseph V. 1983. "The Origin, Goals, and Development of a Clinical Pharmacy Emphasis in Pharmacy Education and Practice." *American Journal of Pharmaceutical Education* 47 (3): 204–10.

Smith, J. Allen. 1979. "The Coming Renaissance in Law and Literature." *Journal of Legal Education* 30 (1–2): 13–26.

Smith, Jesse M. 1981. "Perspectives on Dental Education." *Journal of Dental Education* 45 (11): 741–45.

Smith, Karl A.; Johnson, David W.; and Johnson, Roger T. 1981. "Structuring Learning Goals to Meet the Goals of Engineering Education." *Engineering Education* 72 (3): 221–26.

Snyder, Karolyn J., and Anderson, Robert H. 1980. "Leadership in Teacher Education: A Systems Approach." *Journal of Teacher Education* 31 (1): 11–15.

Snyman, P.C.A. 1979. "A Proposal for a National Link-up of the New Legal Services Corporation Law Offices and Law School Clinical Training Programs." *Journal of Legal Education* 30 (1–2): 43–57.

Speedie, Stuart M. 1980. "A Computer Literacy Course for Pharmacy Students." *American Journal of Pharmaceutical Education* 44 (2): 158–60.

Stark, Joan S.; Lowther, Malcolm A.; and Hagerty, Bonnie M. K. 1985. *Technical Report of a Survey of Faculty in Ten Professional Preparation Fields*. Ann Arbor: University of Michigan, Center for the Study of Higher and Postsecondary Education.

Stark, Joan S.; Lowther, Malcolm A.; Hagerty, Bonnie M. K.; and Orczyk, Cynthia. 1986. "A Conceptual Framework for the Study of Preservice Professional Preparation in Colleges and Universities." *Journal of Higher Education* 57 (3): 231–58.

Stein, Theodore J. 1982. "Child Welfare: New Directions in the Field and Their Implications for Education." *Journal of Education for Social Work* 18 (1): 103–10.

Steiner, Joseph R., and Devore, Wynetta. 1983. "Increasing Descriptive and Prescriptive Theoretical Skills to Promote Ethnic-Sensitive Practice." *Journal of Education for Social Work* 19 (2): 63–70.

Stevens, Robert. 1983. *Law School: Legal Education in America from the 1950s to the 1980s*. Chapel Hill: University of North Carolina Press.

Stillman, Paula L.; Burpeau, D.; Gregorio, Michele Y.; Nicholson, Glen I.; Sabers, Darrell L.; and Stillman, Alfred E. 1983. "Six Years of Experience Using Patient Instructors to Teach Interviewing Skills." *Journal of Medical Education* 58 (12): 941–46.

Stone, Gerald C. 1984. "Survey Reflects Disagreement on 25 Percent Accrediting Rule." *Journalism Educator* 38 (4): 13–16.

Streit-Forest, Ursula. 1982. "Differences in Empathy: A Preliminary Analysis." *Journal of Medical Education* 57 (1): 65–67.

Study Commission on Pharmacy. 1975. *Pharmacists for the Future: The Report of the Study Commission on Pharmacy.* Ann Arbor, Mich.: Health Administration Press. ED 179 187. 60 pp. MF–$0.97; PC–$7.14.

Suess, Linda R.; Schweitzer, Barbara J.; and Williams, Clara A. 1982. "Nursing Students Experiment with Reality." *Nurse Educator* 7 (2): 28–33.

Summers, Robert S. 1984. "Fuller on Legal Education." *Journal of Legal Education* 34 (1): 8–21.

Svarstad, Bonnie. 1979. "Pharmaceutical Sociology: Issues in Research, Education, and Service." *American Journal of Pharmaceutical Education* 43 (3): 252–57.

Sze, William C.; Keller, Robert S.; and Keller, Dorothy B. 1979. "A Comparative Study of Two Different Teaching and Curricular Arrangements in Human Behavior and Social Environments." *Journal of Education for Social Work* 15 (1): 103–9.

Teigiser, Karen S. 1983. "Evaluation of Education for Generalist Practice." *Journal of Education for Social Work* 19 (1): 79–85.

Terkla, Louis. 1981. "Predoctoral Dental Education in the 1980s." *Journal of Dental Education* 45 (12): 789–96.

Thomas, Annette M., and Ship, Irwin I. 1981. "Current Status of Geriatric Education in American Dental Schools." *Journal of Dental Education* 45 (9): 589–91.

Thorpe, J. F. 1979. "A Survey of Product Liability Involvement in Engineering Education." *Engineering Education* 69 (7): 755–56.

Torgersen, Paul E. 1979. "Engineering Education and the Second Obligation." *Engineering Education* 70 (2): 169–74.

Toseland, Ron, and Spielberg, Gil. 1982. "The Development of Helping Skills in Undergraduate Social Work Education: Model and Evaluation." *Journal of Education for Social Work* 18 (1): 66–73.

Trieb, Marc. 1982. "Of Cardboard Cities and Public Politics." *Journal of Architectural Education* 35 (3): 18–21.

Trivett, David A. 1977. *Continuing Education for the Professions.* ERIC Research Currents. Washington, D.C.: ERIC Clearinghouse on Higher Education. ED 135 322. 5 pp. MF–$0.97; PC–$3.54.

Turnbull, Eleanor N. 1982. "Interdisciplinaryism: Problems and Promises." *Journal of Nursing Education* 21 (2): 24–31.

Tymitz-Wolf, Barbara L. 1984. "The New Vocationalism and Teacher Education." *Journal of Teacher Education* 35 (1): 21–25.

University of Oregon, School of Journalism. 1984. *Planning for Curricular Change in Journalism: Report on the Future of Journalism and Mass Communication in Education*. Eugene: Author.

VanderMeer, H. W., and Lyons, M. 1979. "Professional Fields and the Liberal Arts: 1958–78." *Educational Record* 60 (2): 197–201.

————.1980. "What Engineering Faculty Believe about the Liberal Arts." *Engineering Education* 71 (2): 170–72.

Vernon, David H. 1983. "Education for Proficiency: The Continuum." *Journal of Legal Education* 33 (4): 559–69.

Vogt, Donald D.; Montagne, M.; and Smith, Harry. 1981. "Science and Technology in American Pharmacy Practice." *American Journal of Pharmaceutical Education* 45 (3): 232–37.

Vollmer, H. M., and Mills, D. L. 1966. *Professionalization*. Englewood Cliffs, N.J.: Prentice-Hall.

Vonalt, Larry; Andrews, W.; Christensen, L.; and Bayless, J. 1980. "The Mississippi River: Universities and Civil Engineering." *Engineering Education* 70 (7): 762–69.

Von Blum, Paul. 1979. "New Course on Professional Responsibility: The Legal Profession in the Humanities." *Journal of Legal Education* 30 (3): 366–69.

Voris, J. C.; Anderson, Robert J.; and Kimberlin, Carole L. 1982. "Physician and Pharmacy Student Expectations of Pharmacy Practice." *American Journal of Pharmaceutical Education* 46 (1): 37–41.

Wakeland, H. L. 1982. "Preparing Engineering Graduates for International Involvement." *Engineering Education* 72 (4): 276–77.

Walker, Virginia L., and Lowenthal, W. 1981. "Perceptions of Undergraduate Students toward Continuing Education." *American Journal of Pharmaceutical Education* 45 (3): 268–70.

Wallert, James A. Summer 1982. "Broadcast News Education Lags in Technology Areas." *Journalism Educator* 37: 52–53 + .

Warren, Donald. 1982. "What Went Wrong with the Foundations and Other Off-center Questions?" *Journal of Teacher Education* 33 (3): 28–30.

Webb, Rodman B., and Sherman, Robert R. 1983. "Liberal Education: An Aim for Colleges of Education." *Journal of Teacher Education* 34 (4): 23–26.

Weinstein, Harvey M. 1982. "The Integration of Intellect and Feeling in the Study of Law." *Journal of Legal Education* 32 (1): 87–98.

White, James B. 1982. "The Study of Law as an Intellectual Activity." *Journal of Legal Education* 32 (1): 1–10.

Wigton, Robert S. 1980. "The Effects of Student Personal Characteristics on the Evaluation of Clinical Performance." *Journal of Medical Education* 55 (5): 423–27.

Wilensky, H. L. 1964. "The Professionalization of Everyone." *American Journal of Sociology* 70 (2): 134–58.

Willging, Thomas E., and Dunn, Thomas G. 1981. "The Moral Development of the Law Student: Theory and Data on Legal Education." *Journal of Legal Education* 31 (3–5): 306–58.

Williams, Jack W. 1982. "They Train Lions, Don't They?" *Journal of Teacher Education* 33 (3): 31–34.

Williams, Jan R. 1983. "The Accounting Lyceum of the Federation of Schools of Accountancy." *Journal of Accounting Education* 1 (1): 141–45.

Williamson, Kenneth J., and Hudspeth, Robert T. 1982. "Teaching Holistic Thought through Engineering Design." *Engineering Education* 72 (7): 698–703.

Wilson, Brent D. Fall 1982. "Improving Finance Education through Curriculum Planning." *Journal of Financial Education* 1: 47–49.

Wodarski, John S. 1979. "Critical Issues in Social Work Education." *Journal of Education for Social Work* 15 (2): 5–13.

Wright, Keith C. 1981. "Library Education and Handicapped Individuals." *Journal of Education for Librarianship* 21 (3): 183–95.

Wyer, Jean C. 1984. "Procedural vs. Conceptual: A Developmental View." *Journal of Accounting Education* 2 (1): 5–18.

Zagano, Phyllis. 1983. "New 'New Journalism' Course Blends Liberal Arts Tradition with Nuts-Bolts Practice." *Journalism Educator* 37 (4): 42–44.

Zahorik, John A. 1984. "Can Teachers Adopt Research Findings?" *Journal of Teacher Education* 34 (1): 34–36.

Zeichner, Kenneth M. 1983. "Alternative Paradigms of Teacher Education." *Journal of Teacher Education* 34 (3): 3–9.

Zeichner, Kenneth M., and Tabachnick, B. Robert. 1981. "Are the Effects of University Teacher Education Washed out by School Experience?" *Journal of Teacher Education* 32 (3): 7–11.

Zucker, Steven B.; Selby, Gary R.; and Garbee, William. 1980. "A Survey of Career Assistance Programs at U. S. Dental Schools." *Journal of Dental Education* 44 (4): 216–17.

INDEX

A

Accounting
    communication skills, 39
    new fields/techniques, 55, 56
Accreditation guidelines, 79
Accrediting Council on Education in Journalism and Mass
    Communication, 44
Adaptive competence, 48–52, 71
Administrator role, 77
Admissions criteria: medicine, 32
Advanced degrees vs. continuing education, 69
Aged (see Elderly clients)
American Bar Association, 2
American Pharmaceutical Association, 2
Architecture
    as enterprising profession, 7
    career marketability, 54
    clientele, 76
    competence as outcome, 19, 21, 28
    contextual competence, 31
    continuing education, 68
    creative skills, 30
    curricular criticism, 24
    field experiences, 45, 47, 73
    integrative competence, 42
    interpersonal communication skills, 39
    outcomes made explicit, 79
    judgment skills, 41
    professional attitudes, 53
    professional identity, 60, 61
    professional journals, 71
    teaching modes, 50
Art, 7
Articulation: goals/outcomes, 1, 79
Assertiveness training, 38, 39
Association of American Medical Colleges, 2, 7, 49
Attitudes
    as desired outcome, 12, 22, 74
    "becoming professional," 53
    career marketability, 53–57
    caregivers, 38
    faculty views, 28
    liberal arts/professional education, 33
    motivation for continued learning, 67–69
    professional ethics, 61–65
    professional identity, 57–61

views on outcomes emphasis, 16–17, 28
Federation of Schools of Accounting, 39
Field experience, 42, 43–48, 61, 71, 72, 73, 74, 76
First professional degrees
    definition, 5
    degrees granted, 9
Forestry, 7

G

Graduate follow-up studies, 78
Graduate vs. undergraduate professional preparation, 6, 34

H

Handicapped (see Disabled clients)
Health-related fields
    as first professional degrees, 5
    interpersonal communication skills, 37
    client diversity, 71, 76
HEGIS (see Higher Education General Information Survey)
Helping professions, 7, 58, 61
Higher Education General Information Survey (HEGIS), 5, 10
Historical approach, 24, 35, 50
Humanities: contextual competence, 31, 32

I

Informing professions, 7, 58, 71
Integration of theory and practice (see Theory and practice)
Integrative competence, 40–48, 75
Integrity in the College Curriculum, 3
Interdisciplinary approach, 25, 35, 50, 51, 75, 76
International involvement/competitiveness, 51, 56
Internships, 39, 44, 45, 47, 74
Interpersonal competence
    communication, 36–40
    skills, 29

J

Job counseling (see Career guidance)
Journal of Education for Social Work, 15
Journal of Medical Education, 15
Journalism
    as informing profession, 7
    as professional field, 4
    bachelor's degree, 33
    career marketability, 54
    competence as outcome, 19, 28

contextual competence, 31, 32
creative skills, 30
curricular status, 24, 34, 77, 78
degrees granted, 10
field experience, 43, 44, 72, 74
integrative competence, 42
interpersonal skills, 29, 36
professional ethics, 62
professional identity, 58, 59
professional journals, 71
sense of need for future change, 51
student development goals, 27
technological advances, 49
Journals in professions, 14–17, 71
Judgment, 40, 41, 46, 62

K
Knowledge base (see Conceptual competence)

L
Law
as enterprising profession, 7
as first professional degree, 5
attitude toward research, 65, 66
communication skills, 40
competence as outcome, 19, 20, 28
contextual competence, 31, 32
continuing education, 68, 69
curriculum/structure, 23
field experience, 43–44, 72, 74
integrative competence, 42
interpersonal skills, 29
professional attitudes, 53
professional ethics, 62, 63
professional identity, 58, 61
professional journals, 71
sense of need for future change, 51
socialization, 27
student preparation, 6
Legal education (see Law)
Liberal arts
contextual competence, 31, 32–34
cooperation/collaboration with professional studies, 1, 3, 72
enrollment trends, 1
foundation for scholarly concern, 67
lack of focus criticism, 35

prerequisite characteristics, 23, 26
socialization, 27, 42, 55, 57–61, 70, 73, 76
writing skills, 36
Study Group on the Conditions of Excellence in American Higher Education, 1, 5

T
Teacher education
as informing profession, 7
as professional field, 5
attitude toward research, 65, 66
bachelor's degree, 33
career marketability, 54
competence as outcome, 19
contextual competence, 31
continuing education, 69
curricular criticism, 24–25, 77
expanding settings, 55
field experience, 45, 46, 47, 73
integrative competence, 42
interpersonal communication skills, 39
liberal arts coursework, 33–34
professional identity, 59, 61
professional journals, 14, 71
program length, 6
teaching modes, 50
Teaching modes, 50–51
Technical competence, 27–30, 71
Technology: impact on professions, 49–50, 51, 55
Theology: as first professional degree, 5
Theoretical foundations, 19, 24–26
Theory and practice
as form of competence, 40
dichotomy, 43, 44, 46, 74
need for, 2
technology use to fill gap, 47–48
Time factor, 33
Town planning, 41

U
U.S. competitiveness in engineering, 56
U.S. Department of Education: definition of professional, 5
Undergraduate vs. graduate professional preparation, 6

V
Values, 22, 26, 60, 64
Veterinary medicine, 7

Starting in 1983, the Association for the Study of Higher Education assumed cosponsorship of the Higher Education Reports with the ERIC Clearinghouse on Higher Education. For the previous 11 years, ERIC and the American Association for Higher Education prepared and published the reports.

Each report is the definitive analysis of a tough higher education problem, based on a thorough research of pertinent literature and institutional experiences. Report topics, identified by a national survey, are written by noted practitioners and scholars with prepublication manuscript reviews by experts.

Eight monographs (10 monographs before 1985) in the ASHE-ERIC Higher Education Report series are published each year, available individually or by subscription. Subscription to eight issues is $60 regular; $50 for members of AERA, AAHE, and AIR; $40 for members of ASHE. (Add $7.50 outside the United States.)

Prices for single copies, including 4th class postage and handling, are $10.00 regular and $7.50 for members of AERA, AAHE, AIR, and ASHE ($7.50 regular and $6.00 for members for 1983 and 1984 reports, $6.50 regular and $5.00 for members for reports published before 1983). If faster 1st class postage is desired for U.S. and Canadian orders, add $.75 for each publication ordered; overseas, add $4.50. For VISA and MasterCard payments, include card number, expiration date, and signature. Orders under $25 must be prepaid. Bulk discounts are available on orders of 15 or more reports (not applicable to subscriptions). Order from the Publications Department, Association for the Study of Higher Education, One Dupont Circle, Suite 630, Washington, D.C. 20036, 202/296-2597. Write for a publication list of all the Higher Education Reports available.

1986 Higher Education Reports

1. Post-tenure Faculty Evaluation: Threat or Opportunity?
   Christine M. Licata

2. Blue Ribbon Commissions and Higher Education: Changing Academe from the Outside
   Janet R. Johnson and Laurence R. Marcus

3. Responsive Professional Education: Balancing Outcomes and Opportunities
   Joan S. Stark, Malcolm A. Lowther, and Bonnie M.K. Hagerty

1985 Higher Education Reports

1. Flexibility in Academic Staffing: Effective Policies and Practices
   Kenneth P. Mortimer, Marque Bagshaw, and Andrew T. Masland

2. Associations in Action: The Washington, D.C., Higher Education Community
   Harland G. Bloland

3. And on the Seventh Day: Faculty Consulting and Supplemental Income
   Carol M. Boyer and Darrell R. Lewis

4. Faculty Research Performance: Lessons from the Sciences and Social Sciences
   John W. Creswell